CAMBRIDGE PAPERS IN SOCIAL ANTHROPOLOGY

No. 3

MARRIAGE IN TRIBAL SOCIETIES

CAMBRIDGE PAPERS IN
SOCIAL ANTHROPOLOGY

MARRIAGE IN
TRIBAL SOCIETIES

EDITED BY
MEYER FORTES

CAMBRIDGE
AT THE UNIVERSITY PRESS
1972

Published by the Syndics of the Cambridge University Press
Bentley House, 200 Euston Road, London NW1 2DB
American Branch: 32 East 57th Street, New York, N.Y.10022

© Cambridge University Press 1962

ISBN: 0 521 08406 7

First published 1962
Reprinted 1972

First printed in Great Britain at the University Printing House, Cambridge
Reprinted in Great Britain by Redwood Press Limited, Trowbridge & London

CONTENTS

FIGURES

CONTRIBUTORS TO THIS ISSUE

MEYER FORTES. William Wyse Professor of Social Anthropology in the University of Cambridge, author of *The Dynamics of Clanship among the Tallensi* (1945), *The Web of Kinship among the Tallensi* (1949), *Oedipus and Job* (1959), editor, *African Political Systems* (1940), *Social Structure, Essays Presented to Radcliffe-Brown* (1949).

ESTHER NEWCOMB GOODY. Took a B.A. in Sociology at Antioch College, Ohio, in 1954, studied in Cambridge 1954–56, and carried out fieldwork among the Gonja of Northern Ghana 1956–57 on a Fellowship from the Ford Foundation. She completed her Ph.D. at Cambridge in 1961.

JEAN LA FONTAINE. Obtained her B.A. degree at Cambridge in 1953, worked for the East African Institute of Social and Economic Research 1953–55 doing fieldwork among the BaGisu, completed her Ph.D. at Cambridge in 1957, was Commonwealth Scholar at the University of Chicago, 1957–58. Author of *The Gisu of Uganda* (1958), and various papers.

GRACE HARRIS. Received an M.A. from Chicago in 1949, having graduated from the College of the University in 1945. She worked among the Taita of Kenya on a Fellowship from the Colonial Social Science Research Council from 1950 to 1952, completed her Ph.D. at Cambridge in 1955 and has taught at Cambridge, Boston University, Smith College, University of Massachusetts and Brandeis University.

MARGUERITE S. ROBINSON. Took a B.A. at Radcliffe College in 1956, worked at Cambridge University during the year 1959–60 and is now studying for a Ph.D. at Harvard University.

PREFACE

This is the third of a series of occasional papers in social anthropology published by the Cambridge University Press for the Department of Archaeology and Anthropology of the University of Cambridge. We plan to publish further volumes at intervals of about one year. Each volume will be edited by a member of the editorial board and will contain a number of papers arising out of anthropological work carried out in the Department. Each volume will deal, as far as possible, with a single broad topic of theoretical interest. The main contributions will ordinarily take the form of papers based on field research in particular areas and communities, but each volume will also include an introductory paper in which the main theoretical issues referred to in the other papers will be explicitly discussed.

The present issue has been edited by Meyer Fortes, who also contributes the introduction. Professor Fortes wishes to express appreciation of the assistance given by Dr Jack Goody in seeing this issue through the press and of the facilities placed at his disposal by the Director and the staff of the Center for Advanced Study in the Behavioural Sciences, Stanford, California, during a summer visit there.

The fourth number of the series, to be edited by Jack Goody, will use material from centralized political systems in Africa and be concerned with problems arising from systems of succession to office.

We are indebted tó the Smuts Memorial Fund of the University of Cambridge for a grant in aid of the publication of this series.

MEYER FORTES
JACK GOODY
E. R. LEACH

INTRODUCTION

By MEYER FORTES

The papers in the present symposium deal with diverse aspects of marriage. Three give accounts of ethnographical observations in African tribal societies and the fourth offers a re-analysis of data extracted from that treasury of ethnographical riches, Malinowski's Trobriand *corpus*.

So much is now known about the customs and institutions of marriage in all human societies that it might seem doubtful if anything new can be added. Nor are there conspicuous lacunae in the theoretical study of the subject. It so happens that Malinowski, Lowie and Radcliffe-Brown, surely the three foremost authorities of their time on the comparative sociology of marriage, all left comprehensive statements of their conclusions (Malinowski 1929; Lowie 1933; Radcliffe-Brown 1950); and the general principles they set forth do not seem to me to be invalidated by later research. Add the massive investigations of Lévi-Strauss and his colleagues, as well as such compendious recent works as *African Systems of Kinship and Marriage* and the *Survey of African Marriage and Family Life*, and there would seem to be little an ethnographer can now contribute save further illustrations of well-known facts and principles.

Such, indeed, is the main intention of the four essays collected together in this volume. Conceptual and theoretical considerations are kept well under control. But they are not irrelevant; for however particular an ethnographic inquiry may be, direction is given to it by implicit conceptual categories and theoretical criteria. And even so thoroughly explored a terrain as marriage in tribal society may yield unexpected theoretical surprises to a new approach.

An apt illustration occurs in Dr La Fontaine's paper. Like the Taita and some other East African peoples with developed patrilineal lineage systems, the Gisu do not prohibit marriage between agnates outside the range of the minimal lineage. In fact, marriage with lineage kin beyond the prohibited degrees is common. But, says Dr La Fontaine, after marriage the affinal relationship ousts the descent relationship. The individuals are the same people as before. But before the marriage, the husband and his close patrilineal kin defined the wife and her minimal lineage as co-descendants of common patrilineal ancestors. They were therefore vested with rights and duties, entitled to loyalties and regarded with the sentiments that are mandatory for patrilineal kin. Now, after the marriage, their social relations undergo what looks like a striking reversal. Instead, for example, of the familiarity which is normal between kin they must behave with the mutual deference which is obligatory between affines; instead of the unqualified support which kinsfolk must give one another in war, affines may withhold aid if they wish.

The inherent antithesis between kinship bonds and affinal relations is common, probably normal, in all societies in which genealogical connexions between persons otherwise eligible as spouses are recognized and where kinship within fixed degrees is a lawful impediment to marriage. It is an antithesis which epitomizes the cleavage between the domain of kinship and the domain of non-kinship in social structure. What Dr La Fontaine documents is that people cannot be both kinsmen and affines to one another in the same context of social relations. Hence if prospective spouses are kin in their premarital status relations their kinship must be extinguished for them to be able to marry. This is done among the Gisu, and thereupon affinity takes its place.

It is pertinent that this shift is implemented and kept in being, not only among the Gisu, of course, but very generally in African society, by the flow of marriage payments. However, what I want to draw attention to here is the bearing of Dr La Fontaine's observation on a wider theoretical issue. Recent studies of South Indian kinship and marriage institutions (Dumont 1957; Gough 1959) have been concerned with the relative significance of affinal status and kinship in adherence to rules of cross-cousin marriage. The African conception typified by Gisu custom is closely paralleled by South Indian data. [1] To my mind what emerges clearly from both sets of observations is that, in dynamic terms, it is marriage which generates affinal relationship and not vice versa (cf. Goody 1959, for an incisive criticism of Dumont's contrary hypothesis). In formal terms, marriage is the bridge between the kinship side and the affinal side of the dichotomy that is of necessity built into the total genealogically defined domain of social relations which we find in every social system. It is a necessary corollary of the incest law, as Lévi-Strauss has so cogently demonstrated (1949). In other words, there would be no point to marriage ceremonies and legal instruments if the pre-marital status of the spouses in relation to each other and to their relevant kin were already affinal in character.

This brings me to one of the most interesting contributions of this collection of essays. A complex and fundamental problem in the comparative sociology of marriage is that of the regulations, conditions and criteria governing the choice of a spouse and the procedure of espousal entailed thereby. For everything connected with marriage is directed to this outcome.

Marriage, some say, is a lottery; or, as Montaigne says more vividly in his essay 'Of Three Good Women', it is 'a bargain full of thornie circumstances'. In discussing the selection of spouses and the formalities of marriage we are, in effect, asking what kind of bargain is struck, who are the parties to it and what are the rules and circumstances of the bargaining game. I put it this way because it is tempting to describe the process in the language of the Theory of Games, with the simplest two-person zero-sum game as the 'model'. The data are not at hand, in the papers under discussion, to go as far, for instance, as Dr Barth in his ingenious use of this approach in the analysis of Swat Pathan intra-lineage politics (Barth 1959). But Dr Harris's paper, in particular, includes data that do lend themselves to a re-statement on the lines of game theory.

If we consider marriage as an event in a life history it can be treated as a transaction between two parties. In the type of society we are concerned with they consist of the principals—the bride and bridegroom—and certain designated kin of each, determined by jural and moral tenets and rules relating to the status of persons. In connexion with my earlier remarks about affinal relations, it is important to note that these two parties are normally defined as being non-kin within the context of the marriage transaction. The 'game' requires that they be defined as opponents, each aiming at profiting rather than losing by the outcome. Custom gives reiterated expression to this theme, often in the mimicry of ceremony. Characteristically and significantly, the controlling position in each party is held by the parents, notably the father, or a parental collateral, or deputy, of quasi-paternal status.

The 'game' is played subject to a body of rules, conventions, and constraints which, in part, limit and, in part, direct the strategies and tactics of the 'players'. The rules comprise jural and moral ordinances that emanate from the politico-jural domain of social structure and will be enforced by agencies of society. These include the very common rules of incest and exogamy and such special cases as, for example, the Taita rule that marriage is not allowed between the descendants of a common grandfather. They also include procedural rules such as those relating to the sequence of gifts and countergifts in Trobriand marriage, to bride-price negotiations, and so on. An instance of a convention is the permissibility of recourse to elopement in certain circumstances. And a good example of a constraint is the economic need for particular kinds of farming land among the Taita, or for affinal support in gaining political advancement among the Gisu.

To continue the analogy, we can try to determine what are the values at stake, though it is not easy to keep this in line with the 'constant sum' model of the theory. Most anthropologists would agree that the Capital Value is the set of rights in the bride's sexual and procreative capacities and the domestic services that go with them. But our task is complicated by the coupling of this value with the bride-price or other marriage gifts, payments and services. The sum total of marital rights and the marriage prestations constitute a single fund of value from an outsider's point of view. Our problem is to account for the distribution of its components. Bride-price and marital rights move in opposite directions and remain on opposite sides, as between the parties. [2] But they tend towards a balance, in jural terms, and it is of special interest to note, from such data as are provided both by Dr Harris and by Dr La Fontaine, how the balance between the two components is often kept in suspense. This is brought about by arrangements for the transfer of the bride-price and other prestations to be spread out over a period of time, and, concomitantly, for the rights of the husband to be handed over seriatim.

The 'game' is further complicated by the Ancillary Values that are realizable through a marriage in consequence of the status relationships and connexions of the parties. The alliance with a spouse's relatives may be valued for the wealth, influence, political power or mere goodwill it can mobilize. Social geography may be a consideration when, as among both the Taita and the Gisu, the advantages of proximity of residence to a father-in-law with command over land resources have to be weighed against the attractions of an extra-neighbourhood marriage which is attainable without delay for a poor man.

Whether or not he reckons up the alternatives systematically—and doubtless he does not—a Taita suitor and his party have three plans of action to choose from. Dr Harris describes them under the headings of Completed Betrothal, Curtailed Betrothal and Elopement, the last being perhaps resorted to by young men only when the more formal and approved procedures fail. The bride's party, for their part, can either stand out for the first form, compromise on the second, or accept the third with as good a grace as they can muster. They exploit the law that no marriage can be legitimate without the transfer of the bride-price, in whole or in an agreed part, in developing their strategy. That is to say they manœuvre in terms of the kind and amounts of marriage prestations they will accept in return for the marital rights they are obliged to concede. For the Taita, it is tempting to guess that the half-way house of Curtailed Betrothal is likely to be the compromise most acceptable to both parties.

The point of principle need not be laboured any further. A marriage is an event in the career of an individual and in the developmental cycle of families and kin-groups (cf. *Cambridge Papers*, 1, 1958). It comes about by individuals making use of economic resources, social relations, laws and beliefs, in choosing the most rewarding way—within the limits set by social norms—of fulfilling their private purposes. This is the aspect of marriage I have been comparing to the procedures that figure in Game Theory.

But if we are looking at marriage as an institution, the more appropriate questions are where does it fit into the structure of society and what are the ingredients of custom that mark it off as a distinctive institution.

Let us consider, again, the manœuvres to gain a spouse. Before they can begin a choice has to be made. In such famous and voluminously discussed closed or prescriptive systems as those of Australia and of Southern India, this is ostensibly fixed by rules that prescribe eligibility for marriage in advance. A man must marry a cross-cousin, or rather, to put it more generally, a woman who can be placed in a category designated by the kinship term for cross-cousin by virtue of a recognized classificatory rule which, in extreme cases, simply divides all the opposite sex members of one's own generation in the endogamous group into non-marriageable 'siblings' and marriageable 'cross-cousins'. This fixes the structural provenance of spouses quite strictly by reference to their pre-marital genealogical identification and classification. Manœuvres to gain a particular person as spouse are limited in scope and may even be prescribed.

It is quite different in the open (or proscriptive) systems we are dealing with here. In theory spouses can be taken from any genealogically and politically licit group—for instance, one that is not proscribed by rules of incest or exogamy, or is not a member of an inferior caste—in a population that is likely to be large by comparison with that of an Australian tribe or South Indian local caste group. Is the actual selection of spouses in a given generation, or over a stretch of several generations, then purely random or is there some implicit or explicit regularity in it?

Dr Harris and Dr La Fontaine have addressed themselves to this problem. They confirm observations that have previously been made in other parts of Africa, for example among the Tallensi of Northern Ghana (Fortes 1949, ch. xi). Allowing for the bounds set by incest prohibitions and exogamic regulations, which may be implicit rather than explicitly formulated, as, for instance, in the Israeli Kibbutz described by Spiro (1958: ch. xiv), it seems that there is a distinct preferential bias in these open systems. The bias is in favour of marriage within close permissible geographical or social range, rather than far afield. Thus there is a high incidence of inter-marriage between members of geographically neighbouring or socially related families and groups, whether these are genealogically, locally, occupationally or otherwise defined, and the rate decreases along a regular gradient as the spatial or social distance between the parties increases. The inference is that, whatever rationalizations people may give for their choices of spouses, in open systems the odds are large that they will fall within the nearest accessible circle of mates defined as eligible in jural and other customary terms. The same results may come about in closed systems; but this is because eligible spouses are specified by genealogical or ritual rules, or by physical conditions that impose propinquity on spouses, as in an island community.

It should be noted that this tendency is not confined to tribal societies. It occurs to some extent in North Indian castes (cf. Gould 1960), and has been encountered in some segments of western industrial societies. Residential propinquity has been shown to have a strong influence on the choice of spouses in some American cities (cf. Marches and Turbeville 1953, which reviews and adds new data to earlier well-known studies of this propensity). There are cities in which up to 70% of marriages, in certain areas, take place between persons who reside within twenty blocks of each other. Social propinquity, in the sense of class, occupational, educational, religious and such-like solidarity, is commonly believed to influence marriage and many studies have confirmed that this is true for the United States (cf. for example, Centers 1949).[3] It was, of course, a firmly held ideal and practice in Europe, as readers of nineteenth-century novels know, and still prevails in many areas. Among recent studies in Great Britain, Mrs Stacey's description of social life in Banbury shows that there is a distinct tendency towards class and local endogamy among native-born inhabitants of the town (Stacey 1960, App. 7), and this is probably characteristic of similar small towns and villages in England. A more striking example comes from rural Holland where, as Dr Ishwaran's fascinating monograph (Ishwaran 1959, pp. 50ff.) brings out so vividly, marriage is quite explicitly circumscribed by considerations of class, denominational, educational and local solidarity.

I adduce these American and European data for a particular reason. They indicate that the preference for propinquity in the choice of spouses is not due to such accidental factors as the simplicity of economic life or the limitations on freedom of movement due to poor communications or rudimentary political institutions in tribal society. It arises from an invariable concomitant of marriage that is taken into account in all anthropological discussions of the subject but is apt to be ignored by other social scientists. I mean, of course, the structural consequences of the fact that the principals in marriage are normally not isolated individuals but status-endowed persons whose union commits both them and those with whom they have pre-marital social ties to new social relationships. The most general and most important of these are the inescapable affinal relationships. These are critical because it is through them that the structurally discrete conjugal unit is fitted into the external systems of political, juridical, economic and religious institutions and arrangements. Structural propinquity between the parties is conducive to marriage because it facilitates continuity and consistency between the network of status relations in which they and their kin were placed before their marriage and the status arrangements that are the result of the marriage. Local intra-marriage is but a special case of this more general principle. At its simplest, it may make it easier for both the spouses and their kin to manage their mutual affinal relationships without detriment to the loyalties and obligations that persist from their pre-marital social and personal relations.

But by the same token structural propinquity may be associated with wide geographical separation; for different status values may act in what seem like contrary directions to achieve what appears to be the same end of maximizing

6

affinal solidarity. Dr Harris and Dr La Fontaine have some highly instructive data on this subject. The newly married young Taita benefits by living in his wife's father's neighbourhood because this makes it feasible to borrow land from his affines. The father-in-law, in turn, thinks it useful to have his son-in-law close under his eye. The Taita elder, on the other hand, with his established economic and jural position, stands to gain coveted political prestige by marrying into a distant community and making use of his affinal ties to win support abroad. The richest and the poorest among the Gisu both tend to marry far away, but they seek spatially distant affines for contrary reasons. Trobriand chiefs, Mrs Robinson reminds us, follow a policy of taking wives from a wide range of clans so that they may have a wide network of affinal allies and well-distributed sources of supplies.

To choose a spouse with an eye to the in-laws one may become connected with is a common enough practice in many societies. In some cases the aim, avowedly, is to build up or maintain affinal alliances. Marriage then appears as virtually nothing more than an indispensable adjunct to such alliances. Doubtless there are traces of this in, for instance, the marriages of Taita elders. Let cynics make what they wish of the motives and attitudes that may be inferred from such practices. We must remember, however, that they conform to standard patterns in the societies we have been discussing; and their main interest for us lies in the structural principles and customary norms which they represent. The manner in which status position influences choice of affinal alignments has been noted. Prospective affinal alignments and interests in turn decide which of the several jurally permissible modes of espousal is adopted, be it at the demand of the woman's party or merely by their acquiescence. This is where the game-like manœuvres play a part. And in passing it is worth noting how widely espousal by elopement is conceded. The reason is simple. It is a kind of escape mechanism. It enables marriages to be achieved when the principals are in all respects well suited and lawfully eligible but adventitious impediments stand in the way of orthodox procedure, for example when the jural superiors of one or the other are unjustifiably recalcitrant or when the suitor is handicapped by poverty. This relates to the basic limiting fact in marriage. In tribal societies it is normally accepted that every adult has a right to get married. It is regarded as a necessary attribute, not only of maturity, but of citizenship, in the sense of membership of the widest political community. A parent or any other person who uses authority derived from his domestic or descent status to obstruct this right without just cause may incur public censure. The *fait accompli* of an elopement may be as welcome a way out for the responsible parent as it is for the young couple.

The issue of status is central. To adapt (without disrespect to its distinguished author) the most hackneyed of all sociological aphorisms, marriage could be briefly defined as the sanctioned movement from the filial status of son or daughter to the conjugal status of husband or wife. This holds, in the broadly descriptive sense, at any rate, for first marriages. And first marriages are decisive both for the spouses, for the domestic groups from which they move, and for those which they eventually start. A person's first marriage constitutes a critical, that is an irreversible change of status, one of the most important in the life cycle. Dr Goody's study provides an insight into what this means. A Gonja woman's first marriage creates once and for all the inextinguishable and irreversible status of wife for her. Frequent divorce and remarriage is customary among the Gonja. But later marriages do not add to or subtract from the uxoral status gained by a first marriage. This is symbolized and sanctioned by the requirement that a woman must be ritually freed from the sexual control of her first husband when he dies, no matter how many husbands she has had since. This concept of uxoral status is found in other parts of Africa (e.g. among the Hausa: cf. M. F. Smith 1958) and elsewhere. I would guess that it is implied in the Trobriand manner of establishing a marriage and in such nuptial ceremonies as the Nayar *tali* tying rite. In structural terms one might say that first marriage establishes the husband–wife constellation as an entity which is maintained through the entire life of the partners as if it were ideally the same, regardless of any permutations of the members of the unit. This is analogous to leviratic marriage, if it is thought of as the original marriage of the widow continued with the aid of a new incumbent of the office of husband, primarily in his physical aspect, as sexual and economic mate.

Dr Goody's observations confirm what we know from other sources, that the significant feature for which first marriage is thus jurally and ritually singled out is the sexual roles it creates. Anthropologists agree that what distinguishes the conjugal relationship uniquely from all other dyadic relationships, and isolates it as the core of the domestic domain, is the exclusive, or at the minimum privileged sexual rights and claims of the spouses on each other. These rights and claims pertain to socially responsible procreative sexuality as opposed to the irresponsible juvenile and adolescent sexual indulgence which is often condoned, if not freely allowed, pre-maritally. These rights may be delegated (e.g. by a sterile husband), distributed (as in polyandry), split up into a bound moral and symbolic element and a free physical element (as among the Nayar) or transposed in context. This does not alter their significance as the distinctive feature of the conjugal relationship. For it is by entering legitimately into conjugal sexual relations that the transition in status—not, be it noted, in physical maturity—from daughter to wife and son to husband is effected. This transition is accomplishable only once and for all in a person's lifetime, and that only with the concurrence of society—or rather, to put it more exactly, with the necessary jural authorization.

INTRODUCTION

Dr Goody's account shows that Gonja social structure generates very divergent pulls on a person, and so disperses all social relations both temporally and spatially. The result is that marriage inevitably becomes a very unstable partnership. But this applies only to particular marriages. The institution itself, in essence the jurally validated conjugal relationship, is not thereby annulled or even diminished in structural importance. As in all societies, a precise demarcation between unmarried co-habitation, even if it imitates marriage in all particulars of residence, housekeeping, sexual association and procreation, and true, that is legal marriage is maintained; and this is aptly symbolized in the once-for-all status of spouse conferred by first marriage. It is consistent with the Gonja adaptation of the form of marriage to their peculiar economic and political conditions that *de facto* marriage should be regarded as redundant for women past child-bearing and therefore easily terminable. There is no other legitimate way in which a woman can divest herself of the many contingent duties and responsibilities of the conjugal bond. This is jurally effective because, as Dr Goody demonstrates, the woman is able to resume her filial status in this situation.

My argument implies that the conjugal relationship derives from the marital status of the spouses, that is from the rights and duties, claims and capacities that are conferred on them from the outside, so to speak, I mean from the politico-jural domain. I stress this because it is easy to fall into the error of regarding marriage as a purely domestic matter. That it is not so is evident from the rule that the rights and duties of spouses, once authorized, must be respected by all others, hence the common practice of imposing jural penalties for adultery.

No aspect of marriage has more frequently been described than the ceremonies in which jural and religious sanction as well as social recognition is accorded to it. And none of them is so well known as those by which a bride-price and other marriage gifts are transferred. The African forms of such transactions have been authoritatively elucidated by Dr Lucy Mair and the other contributors to the *Survey of African Marriage and Family Life* (Phillips 1953). The general view is that these transfers, whether they take the form of valuables, livestock, money, labour service, or largely symbolic goods, certainly in the circumstances typical of societies with a patrilineal descent organization, signalize the transfer to the husband of marital rights over his wife and parental rights over any children that will be born to her. The papers in the present volume all give some attention to these prestations; and they suggest some comments on current views.

Marriage payments and gifts appear to consist of two constituents, a Prime Prestation and Contingent Prestations. The Prime Prestation is stipulated by the marriage laws. It is normally fixed in kind and amount, and is often restricted to the context of marriage as regards its disposal by the recipient

9

(e.g. it is earmarked for the bride-price of the brother of the girl for whom it is given or is offered as a sacrifice to ancestors to announce the marriage). It is the part of the marriage payments which constitutes the *sine qua non* for lawful marriage and which is, therefore, strictly speaking, the sole jural instrument for the transfer of marital rights. Thus it is the part of the marriage payments which stands for the nuclear sexual and parental rights and relationships of the spouses and thus corresponds to the Capital Value in marital rights. Bargaining cannot enter into this. For no matter what its economic worth may be its significance lies in its binding power as a jural instrument. That is why it is returnable when a marriage is terminated by divorce, and can more reasonably be equated with a pledge than with a purchase price.

The Contingent Prestations have a different meaning, even when they are made up of the same kinds of goods or services as the Prime Prestation. They are often open to bargaining and may be partly or wholly counterbalanced by reciprocal gifts or services from the recipients. This is understandable, for they are not a jural instrument for the transfer of rights but a means of winning and preserving the goodwill of those with the power to transfer marital rights. There is an element of barter in them. In other words, they are the medium through which affinal relations are established and maintained. That is why they are often, if not normally, spread out over time and may be linked with the fortunes of the family. They correspond to the Ancillary Values realized in marriage.

The distinction I am drawing has some interesting corollaries. Clearly it is the Prime Prestation that mediates the movement of the spouses from their pre-marital to their conjugal statuses. But the existence of affinal relationships presupposes that the pre-marital statuses of the spouses are not entirely extinguished by their marriage. If marriage were completely to wipe out a person's filial and sibling status, that is to say his or her pre-marital kinship ties, then neither spouse (nor, by derivation, their kin) could have affinal relations with his or her spouse's kin. Conjugal status does not replace filial status, it is added on to it; and their potentially conflicting co-extension is regulated by arrangements which segregate their respective fields of operation.

It is in this connexion that such incidental features of marriage as co-residence and common housekeeping are relevant. Transfer of the critical marital rights focused in the sexual relationships of the spouses necessitates only the relinquishment by parents of their control over their child's sexual and procreative capacities. It does not require them to give up all other claims on and rights over their child. They may be entitled to hold on to some domestic services from their child and to his or her physical presence in their home at times when the spouse's rights are not thereby infringed. That is why first-married spouses, in some societies, continue to reside with their respective parents until they themselves become parents and only then acquire a status that entitles them to set up in their own home. It is here that the gifts, payments or services which I have designated Contingent Prestations are sometimes brought into play as a means of inducing a wife's parents and kin to give up their residual rights and claims on her and permit her to join her husband in their own home.

And there is yet another side to marriage gifts and payments. This is very well brought out in Mrs Robinson's essay on Trobriand marriage. As I remarked earlier, the chief responsibility for these prestations rests with the parents of the spouses, though they normally go from the parents and selected kin of one spouse to the parents and selected kin of the other. This seems self-evident in a patrilineal or patrifilial system, where jural control over an unmarried person is vested primarily in the father. In this situation marital rights can be established only with the consent of the fathers of a prospective husband and wife; and this is signified by the bridegroom's father when he undertakes to hand over the Prime Prestation of the bride-price and by the bride's father when he agrees to accept it.

Mrs Robinson demonstrates that the father's consent and acquiescence (especially the girl's father's) is essential for marriage in the Trobriand Islands. This seems curious, at first sight, in a matrilineal social structure. But the same holds also for matrilineal systems in other parts of the world, as Mrs Robinson points out. Thus it raises important theoretical questions. Some of these are touched upon in both Mrs Robinson's and Dr Goody's papers. I will make only one comment. In matrilineal systems, as is well known, a woman's husband does not acquire full jural control over her children by him. But he does have moral claims, backed by ritual sanctions, on their affection and loyalty in recognition of the responsibility he exercises in their upbringing. It might be argued that this is sufficient to account for the requirement of a father's consent to his child's marriage and that the obvious way for him to signify this formally is through the medium of marriage gifts. But Mrs Robinson shows convincingly that the Trobriand father's role is not as passive as this view would imply. He plays too decisive a part in both the giving and the receiving of marriage prestations. He appears almost to have a right of veto in regard to his daughter's marriage, which is curious if not, on the face of it, anomalous, in a matrilineal family system.

Mrs Robinson associates the recognition given to the father's authority with his status by complementary filiation. Clearly he has power and some rights in relation to the basic attributes of marital status, that is, sexual and procreative potentialities. And the reason for this is not far to seek if we consider complementary filiation from the parents' side. A matrilineal father is his children's moral mentor. He, therefore, is the guardian of their sexual development during childhood, a matter of special importance for the daughter. [4] For a woman to be able to enter licitly and securely upon the adult sexual role required of her in the conjugal relationship, she must be free to give up her childish sexual role and the dependent relationship to her father implied in it. This is essential for her movement from filial to conjugal status to be properly accomplished. But it can be brought about only with the consent and goodwill of her father. This is formally documented in the prestations which dramatize the investiture of her husband with his conjugal sexual rights. It is valuable to have this aspect of the patrifilial relationship brought to our attention in the setting of a matrilineal family structure and shown to be most conspicuously evinced in the transactions of marriage. The father's control over his daughter's sexual and procreative capacities in patrilineal family systems has frequently been described. But Mrs Robinson's study prompts the suspicion that we are still far from a satisfactory theoretical understanding of what lies behind these practices. We need to know much more about the feature that is descriptively complementary, in the patrilineal setting, to the matrilineal father's role in his child's marriage—I mean the mother's brother's role. It is curious and surely significant that mother's brothers often have a jurally effective voice in the marriage of a sister's child in patrilineal systems, this being symbolized, as usual, in their share of the marriage prestations, both as donors and as recipients.

These comments do not exhaust the theoretical problems that arise in the essays of my co-authors. They are intended merely to show that doubts about the possibility of adding anything new to the theoretical analysis of marriage in tribal society are wholly unfounded. In spite of their self-imposed limits, the authors of the essays all pose new problems and suggest fruitful hypotheses for further research. It would be most interesting to see what general principles someone skilled in the modern Theory of Games could elicit from such data as have here been presented. It would also, I believe, well repay the effort, if someone were to undertake a more rigorous analysis than has yet been attempted of the correspondences between the values at stake, the prestations required, and the claims and rights created and transferred in marriage. Enough is known to justify the conclusion that these correspondences are minute and particular, not gross and general, and that the prestations discriminate jurally, and often ritually as well, between the critical and irreducible elements of marital status and the contingent elements.

NOTES

[1] Cf. Dumont, p. 27, 'The opposition between kin and affines takes on a spatial aspect; there are kin places and affinal places....'

[2] Cf. the well-known African maxim that the bride-price must not be where the bride is.

[3] The apparent inconsistency between these quasi-endogamous tendencies and the scale of social mobility in western society has received much attention in various countries. It seems that the findings are open to divergent interpretations. I refrain from discussing this question any further as it is only of marginal relevance to my purpose. It is authoritatively dealt with in Lipset and Bendix, 1959, ch. II.

[4] We should recall, in this connexion, the contrast Malinowski frequently emphasized between a brother's strict exclusion from concern with his sister's sexual life and a father's permitted interest in her love affairs and marriage, among the Trobrianders.

CONJUGAL SEPARATION AND DIVORCE AMONG THE GONJA OF NORTHERN GHANA[1]

By ESTHER N. GOODY

In analysing the manner in which Gonja marriages are ended, and the frequency with which this occurs, my main concern is to distinguish the *pattern* of divorce which characterizes this society and to trace the ways in which this is related to other features of the social system. Specifically I shall deal with such problems as: who initiates divorce, at what point in a woman's life divorce is most likely to occur, the reallocation of rights and obligations which follows and to some extent defines divorce, the alternative roles which are available to adult women, and the spatial correlates of divorce. In conclusion it is suggested that to assume that divorce is necessarily a 'social evil' or 'an index of a state of anomie' may obscure the fact that in some societies marriage is in practice relevant only for a given stage of the life of one or both partners, and not an indissoluble bond 'till death do them part'.

The Gonja state, a loose federation of largely autonomous Divisions, lies just north of the limits of the old Ashanti kingdom and extends across the entire breadth of the northern region of Ghana. The population of 84,415 is distributed over an area of 14,469 square miles in a density ranging from four to nine persons per square mile. [2] The open stretches of orchard bush are occasionally relieved by stream beds lined with dense vegetation and, around the major rivers, the Black Volta along the western boundary, the White Volta which flows through the centre of the state, and the Volta proper which forms a part of the southern border, hills covered with forest growth appear.

The Gonja live in scattered compact villages of from sixty to several hundred people, many of which are situated along the old North–South trade routes over which passed the gold and kola nuts from the south that had been exchanged at the borders of the forest country for slaves, cattle and salt of the desert and the tsetse-free northern plains. The villages are situated from five to fifteen miles apart, although a few are even further from their nearest neighbour, while around the Divisional capitals several villages may cluster within a 10 to 15 mile radius. Land around these permanent villages is not 'owned', for there is sufficient for all to farm. The system is one of 4 years' cultivation followed by a long and indefinite period of fallow. The staple crops are yams, millet, guinea corn, maize and cassava. Cattle are kept in small numbers where tsetse allow, and adult men generally own a few sheep, goats and chickens.

14

SEPARATION AND DIVORCE AMONG THE GONJA

Gonja traditions place the origin of the state in the seventeenth century, when a band of Mande horsemen and their Muslim advisers conquered the several groups of indigenous agriculturalists and settled down to live among them. The different territorial segments of the state, or Divisions, were apportioned out among the sons of the founder, NdeWura Jakpa. The descendants of these Divisional chiefs continue to share among them authority over the villages of the original Division, the office rotating among the two, three or four segments of the ruling family. Several of the Divisions supply in turn, in the same fashion, the paramount chief of the Gonja state, the YagbumWura.

The Ruling group, the Ngbanya, descendants of the conquering Mande, make up one of the three social estates into which the population of Gonja is divided. The Muslim estate is the smallest of these, although it consists of several patronymic groups which tend to be localized in or near the Divisional capitals. Muslim office-holders act as religious advisers to Divisional chiefs and to the paramount, and have formal duties in the enrobing of chiefs and in the annual Damba ceremony at which the political constitution of the Division is acted out and reaffirmed.

The third social estate is made up of several Commoner groups with differing cultural and linguistic affinities. There are Commoner groups who speak dialects of the Mossi, Grusi, Gurma and Senufo subgroups of the Gur languages while others speak, as do the Ngbanya and many of the Muslims, dialects of the Guang subgroup of the Kwa languages. All members of the Ruling estate speak a single Guang dialect, Ngbanyito, but those whose Divisions contain Commoners speaking other languages or dialects are bi- or tri-lingual. These Commoners appear to have had acephalous political systems; their office-holders today are Earth priests (*tindaana*) and shrine priests (*kagbirwura*).

Although Commoners and Rulers are pagans, except for a few converts to Islam in the larger towns, Muslim elders are often called in to officiate at life crisis ceremonies. This is not held to be vital for the efficacy of the ceremony, but is thought to give added merit to the occasion. A member of the Ruling group who has been brought up in the ways of Islam (*e bu bori*—'he prays to God') must give up public observances on taking office. The authority of religious and political leaders is conceived to be of a separate and complementary nature, and neither may usurp the power of the other.

As this suggests, the Gonja political system is far from being a despotic one. In addition to the Muslim offices, and to the minor Ngbanya chiefships, there are positions in each Division held by Commoners. Vested in certain Commoner kin groups are offices pertaining to the Earth or to powerful shrines. Other Commoners hold office through maternal filiation to the Ruling group. These Sister's-Son chiefs cannot succeed to the Divisional chiefship, nor pass on their positions to their sons, for membership in each of the social estates

15

is based on agnatic kinship. A man belongs to the estate of his father. Yet a Sister's-Son chiefship may carry with it considerable power. Some villages are traditionally placed under a Sister's-Son chief, and often a Divisional chief will take as his closest adviser and confidant a man who holds one of these chiefships. For such a man has been given office as a personal mark of favour, not, as with members of the Ruling estate, as a matter of birthright. And further, this office is terminal; there can be no promotion and a Sister's-Son chief has nothing to gain from participating in court intrigue, while for a member of the Ruling estate a minor chiefship is but the first step on a ladder which may one day lead to the paramountcy.

While estate membership, and thus succession to most offices, is determined by agnatic filiation, those who share rights in the same office do not otherwise form a corporate descent group. They are unlikely to reside together, property does not necessarily pass between them, and jural authority is vested not in the senior member of a group of agnatic kinsmen, but partly in the head of the compound in which a man is living and partly in the eldest of his father's classificatory siblings, [3] who may be a maternal, or paternal half sibling, or a cross or parallel cousin of the father. Further, considerable ritual authority and some rights to property are vested in maternal kin. Thus while agnatic descent is important in determining rights to office, for other purposes the full range of an individual's kinsfolk are significant. I have considered the system to be bilateral or cognatic. Neither in terminology nor behaviour are there recognized limits to the extension of cognatic kinship ties. Where time and distance have rendered connexions unknown, and distant kinsmen strangers, kinship, except in a vague residual sense, lapses.

Marriage is the normal state for all adults in Gonja society during the active middle years of life. Polygygny is permitted but not widely practised. Out of a total of 197 adult males of two central Gonja villages, [4] 13% were unmarried, 69% had one wife, and 18% had two or more wives.

There are no restrictions placed on the intermarriage of members of any of the three estates and a consideration of current marriages in the village of Buipe, where all three estates are substantially represented, indicates that marriages between estates frequently occur (Table 1).

Table 1. *Married women in each estate with husband of Ruling, Commoner and Muslim estates*

Wife's estate	Husband's estate			Total	
	Ruling	Commoner	Muslim		
Ruling	1 (10%)	5 (45%)	5 (45%)	11 (100%)	
Commoner	8 (24%)	12 (35%)	14 (41%)	34 (100%)	
Muslim	4 (20%)	6 (30%)	10 (50%)	20 (100%)	
Total	13	23	29	65	

Nor are there either formal or actual territorial restrictions on marriage. In a group of thirty-five men whose fathers were born in Buipe, about one-quarter had married women whose fathers were also from Buipe;[5] another quarter had taken wives whose fathers came from other villages in Buipe Division, while the remaining half had married women whose paternal villages lay in other Gonja Divisions (see Table 2).

Table 2. *Marriages of 35 men whose fathers were born in Buipe, by residence of wife's father and distance of wife's father's village from Buipe*

	Wife's father from			
	Buipe	Other villages in Buipe Division	Other Divisions	Total
Number	9	9	17	35
Percentage	26	26	48	100
Average distance from Buipe in miles	0	14·7	43	

While there are variations in the ceremonies typical of each estate, in central Gonja there are several features common to all. In all cases it is the transfer by the groom's representative to the father or guardian of the bride of twelve shillings[6] and twelve kola nuts which formally legalizes the union. No more substantial payments of bridewealth or dowry change hands, although gifts from a man to his sweetheart are an important part of courting. A man is also expected to make occasional presents of grain, meat, palm wine, and small sums of money to the bride's family during the courting period and in the case of an important chief or elder these may be worth, in all, several pounds. Such gifts are necessary to win consent to the match but not to make it legitimate. Courting gifts have no bearing on the legitimacy of children, and are not reclaimable on divorce.

At marriage a woman goes to join her husband in whichever compound he may be living. As a man may be resident with either maternal or paternal kin this cannot be characterized as patrilocal marriage; the term virilocal is more appropriate. The Gonja do not recognize the sororate, and, indeed, prohibit a man from marrying two sisters or first cousins. So strong is the feeling that no man should marry twice into the same kindred (save possibly his own) that I have known a youth to be dissuaded from marrying the daughter of a woman who had briefly been the wife of a paternal uncle, although there was no issue of that union. This prohibition on marrying twice into the same kindred continues after the death of the original spouse. Thus there is no form of levirate or widow inheritance, and on the death of her husband a woman of marriageable age returns, after a suitable period of mourning, to her natal kin. In fact, elderly widows also make this move, a practice which has important implications for Gonja divorce. It is true that Muslims speak of inheriting the wife of an elder patrilateral parallel cousin, but only one instance of this was recorded. With this single exception, rights over women may be said to be completely individualized.

The rights over women which are transferred at marriage are essentially rights to services, economic, domestic, ritual and sexual. Each married woman is allotted a plot in her husband's farm in which to plant the beans, okra and peppers which are her responsibility. In addition she is expected to contribute labour at certain times in the agricultural cycle. But men are the farmers; women help but do not farm. Their main concern is with the care of husband, children and the compound, and the daily round is occupied by trips for firewood and water, or to the farm to fetch produce or condiments, the washing of clothes and the preparation of food.

All important ritual offices and positions are held by men. Mallams and Limams, tindaanas and shrine priests act as representatives of the community with respect to supernatural forces of various sorts. However, in the sphere of domestic ritual, while men still occupy the central roles as heads of compound and kin groups, women also have a place. This is due to the fact that most domestic rituals and *rites de passage* include as a central rite the preparation and sharing of a sacramental meal. Both preparation and distribution of these meals are left to women, and it is often a wife who is specified as the proper person to direct operations. To the extent that domestic rituals focus on the preparation and sharing of food, the wife's domestic services become ritual services.

Rights *in uxorem* among the Gonja consist, then, of economic, domestic, ritual and sexual services. With regard to the latter, a husband has prescriptive rights in his wife's sexuality while they are living together, and may claim a fine, [7] and administer a beating to an adulterer caught *in flagrante delicto*. Erring wives, although they may be beaten by an irate husband before the neighbours can stop him, are not legally subject to physical chastisement or monetary fine. Adultery, unless it is recurrent and ostentatious, is seldom the sole cause of divorce.

Rights *in genetricem* in Gonja are extremely complex and can only be roughly summarized here. Briefly, they are coextensive with ties of biological consanguinity and are never defined by socio-legal fictions. Thus the *pater* is always the *genitor*, whether the child is born before his mother's marriage, of an adulterous union, or in wedlock. By *pater* here is meant the man from whom a child traces his paternity and thus his relationship with paternal ancestors, derives his position in the community with respect to territorial and political (estate) affiliation, from whom, and through whom he has the right to claim support in litigation, medicine in time of sickness, and food in time of hunger, and through whom he has rights of inheritance in masculine property. [8] This is not to say that a child is necessarily reared by his *pater*. Indeed, in Gonja this is frequently not the case, for two sorts of reasons. On the one hand, children may be reared by their mother's husband although he has no rights in them and they none in him, because of the latter's tie with their mother. Conversely, kinsmen of either parent, in whom reciprocal rights *are* vested, frequently act as foster parents. Thus it is not the distinction between *pater* and *genitor* which is important for understanding individual life histories as well as Gonja social structure, but rather that between the *pater-genitor* as parent, and a kinsman, or occasionally a step-father, as foster parent. That is, the individual who acts as the socializing agent must be identified and, where necessary, distinguished from the *pater-genitor*. [9] In Gonja one must inquire not only 'Who bore you?' (*wane kurwe fo?*) but also 'Who reared you?' (*wane belo fo?*). [10]

Rights *in genetricem* are tied to biological parenthood, but they are to some extent shared by the siblings, parents, and parents' siblings of the biological father and mother. Rights of this latter sort may be termed derived rights, and although latent for most children for most of the time, they are made explicit in the institution of fostering. [11] In the village of Buipe at the time the census was made, approximately 18% of the children of suitable age were living with foster parents. About half of these were girls and half boys.

At marriage the Gonja husband acquires exclusive rights over his wife's sexuality. This makes it highly likely that she will bear children of whom he is the biological father. In this sense a husband obtains rights *in genetricem* through marriage. He cannot, however, be accepted as *pater* of any child of his wife's known to have been begotten by another. This rule is often phrased in terms of the importance of restricting succession to office to direct descendants in the male line. Its observance is ensured by strong supernatural sanctions, for it is a man's own immediate ancestors, both paternal and maternal, to whom he turns for help in crises. Since the ancestors are not only uninterested in, but powerless over, mortals to whom they are not related, it is held to be useless to seek assistance from a dead step-father who is not a kinsman. The situation is rendered more complex, and more compelling, by Gonja beliefs about the way the ancestors behave. These hold that a man who has offended them may be punished through his children or those of his collaterals. Thus when a person suffers misfortune or falls ill it may be due to sins of his kin rather than to anything he has done or omitted to do. The relevance of this for true declaration of paternity lies in the fact that most children are ill at one time or another, and if a man or his wife should be trying to pass a child off as the husband's when this is not so, danger to the child tends to be interpreted as an expression of the anger, direct or indirect, of the true paternal ancestors. These must then be acknowledged, and in the case of a minor, the father or a paternal kinsman found to approach them on the sick person's behalf.

It is thus in a very limited sense that rights *in genetricem* may be said to be transferred at marriage. Strictly speaking, it is the right to beget children, and to restrain other men from doing so, which marriage conveys to the husband. But physiological paternity alone can convey rights over the children themselves. This being so, it is not surprising to find that the Gonja recognize no circumstances under which one man may be deputed to beget children for another. The suggestion that this did occur among certain peoples was met not so much by disbelief as with a lack of understanding. This view is perhaps related to the fact that the Gonja hold that it is the man who places a child in the mother's womb for warmth and protection during the early stages of growth—the woman nourishes it, but does not contribute to the actual formation of the foetus.

It has seemed important to go into such detail about rights *in genetricem* in part because it has been suggested that marriage could be defined in terms of the admission of children to 'full birth-status rights' in their society (Gough 1959). It is difficult to see how the Gonja child born out of wedlock suffers a limitation of his 'birth-status rights' in his society, excepting in so far as he is liable to be taunted by his peers. [12] As I have indicated, rights normally derived through the father are granted such a child if his father is known and will acknowledge him. Rights derived through the mother are in any case not affected. [13]

Yet it would be totally incorrect to suggest that the Gonja do not recognize marriage. Lovers who are not married according to the traditional rites are referred to as *jipo*, as are a courting couple who have set up housekeeping together for a trial period. Between *jipo* no rights may be said to obtain; for example, there is no right of compensation for the woman's adultery. Claims based on the rights which vest in marital partnership may be informally pressed. A man may question his lover about an extended trip to the bush latrine, or complain because the soup is tasteless. But he cannot appeal to her kinsfolk to intervene on his behalf and any show of force or anger would quickly end the union. Further, domestic arrangements based on the *jipo* relationship are, and are seen as being, temporary. Once a couple who are *jipo* has settled down together in the sexual and domestic relationships which are also the basis of marriage and of the household, marriage rites tend to be celebrated within a few months. For marriage itself may be so easily ended that there is no advantage in failing to regularize the union. The three cases of trial domestic establishments which I actually observed all involved men and women in their late twenties or thirties; the women in each instance had with them young children of previous marriages. In two cases the couple later married. I left the village before the last pair had reached a final decision.

SEPARATION AND DIVORCE AMONG THE GONJA

There is an additional reason for considering at such length the type of rights transferred at marriage. This has to do with the definition of divorce as it operates in this society. For basically it is the withdrawal of marital rights which constitutes effective divorce. In Gonja rights acquired at marriage are essentially rights to specific services. There are no rights of any substance which either spouse holds over the other when they are separated, for services inevitably tend to lapse. Thus marriage is closely bound up with co-residence and a separation which lasts for any length of time results in the withdrawal of marital rights, which is in fact divorce. In the discussion of divorce procedures and the pattern of divorce which follows, the difficulty in distinguishing between divorce and separation is treated at some length. Before turning to this problem, however, I want first to consider some data on the frequency of divorce in central Gonja. For the incidence of divorce, and specifically what might be called patterns of divorce, are the main concern of this paper. Pattern is here used to refer to the fact that there are features of Gonja divorce which tend to vary together. It would be possible to isolate different 'types' of divorce from the same material. Such an approach would, however, fail to give adequate emphasis to the inter-relatedness of the factors involved. Specifically, by pattern is meant: (1) the time at which a divorce occurs, here the point in a woman's life, and not the stage of a marriage; (2) the manner of bringing about the dissolution of marriage; (3) the role which the woman adopts as an alternative to that of wife in the previous union; and finally, (4) the consequences for those involved, and on a different level, for the society as a whole, of the ending of one set of relationships and the replacing of these by a different set.

The first factor, and the one which most nearly approximates an independent variable, has to do with the time at which divorce occurs. As Fortes notes in his discussion of the stability of Tallensi marriage (1949a: 84–7), early marriages uncomplicated by the birth of children may be lightly treated as experimental where later, fruitful unions have a greater tendency to be stable. For an understanding of the Gonja situation it is important to distinguish not only between a high rate of early divorce and a consistently high divorce rate, but also between frequent divorce during the years of active child-bearing on the one hand and a high rate of divorce in old age on the other. [14]

I take as a unit of reference here the life span of a woman rather than using stages in a marriage, because a consideration of the former seems to throw more light on the significant variables. I am thus concerned with the effects of the dissolution of marriage during the early phase of a woman's marital career before she bears children, or when she has but one or two very young children, as compared with the correlates of divorce during the middle, child-rearing phase, and again with those of the last, post-menopause phase when her children are adolescent or adult and when child-bearing and sexuality are no longer primary considerations. For Gonja marriages are ended easily and frequently in each of these phases, but with quite different consequence for the actors and for the social structure within which they operate.

Dissolution of marriage may come about through formal divorce, elopement, separation, or death of husband. The last of these becomes, of course, increasingly likely as a woman grows older, and its consequences vary depending on the wife's age and the ages of her children when she is widowed. Among the three remaining possibilities, those among which the actors have a measure of choice, there is also some variation with the wife's age. Formal divorce is in any case rare and I have too few instances to indicate a trend. Elopement is also infrequently resorted to, but in the nature of the situation is limited to the early and middle periods of a woman's adult life. Women past the age of 50 seldom if ever remarry in any case and are thus unlikely to take this method of ending an unwelcome union. Elopement is more often resorted to by the adolescents who in this way seek to escape the matches arranged for them by parents or guardians. For older women, parental and fraternal authority are not determining factors and the more usual practice of the wife returning to her natal home and remarrying from there is not likely to be frustrated by intercession of her kinsfolk on the husband's behalf. The most common form, gradual transformation of an extended separation into a *de facto* divorce, may occur at any time in a woman's life and is frequently resorted to as old age approaches.

When a young or middle-aged woman leaves a husband, it is almost without exception to marry again within at most a year or two. Thus one husband is substituted for another and the role of wife although interrupted is not abandoned. This is underlined by the fact that there is a marked tendency for women to bear children to each man to whom they are married (Table 8, p. 27). As women reach late middle age the likelihood of a divorce or separation being followed by remarriage decreases until, in a sample of 91 adult women, of the 19 who were over the age of 50, only four were married (Table 9, p. 37). Where widowhood, divorce, or conjugal separation are not followed by remarriage, a woman no longer engages in those tasks and activities, domestic, sexual and reproductive, which are associated with the role of wife. Specifically, she no longer lives with a husband, but rather with kinsfolk. Among the Gonja such a woman is said to be resident as sister, or very occasionally a father's or mother's sister. The implication of this change of roles will be discussed in detail below.

The last of the factors to be influenced by the time at which a divorce occurs has to do with the nature of the relationships derived from the marriage, and by extension, with the consequences of the marriage and the divorce for the social structure itself. Frequent divorce during the early years of marriage, particularly before the birth of children, is consistent with high overall jural and conjugal stability of marriage. Divorce in this phase of a woman's life approximates to 'experimental marriage' in that there are no lasting consequences to either partner. Where stable marriage is the general rule, a woman may subsequently settle into a lasting union as easily as though it were her first. The importance of distinguishing a pattern of easy early divorce from frequent dissolution of marriage during the middle years of active child-bearing lies in the different sorts of sibling ties which arise as a consequence. For where, as in Gonja, many women have children by each of two or three successive and unrelated husbands, dispersed groups of maternal half-siblings are common. A further important feature is the fact that once children have been born, the dissolution of a conjugal union can no longer terminate all relationship, for the couple is permanently united through parenthood, through their claims on and obligations towards their children.

The regular dissolution of marriage when the wife reaches old age has yet other correlates. Since at this point divorce is not apt to be followed by remarriage, no new maternal siblings will be added to the existing group. For an elderly woman the alternative to remarriage is residence as a sister. This leads to the drawing together in old age of sibling groups whose members have been scattered and forces their children to recognize the separate identity of each parent and his or her respective siblings.

In the sections which follow, I shall discuss first some measures of the frequency of divorce and remarriage. Next I shall consider the various ways in which marriage may be ended. The next section deals with divorce in old age, which is discussed in considerable detail as it constitutes one of the distinguishing features of Gonja social organization. Finally I shall consider briefly the implications of the Gonja pattern of divorce for the wider social system.

It is today widely accepted that no discussion of divorce should be presented apart from adequate data on the incidence of divorce (see Barnes, 1949). If this is generally true, it is that much more important where, as in the present case, an attempt is made to relate patterns of divorce to other characteristics of the society. However the data at my disposal are limited in both quantity and detail. In presenting this material I have broken it down into categories based on age, estate membership, etc. in order to illustrate where possible trends and tendencies even though the numbers are too small for proper statistical treatment. I have done this because it appeared that some documentation was better than bare unsupported generalizations, and not because I thought that the numerical material was, by itself, adequate to prove the argument. Because this is so, and because the figures are small enough to require the use of correction factors in every case, and in several too small even for this, no attempt has been made to apply tests of significance. In any case those I would have used require assumptions about the randomness of the sample which are not warranted here.

The material on marital status and residence of elderly women presented later in this chapter is derived from a complete count of the village of Buipe, which has a population of 350. However, it proved impossible to use census data for information on the divorce rate because the accurate information necessary for this more complex inquiry cannot be elicited on superficial contact. The censuses were conducted on a single day so that the replies to the question 'who slept in this room last night?' would have a uniform meaning and not be complicated by the coming and going of visitors and the regular shifts of co-wives. It has repeatedly been my experience that the number of husbands a woman admits increases directly with the rapport of the observer's relationship with her. Thus, one of the women I knew best toward the end of my time in the field had told me at length of her various marriages, where they took her and how they came to be dissolved. Yet quite by accident I learned from someone else that she had been married for about two years to still another man. It is true that she had her reasons for not wishing to remember this marriage, but she is unlikely to be unique in this.

The following tables are based on records made on all the Busunu women who came to us seeking medicine. [15] The fact that they had sought us out and wanted something from us made them more patient with detailed questioning than where the reverse was the case. Some comments are in order, however, as to the nature of the sample. Only women of 18 and above are included and more than half of these are 30 years of age or under. This does not represent the distribution of this age group in the population as a whole. There are two reasons for this imbalance. In the first place it was our experience in all three villages studied that people were more eager to seek medicine for young children than for themselves. Women under 30 are somewhat more likely to have young children than are older women. Secondly, young adults were, not surprisingly, less suspicious of Europeans and their ways, and came to us more frequently than did their elders. There are obvious disadvantages in basing an analysis of divorce on a sample heavily weighted in favour of young women. However, enough older women are included to show clearly that trends continue through a woman's life. And in any case I feel the disadvantages are more than balanced by the fact that fairly detailed information is here available on 55 women not arbitrarily selected. There were no Muslims in the sample, since there were few in Busunu.

Table 3. *Women in each estate and in total sample who have had one and more than one husband*

Estate	One husband		Two or more husbands		Total	
Ruling	9	(64%)	5	(36%)	14	(100%)
Commoner	27*	(66%)	14	(34%)	41	(100%)
All	36*	(65%)	19	(35%)	55	(100%)

* Figure includes two women divorced and not yet remarried.

Information on the marital histories of 55 Busunu women is summarized in Tables 3 to 8. Considering first in Table 3 women of all ages by estate, it appears that there is no important difference in the proportion of women in each estate who have remarried. About one-third in each group have had more than one husband.

Table 4 indicates that, as would be expected, there is a direct relationship between age and proportion of the women in the population who have remarried. While less than one-third of the women 30 or under had remarried, half of those over 40 had done so.

Table 4. *Women in total sample in each age group who have had one and more than one husband*

Age (years)	One husband	Two or more husbands	Total
–31	23* (70%)	10 (30%)	33* (100%)
31–40	9 (64%)	5 (36%)	14 (100%)
41–	4 (50%)	4 (50%)	8 (100%)
All ages	36	19	55

* Figure includes two women divorced and not yet remarried.

Table 5 compares women of the Commoner and Ruling estates as to the number of husbands for each age group.

Table 5. *Number of husbands of 55 Busunu women by estate and age of wife*

	Estate						
	Ruling		Commoner		All		
Age (years)	1 husband	2 or more husbands	1 husband	2 or more husbands	1 husband	2 or more husbands	Total
–30	5	1	18*	9	23*	10	33*
31–40	3	2	6	3	9	5	14
41–	1	2	3	2	4	4	8
All ages	9	5	27*	14	36*	19	55
	14		41		55		

* Figure includes two women divorced but not yet remarried.

Of the 41 Commoner women between the ages of 18 and 60, 14 or 34% have been remarried at least once. Two more are currently separated and not yet remarried, but as both were under 30 and not infirm, remarriage for them is but a matter of time. Of the 14 who have remarried, 12 have had two husbands and two three husbands. Of the 14 women of the Ruling estate between the ages of 18 and 60, five or 36% have been remarried at least once, two have had two husbands, two three husbands and one four. Inspection of this table suggests that the likelihood that older women will have remarried more frequently is more pronounced for women of the Ruling estate than for Commoner women. The figures here are too small to warrant the reckoning of percentages, but the fact that women of the Ruling estate who have remarried had, in all, more husbands than Commoner women supports this conclusion. The Gonja themselves say that women of the Ruling estate are more apt than others to have a succession of husbands.

Tables 3 to 5 have considered frequency of remarriage, whether this was occasioned by death or divorce. Information as to how each marriage was dissolved is available for only some of the women and numbers are too small for detailed analysis within age categories. Tables 6 and 7 contain the available data.

Table 6. *Manner of dissolution of marriage*

Number of husbands and how marriages ended

| Estate | 2 husbands | | 3 husbands | | 4 husbands: 2 death, 2 divorce | 2 and 3 husbands: NA how separated | Total |
	death	divorce	1 death 1 divorce	2 divorce			
Ruling	1	1	.	.	1	2	5
Commoner	4	3	1	1	.	5	14
Total	5	4	1	1	1	7	19

Table 6 is based on the 19 women in the sample who had remarried at least once. The 12 for whom there is information are grouped by estate and the number of remarriages. There is no apparent difference in the pattern observable for women of the two estates. It is worth noting, however, that multiple remarriages are not necessarily the outcome of a series of divorces. It is impossible to make a general statement on the basis of such low numbers, but observation bears out what the figures at least suggest. That is, that apart from the differences associated with estate membership, women do not fall into two clear groups, one of which tends to form stable unions and the other of which is divorce prone. Table 7 considers the seventeen broken marriages recorded in Table 6 by the cause of their dissolution and whether the wife belonged to the Ruling or Commoner estate. Nine, or slightly over half of the marriages, were dissolved by divorce. And again there is no apparent difference for the women of the two estates.

Table 7. *Relationship between estate and manner of dissolution of marriage*

| Manner of dissolution of marriage | Estate membership | | |
	Ruling	Commoner	Both
Death	3	5	8
Divorce	3	6	9
Total	6	11	17

The last table in this group, Table 8, deals with a problem which is important both for the analysis of the significance of remarriage and for the interpretation of the tables themselves. In this table, the number of husbands reported by the women in the Busunu sample is compared with the number of husbands to whom they have borne children. There is an incidental finding here worth commenting on. One suggested cause of divorce (Fortes 1949a: 87) is barrenness. Of the nineteen women who had remarried, only three had never borne children. Of these, one had been twice widowed and two once divorced. The latter number represents only about one-tenth of those who have remarried and I think it may be said that although barrenness is a contributing factor, it is not among the primary causes of divorce in Gonja.

Table 8. *Number of husbands to whom each woman has borne children and reported number of husbands*

Number of husbands to whom living children borne	Reported number of husbands					
	One	One divorced	Two	Three	Four	Total
0	1	.	2	1	.	4
1	32	2	2	1	.	37
2	.	.	9	.	1	10
3	.	.	.	2	.	2
Information incomplete	1	.	1	.	.	2
Total	34	2	14	4	1	55

The essential fact which emerges from this table is the correspondence between the number of husbands women have and the number to whom they bear children. And here it is important to remember that the sample is heavily biased in favour of young women whose child-bearing careers are incomplete. Some who have not yet borne children to their present husbands may still do so, and some will marry and bear children to future husbands. If we consider all the women in the sample for whom we have information on children born of each marriage, we see that 45 out of 53, or 85%, have borne children to each husband. If instead we consider only those women (on whom information is available) who have been married at least twice and who have ever borne children, we find that 11 out of 15, or about three-quarters have borne children to every husband married.

This has two important implications. In the first place, it is possible that women are more apt to report marriages in which they have borne children and this is indeed borne out by attempts to obtain detailed marital histories. In some cases additional, childless, marriages were mentioned in later interviews. To the extent that this is the case, the actual frequency of remarriage is higher than indicated by the data here reported. At the same time this would mean that the figure of 61% [16] of all successive marriages as fertile is too high. This is probably correct. Even so, the figure is high enough to have important implications for the composition of sibling groups. For of the 55 women in the sample, 12, or 22%, have had children by more than one husband. If we take the figure of 50% for the frequency of re-marriage of women over 40 (see Table 4), then assuming that the proportion of fertile marriages to all marriages remains the same we find that 30% of all women over 40 may be expected to have borne children by more than one husband. While it is true that fertility declines with age, it is also the case that women do not remarry once they are past childbearing. The assumption is only partially warranted and the 'true' proportion of women bearing children to more than one husband probably lies somewhere between 22 and 30%.

Ties of siblingship are of great importance to members of all three estates, and of these, the ties between children of the same mother are undoubtedly the closest after those linking full siblings. This is so in Gonja in spite of the fact that fathers of maternal half-siblings are necessarily unrelated and may live in widely separated villages. It is a characteristic of a woman's successive marriages in Gonja that children tend to be born of each marriage; this was so in 61% of the cases in the Busunu sample.

Briefly, then, Gonja women of the Ruling and Commoner estates, and observation suggests those of the Muslim estate as well, tend to leave their husbands relatively frequently. They do so not only as young women but throughout their lives, and both before and after they have borne children of a marriage. In fact there is a tendency for women to bear children in each of two or more successive unions.

It has been suggested that certain variables may be found to be related to the time, the point in a woman's life, when divorce occurs, and thus that a divorce rate should be time-specific. To recapitulate, these variables are: (1) the manner of dissolution of a marriage; (2) the alternative roles adopted by the ex-wife; and (3) the consequences, both for those immediately concerned, and for the social structure as a whole.

On the basis of Table 4 it appears that about half of the women over 40 have had two or more husbands, and Table 7 indicates that for women of both Commoner and Ruling estates about one half of those who remarry do so after a divorce and the others following the death of the previous husband. Thus it may be said that roughly one quarter of the women over 40 have been divorced and remarried at least once. Of the three ways in which marriages may be ended, formal divorce, elopement and conjugal separation, by far the greater number are terminated by the latter. For while there is a notion of formal divorce, this is seldom resorted to, and then almost always by the husband. Divorce in this sense is brought about by the simple statement, 'I refuse you, you are no longer my wife' (*N'kine fo, lelingeri m'etche mina la fo*). Alternatively, if a man is very angry he may break the large water pot which stands at the back of his wife's room. It is said that when this is done, reconciliation is impossible.

The formula of renunciation resembles the traditional Islamic means of bringing about a divorce (Trimingham 1959), but although this may have been its origin the similarity is but superficial. There is no notion of repeating the refusal more than once, a triple declaration is no more or less binding than a single utterance, and it is always subject to negotiation; for women are as free to refuse their husbands as are men their wives, and no Muslim official is concerned in the proceedings at any point. While it is often said of a couple who have separated 'he refused her' or 'she refused him', this usually turns out to be the equivalent of 'she left him', or 'he threw her out'. The latter is very rare. Men seldom actually tell their wives to go, although through surliness, neglect or the open favouring of a co-wife they may just as effectively drive them to leave.

Where these usages are followed it is meaningful to speak of divorce and remarriage. But remarriage may occur by elopement without any form of intervening divorce. Elopement, in the sense of going without ceremony from parents' or husband's house to a domestic and sexual union with a man thereafter called 'husband' (*n'kul*), is rare. In such a case the marriage kola nuts are sent to the wife's kin, but not until after the household has been established. Elopement is occasionally resorted to by a young couple whose parents have other plans for them. Such a pair may find it expedient to settle in a distant village for a few years until their parents grow accustomed to the match. This was the course adopted by Mahama and his bride, and when they returned home after 18 months their kin were so pleased to see them that they helped to build the young wife a room and installed her there with full ceremony. Occasionally a mature woman will simply leave the bed and household of her husband and settle down with a different man. Legal action does not appear to be sought in either kind of elopement, although the latter type is held to be highly improper [17] and the new husband renders himself liable to retribution by sorcery.

The third method of ending marriage, conjugal separation, is the most common of all, barring death. Since marriage is virilocal, separation must be initiated by the departure of the wife. She may leave in a huff after a domestic squabble, or she may simply go for a routine visit to kinsfolk. When such an absence is prolonged until either the husband has ceased to beg for her return, or she gives up waiting for him to send for her, the marriage is effectively at an end. In neither case is a formal renunciation necessarily involved. If the woman is not yet past the menopause the most common indication of the conclusion of the period of conjugal separation is her marriage to another man. For an older woman there is no end to this period, and the separation becomes terminal, that is final. The following two cases are typical of many, many others.

Ndembu, the 30-year-old Commoner, wife of Lansa, a member of the Busunu Ruling estate, had for several weeks been restive and casual in the performance of her wifely tasks and when her husband finally beat her for refusing to heat his bath water, she took their 18-month-old child and went to her father in the nearby village of Etcheboinyang. 'Her father is an old man and irritable', Lansa said, 'and if I go there and beg her to return he will abuse me. Besides, she ran there once before and I had a difficult time getting her to come back. This time I will leave it.'

The story of Miama of Buipe illustrates other factors in this situation. She was, when I knew her, an elderly woman of 65, but in describing her early life she told me how she had gone with her father to a village near Bole when he was appointed Limam there. From there she married the chief of a neighbouring village and bore him two children. When later she returned to Buipe for her father's funeral her husband failed to send someone to accompany her back to his village. Her people prevailed upon her finally not to think any more of him but to marry a local man, which she did, going to live with him in Morno a few miles away. After the birth of her daughter there, she came, as is the custom, to her maternal home for several months and never returned to her husband. When the child reached the age of seven her father came for her, but the girl visits her mother from time to time.

Miama could have returned to her first husband without being sent for if she had really been eager to do so. Similarly, her failure to rejoin her second husband in Morno was a matter of her own preference. In each case she used a visit to her kin as an excuse to initiate a separation which time and later ties and interests finalized. But neither of Miama's marriages, nor that of Ndembu discussed above, could be said to have ended by divorce in the sense of a formal refusal of one spouse by the other.

The prevalence of simple conjugal separation followed by remarriage as a means of ending a marriage suggests that a formal termination of or retransfer of conjugal rights is not of great importance to the Gonja. And it was emphasized in the discussion of rights transferred at marriage that these in any case consisted of rights to services, domestic, ritual and sexual, which depended for the most part on joint residence. Hence physical separation effectively terminates those rights which are most characteristic of marriage. Rights *in genetricem* are in any case confined to those related by blood, and extend through genitor and genetrix to the kinsfolk of each. The fate of the parents' marriage does not affect rights in their children and through them the parents continue to be related even after their marriage is at an end.

The problem of the continued relatedness of divorced persons must be considered in some detail, as it is relevant not only to any definition of divorce, but also to any distinction between the effects of divorce before and after the birth of children. For there is a limited sense in which the marital relationship is never completely dissolved between any two partners.

A previous husband retains no rights whatever *in genetricem*, that is, with respect to future children of his wife. Similarly, his rights to her domestic services lapse entirely with a wife's departure. [18] If she returns to a previous spouse he resumes his rights in her services without ceremony whether or not their separation followed a formal refusal (divorce), or whether the woman has married again in the interim. On the other hand, if she remarries, the new husband enjoys rights to her services equivalent to those held by the first. Sexual rights are even more vaguely defined. There is a sense in which a man's claims on his wife's sexuality persist even after her remarriage. Thus when her husband dies, a woman must undergo a ritual bath in protective medicine (*jobuni*) to safeguard her from the jealousy of his spirit. All of a man's widows do this as a part of the 3-day funeral ceremony. But in addition, any previous wives will be informed of the death, and even those who have since remarried should return to the village where their former husband was living and be ritually bathed.

This persistence of sexual jealousy after the jural dissolution of a marriage is discussed again below. But first there is a curious limitation on the widow's obligation to bathe which merits consideration. This has again to do with the apparent persistence of rights after divorce. For a woman is not held to be fully widowed by the death of a second husband if the first is still living. Although she participates as a widow in the funeral rites she does not in this case bathe in protective medicine. For, I was told, if the first husband is still living, the one who has died can do nothing since he knows he does not 'own' her. That is, although the second had full rights of sexual access, these were seen as rights of 'use' and not of 'ownership'. I was unable to discover any positive correlates of such 'ownership' rights, in that a first husband appears to have no more control over his wife while their marriage endures than does the successor in his turn. It is in fact, I suggest, a matter of recognition of prior claim. As such it is the representation on the supernatural plane of the situation where a deserted husband has no redress if his wife leaves him to return to an earlier spouse. [19]

Indeed, as the rite of bathing the widow in protective medicine suggests, a man's interest in his wife's sexuality persists even beyond the grave. For it is specifically to fear of the sexual jealousy of the ghost that the need for these ritual precautions is ascribed. The bathing, which ought to form a part of the 3-day funeral, should later be repeated before a widow enters into a new union. On this second occasion her prospective husband also seeks the protection of the medicine. While the rite is occasionally omitted from the funeral ceremony it is said to be scrupulously observed prior to the widow's remarriage. Grunshi (a member of the Busunu Ruling estate) and her friends considered that Akua's son was still-born because Akua had never bathed in protective medicine following the death of her husband. And although she had not remarried, but become pregnant by one of a succession of lovers, it was her failure to bathe, and not her unmarried condition which was to blame.

This persistence of sexual jealousy even after a union appears to have been jurally terminated is institutionalized in the rival (*kadata*) relationship. Any two men who have at any time courted, had sexual relations with, or been married to the same woman are rivals, and it is assumed that whenever they meet they will quarrel. Rivals are scrupulously careful never to eat together lest one poison the other, and members of the next generation must never attend a sacrifice to the spirit of a father's rival. The Supini Wuritche of Busunu was, when I knew her, unmarried. Two of her former husbands lived in the village still, and she visited one or the other of them frequently. I was warned, however, that my friendship with both these men would lead to trouble, for they were rivals and each would suspect me of favouring the other in conversations with their former wife.

While a marriage lasts, the husband has exclusive rights over his wife's sexuality and any man who infringes these is liable to an adultery fine. However, I have no record of an adultery fine being awarded except where the offence was committed while the woman was actually living with her husband. This supports the conclusion mentioned above that for the Gonja marriage is inseparable from co-residence. The people themselves do not describe marriage this way. They say that a man who succeeds in getting another's wife to come to him may have to pay a fine to her former husband. The Buipe KagbaapeWura spoke repeatedly of his intention of suing the present husband of his estranged wife, Dongi, and Aboker was vehement in his insistence that he would demand payment from Akua's prospective husband, in spite of the fact that he himself had sent her away. Yet neither threat was carried out during the five months I was in Buipe, and I know of no successful claim of this sort. It seems more probable that such threats are a reflexion of the very vagueness with which rights *in uxorem* are defined. Because a husband has the undisputed right to claim payment if his wife commits adultery while she is living with him, and because a separation may be resolved either by divorce or reconciliation, it is difficult for a man to accept the fact that in leaving his house a wife removes herself from his jurisdiction, and that thereafter her lover is not in fact responsible to him.

In this situation, where although a deserted husband feels that he has been wronged, he can make no successful claim at law, it is not surprising that redress is sought through supernatural agencies. For retaliation against a man who 'steals' one's wife by elopement is said to take the form of causing his illness or death by the use of medicines (*kuderu*). And this is justified by the certainty that no woman would leave her husband suddenly and by stealth unless her head had been turned with medicines. It is partly in order to protect themselves against unscrupulous rivals that men are thought to learn the arts of witchcraft and sorcery (*egba*) which enable them to know the use of medicines for killing and injury. A wronged husband who obtains revenge by these means is held to be within his rights and is not subject to control or retaliation by the community.

The possibility that an estranged wife who has remarried may some day return to her first husband is a real one, and older men particularly speak hopefully of it. Akuro's wife, Nyomba, had left him for a Mossi man some 15 years before, the four young children remaining with their father. When, during my stay in Busunu, she returned to greet her grandfather, Akuro did his best to persuade her to rejoin him. I was told that had she agreed, she would have been fully reinstated and nothing further said of the years between. He talked for days about her ingratitude in refusing, and her lack of maternal affection for her children, who, he said, had grown up as orphans (*kamunibi*) in the absence of their mother. And in Buipe, the elderly KagbaapeWura continued to speak of Dongi as his wife although she had remarried and borne children by another man with whom she was still living. When she was brought to a nearby village by her mother's death he sent a succession of messengers to greet her and finally went himself to beg her to return to him. Her refusal did not finally discourage him and he continued to talk about 'my wife Dongi' as though she were absent on a visit.

Some wives actually do return. Pantu was complaining about his wife leaving him for a man in another village, but when l asked if he would take his rival to court, he explained that he could not very well do so as it was to this man that she had previously been married. Or widowhood may precipitate the reunion. When Hawa's husband died in Busunu, there was speculation as to whether she would now return to her first husband in Langanteri whose children of 7 and 9 she had with her. But he too died before she completed her mourning period and she eventually went to her mother with the children of both marriages.

That there is a sense in which a man's rights in his wife's sexuality persist after divorce is indicated by the fact that all previous wives, even those who have remarried, are considered to be in danger from the jealousy of a husband's ghost. The fact that a former marriage can be resumed without ceremony is a further indication that all ties are not severed at divorce. These persisting, if minimal, rights almost certainly derive from the casual way in which most marriages are ended and the vague manner in which the transfer of marital rights is accomplished.

There are additional links which persist between a divorced couple if there were children of the marriage. Where this is so, an estranged wife, even though she has since remarried, may be called upon to prepare a sacrificial meal for her husband's ancestors if no other wives are available to perform this task. The welfare of her children is involved since ancestors often vent their anger on the offspring of those who have offended them, and no further sanction is necessary to secure her co-operation. That it is necessary from the husband-father's point of view is a function of the ritual significance given to the domestic role of a wife in preparing food. Further, it reflects the fact that once there are children of a marriage, to the roles of husband and wife are added those of father and mother. Whatever is the fate of the conjugal union, the ties of parenthood remain. Thus the husband's ancestors are seen as demanding the presence of the 'mothers' of their descendants, regardless of whether or not they are still 'wives'.

The persistence of the parental roles is also indicated by the fact that both parents and the kin of each continue to have an interest in and claims on the children even after a marriage has been ended. These diffuse claims on children of a marriage and the reciprocal claims of the children on their dispersed kin are expressed in the institution of fostering. Divorce does not nullify these claims. Indeed, it may for reasons of convenience activate those which otherwise would remain latent. A woman going to a new husband may hesitate to take with her all of several young children, yet be reluctant to relinquish her right to the custody of any who are still too young to fend for themselves. Or the father who has kept with him the older children of a dissolved marriage may wish to avoid leaving the smaller of these in the care of his other wives lest they give preference to their own. Under these circumstances, or other similar ones, some form of fostering is often resorted to. Yet whatever the residence of children after their parents' divorce, the full range of kinship bonds, those dependent on the mother, and those derived through the father, continue to be of significance throughout life.

Rights to custody of children on divorce are not precisely defined. Young children in any case will accompany their mother, and older girls are likely to do so. Boys past the age of six or seven are more apt to remain with the father than to go with their mother when she enters a new marriage. But the claims of the kin of both parents to foster children, and hence the availability of a mother substitute among paternal kin and of a father substitute among the mother's relatives to some extent balances this tendency to divide the older children along lines of sex. Particular arrangements vary depending on the age and sex of the children and the availability of foster parents. The most constant feature of the residence of children at their parents' divorce is that the sibling group tends to be split up. Neither parent is likely to agree to the other retaining all the children.

It is important here to distinguish between rights to custody during childhood and reciprocal claims regarding members of the junior generation as these reach adulthood. The Gonja situation is close to being the mirror opposite of that which obtains among the matrilineal Ashanti. Among the Ashanti, the father is recognized as having the right to rear a son to adulthood, and this is backed by the supernatural sanction of the *ntoro* (Rattray 1929: 8ff.). Once he has helped a son to marry, however, the father's formal obligations to him are ended, and it is the mother's brother who assumes these and with whom the youth goes to live, if not immediately, then at his father's death. Among the Gonja, where a mother's brother has been acting as foster parent to his nephew, he is responsible for the latter's care and education until he reaches adulthood. The mother's brother's authority is explicitly enforced by reference to the particular danger attendant on angering maternal ancestors, who alone are held to be able to kill. It is the duty of the mother's brother to provide a wife for the nephew who has been his charge. Once this obligation is fulfilled the youth is free to return to his father's house and many do so at that time. If, however, the two men are close, the nephew may remain until his foster parent dies before returning to his paternal home.

The Gonja are adamant about the inevitability of a man's eventual return to his father's village. My data on residence suggests that although this move is frequent it is by no means always made. However, the important fact here is that the identification between a man and his son is held to be ultimately stronger than that between the nephew and his maternal uncle, even where the latter relationship has been the most active in adolescence and early adulthood. The point to be emphasized in the context of the residence of children on divorce is that whatever arrangement is made for boys during their childhood and adolescence, as adults they are expected to return to their agnatic kin. For it is only by reasserting their identification with them that full status in the political, and in some cases, in the ritual, sphere may be realized.

Yet even when a man lives among his paternal kin, those to whom he is related through his mother continue to be of importance to him. He is bound to them by reciprocal obligations for support in times of crisis, their links through common ancestors may expose them to common supernatural threats which must be jointly met, and, most tangibly, it is through uterine links that a man's rights to inherit property often pass. And as has been indicated, he has rights, defined in terms of fostering, in the children of his 'siblings'.

In short, since the kin of both parents continue to be of vital interest throughout life, the termination of affinal relationships at divorce does not simultaneously involve the ending of all relationships between the divorced couple. They and their kinsfolk continue to have a joint concern in the children of the marriage. That is, the ties of kinship created with the birth of children continue to bind their parents after divorce.

Spouses who have separated and remarried may continue to refer to one

35

another as husband (*n'kul*) and wife (*m'etche*). These terms have a wide extension during the active phase of marriage, being applied to all the spouse's siblings of like sex, real and classificatory, unless, as with marriage to kin, a kinship term is more appropriate to the speaker. Where children have been born the termination of a marriage does not change the more inclusive usage. Thus on inquiring as to why Seidu, my cook, referred to one of the senior Busunu women as *m'etche* (my wife) I was told that she had once been married to his father's sister's son and had borne him a child. This boy remained with the father, and his mother subsequently remarried. Yet Seidu continued to think of her as the wife of his 'brother' and the mother of his 'son'.

TERMINAL SEPARATION

Divorce in Gonja is easily brought about by either partner, although most frequently initiated by the wife. It appears to be a relatively common occurrence at all stages of a woman's adult life. While young women do leave their husbands before any children are born, or when they have only one or two small ones, it also happens regularly that more mature women with older children leave one spouse for another. However, as a wife approaches old age it becomes increasingly likely that she will leave her husband to settle with kin. [20] In the early and middle stages of a woman's life, marriages tend to be ended by separation which becomes finalized by a subsequent marriage rather than by a legal divorce. When an older woman separates from her husband, however, it is highly unlikely that she will remarry and her status continues that of a 'separated' rather than a 'divorced' woman. Since separation in old age is so uniformly final it is designated 'terminal separation' to distinguish it from the separation which is in fact a transition between one marriage and another. Men, it must be noted, continue to take wives as long as they can persuade women to marry and stay with them. They generally remain married until a more advanced age than women, although elderly men, except for chiefs, are often single.

That elderly women tend to live with kin rather than with a husband is an empirical fact. In Buipe, of 19 women over 50, 15 were living with kin while four were living with husbands (Table 9). All of those with kin had been married. Eight of the 15 had husbands living, while six were widows at the time of the census. [21] Significantly, the four women in this age group who were still married were all of the Commoner estate, providing corroboration for the prevalent feeling that marriages to Commoner women are more apt to be stable and of long duration. No woman over 50 in Buipe at the time of the census who belonged to either the Muslim or Ruling Estate was still living with a husband.

The withdrawal from married life represented by a woman's separation

Table 9. *Residence of adult women in Buipe with kin or husband by estate and age**

Estate	Age (years)			Total
	−30	31–50	51–	
Ruling				
Living with { Husband	7	3	0	10 } 14
Living with { Kin*	1	1	2	4
Commoner				
Living with { Husband	18	10	4	32 } 42
Living with { Kin	3	1	6	10
Muslim				
Living with { Husband	11	10	0	21 } 35
Living with { Kin	2	5	7	14
Total	42	30	19	91

* There were no cases in which widows were living with their dead husband's kin. Thus 'kin' refers to a woman's own kin.

from her husband in old age does not, however, have the status of an explicit cultural norm. Unlike other customs which influence the patterns of residence and the developmental cycle—the prohibition against a widow remarrying in her husband's kindred, the custom of fostering children and the convention that a son returns eventually to his father's kin—this was never discussed as though it were generally expected behaviour, or even formulated as something 'we Gonja do'. Nevertheless, both observation and census figures show that it *is* something Gonja do. [22]

There are three problems to be considered in connexion with the practice of terminal separation. The first has to do with the circumstances which seem immediately to precipitate it, and the manner in which it is initiated. Secondly, there is the question of what features of the social system are associated with and facilitate separation. And finally, we must ask what the implications are in terms of residence patterns and the developmental cycle, and for the social system as a whole.

In the instances of terminal separation which I observed or was able to inquire into in detail, both in Buipe and elsewhere in central Gonja, there seemed to be three sorts of immediate cause. Most dramatic were witchcraft accusations; in the three villages studied there were four older women who had been forced to leave their husbands for this reason. There were other instances of women living with kin on this account, but, being younger, they remarried or, in one case, the husband regularly visited his wife and children in her village during the dry season. Thus, if a woman is accused of witchcraft in her husband's village and is forced to leave, this need not terminate the marriage, and if it does she may still remarry. But when older women return to their kin in this way, they are unlikely to remarry and the separation becomes terminal.

Another immediate cause is illness. The first response to ill-health is the pragmatic one of procuring the appropriate medicine. This it is a husband's duty to provide. Should it prove ineffective, diviners are consulted and it frequently turns out that more powerful medicine may be had from the woman's kin. The sequence is a regular one. The husband's aid is first sought and then, if this fails to bring relief, even long journeys are undertaken, regardless of the weakness attendant on protracted illness, in order that the help of kin may be secured. Indeed, in some cases the cause of the illness is held to be bound up with the residence in the husband's house. Since the elderly are increasingly subject to infirmities, this greater efficacy of treatment by kin is particularly apt to serve as the initial reason for the separation of an older woman from her husband. Although her intention may not have been to make a permanent break, failure to make a complete recovery is apt to be construed as cause for remaining with kin, rather than as an indication that their medicinal resources are not in fact superior to those at the husband's disposal. Conversely, younger women with young families who appear to be happily married tend to return to their husbands in spite of the lack of success of therapy by kin. Increasing illness and infirmity of a husband may also precipitate a separation at this time if his ability to support a wife is affected. For although a woman's 'brothers' are obliged to supply her with food if she is in need, this is not binding upon them so long as she lives with a husband. While they may help to support a married sister, they can refuse on the grounds that their duty is not to feed her husband and his other dependants, but only toward their sister and her children. For as long as she is in her husband's house the food she prepares goes to feed everyone there. If she wishes to claim her brother's support as a right, a woman must go and live with him.

In citing polygyny as one of the factors precipitating terminal separations it is clear that it is so only under special circumstances. For many polygynous unions last for several years, and some women say that they prefer them, as domestic tasks are less onerous when shared. But where a second wife is brought in to join a domestic unit which has for many years been based on monogamous marriage, it appears that this may have a directly disruptive influence on the first marriage.

In each of two cases where this sequence of events occurred, the first wife was mother of well above the average number of living children, in one case seven, and in the other eight, a circumstance probably not unrelated to the fact that also in each case she had lived for at least 20 years as the sole wife of the father of her children (see Dorjahn's Temne study). Twenty years of a stable monogamous marriage and the rearing of a large family would seem to lower a woman's tolerance for sharing her position with a co-wife. Significantly, the son of one of these women described his mother's

38

fate thus: 'My father drove her out. For 20 years she lived with him and cooked for him and then he drove her away by taking another wife.' He and his brothers are very bitter about this conduct of their father's. The details of their elaborate efforts to dislodge their mother's successor lead one to sympathize with the lot of the step-mother.

The second case is a particularly striking one to me because, of all the couples I knew in Gonja, I would have said they were the least likely to separate. Nyiwuleji's wife, Nana, herself one of seven full siblings, had eight living children, the youngest twins of just under one year, and the eldest just become a father. Superficially, this case differs from the previous one in that the break occurred during the courtship of the second wife, before her actual introduction into the household. Significantly, it followed a quarrel about the rights over disposal of yams grown on Nyiwuleji's farm.

Now all husbands know that their wives try to put aside a portion of the farm produce allocated for domestic consumption. This they sell in the village for pin-money and, provided the family has sufficient to eat, nothing is said. It is impossible to sort out from the allegations and counter-allegations of this quarrel whether Nyiwuleji chose to take issue with behaviour he would ordinarily have tolerated, or whether Nana really did go too far. Probably there were elements of both. For a wife of a long-standing monogamous union comes to assume a community of property and interests with her husband which is not in fact justified and in a way which would be impossible if this were constantly challenged by the competing claims of a co-wife. In the same way, I suspect, she comes to assume an exclusive right to his affections which grows out of their close relationship but which is not supported by the jural norms of the society. For these positively sanction plural marriage for men, and accept their affairs as long as these do not involve adultery with the wife of another.

Thus when a man in Nyiwuleji's position contemplates converting a mono-gamous domestic family into one based on plural marriage, he may, as Nyiwuleji apparently did, feel that he must see that his first wife does not exceed the limits of a wife's prerogatives. For, if a second wife also took such liberties, as a husband he would be bullied if not impoverished. And to deny one wife what is allowed another is out of the question. Similarly, Nana seems to have said, in effect, if I stay it must be on the same basis as before, otherwise I go. And if, as I have suggested, these 'same terms' include sole claim to a husband's resources and affections, her terms are clearly impossible. But as this is not an accepted basis for complaint in a polygynous society, the actual break occurs on some other pretext.

The extra-marital affairs of young married men may also occasion quarrels if the wife comes to know of them. Again there is no legitimate basis for complaint within the society's norms. But the wife nevertheless feels herself slighted and may refuse to cook for a week or two as a mark of her displeasure. If she has been looking for an excuse to leave, this will do, but ordinarily a husband's affairs do not lead to the departure of a young first wife. Nor does the introduction of a second wife, otherwise there would be no polygyny, but rather, serial monogamy. But where the first wife is an older woman, and particularly where for a long time she has been an only wife, the tensions arising from the transition to plural marriage tend to precipitate a separation.

I have discussed witchcraft accusations, the increasing illness and infirmity of old age, and the taking by the husband of additional wives where the union has previously been monogamous, as some of the apparently immediate causes of the termination of marriages when the wife reaches old age. This return of a woman to live with her kinsfolk as old age approaches, and her consequent withdrawal from married life, is well-nigh universal among women of the Muslim and Ruling estates and frequent with Commoner women, as indicated in Table 9. In citing the immediate precipitating causes I have interpreted this pattern from the actor's point of view. One woman could not remain with her husband because there she was considered to be a witch. Another found that in order to obtain proper treatment for illness she had to seek the medicines of her kin. And still another resented her husband's taking a second wife. Yet witches, illness and polygyny occur in many societies where a woman expects to live out her life in her husband's house. In order to deal meaningfully with the question of why terminal separation is a significant feature of Gonja social organization, we must consider how other aspects of the social system function in such a way that as a woman approaches old age these crises are resolved by termination of marriage.

Here the absence of the levirate or any form of widow inheritance is undoubtedly a key factor. This operates in two ways. On the one hand, a woman knows that should her husband die first, she will in any case return to her kin in old age. Although her husband's kin have an obligation to support her if she wishes to remain with them as a dependant the majority of widows return to kin. As one woman put it, 'If I stayed there they would have expected me to fetch water, carry firewood and cook for them. But here in my brother's house I can sit in the shade of my room and spin thread for my shroud in peace.' If she has any kin who are able to do so, a widow will exercise her right to claim support from them. And such a claim may not be denied without risking the ire of the ancestors. In this situation, for a woman to withdraw from a marriage which she no longer finds rewarding is but to anticipate the inevitable.

But this course would be impracticable if the role of divorced sister were not a recognized one in Gonja society. That it does receive recognition is made inevitable by the return of widows to their kin, and the fact that women past child-bearing age are not wooed, and hence become the responsibility of their kin.

Here it must be noted that men do not, as a rule, encourage an ageing wife to leave. Even when she can no longer bear children and has ceased to be interested in sexual relations, a wife is valued as a companion and for the domestic services she renders. Furthermore, it is hard on a man's self-esteem to lose a wife, whatever her age, and the older he gets the less complaisant he is about it, for he knows it will be hard to find another. Today it is the old men who complain most bitterly about the difficulty of persuading modern girls to accept arranged marriages, 'For how else are we to find wives?', they say. 'If we court a girl, it doesn't matter how many gifts we give her, she will take them and then marry a young man.' The regularity with which men express regret when their older wives desert them leaves no doubt as to their feelings. Let me cite but a few of the many confirmatory instances. Earlier in this paper I described how the KagbaapeWura still hoped that his estranged wife, Dongi, would consent to return to him. Yet this woman was at least 45 and if she did return could not be expected to remain for more than a few years. Then there is the concession made by the chief of Busunu to his 12 wives when he begged them to remain with him until his death, saying that he did not care if they took lovers so long as they stayed in his house to cook for him. [23] Or again, neither the Chief's 'sister', Supini Wuritche, nor her two ex-husbands in Busunu were married at the time I knew them. Each man complained that since she had left him, he had been wifeless, and each strongly resented the other as a possible obstacle to securing her return.

But whether or not men are glad to see the last of elderly wives, the fact remains that in Gonja these women may and do return to their kin in old age and that this is in direct contrast to the pattern reported for the LoWiili (Goody, J. 1956) and the Tallensi (Fortes 1949a), patrilineal peoples living to the north. The matrilineal Ashanti to the south, however, follow much the same practice (Fortes 1949b). There, also, terminal separation is associated with a relatively high divorce rate, but in Ashanti it is one facet of a traditional system in which many marriages were duo-local, the husband and the wife each residing in their own lineage compound, with the wife visiting her husband at night and sending him food when her turn comes to cook. Further, while the ideal is for sons to grow to manhood in the father's house, on his death or before they tend to join their mother's brothers and assume their roles as adult lineage males. As soon as her sons are able, they are expected to build their mother a house of her own which becomes the nucleus of a potential matrilineage segment. It is, Fortes contends, a desire to consolidate her position as founder of a segment of her matrilineage that leads the ageing Ashanti wife to separate from her husband and live with her brothers or sons.

No such explanation is possible for terminal separation among the Gonja, for no lineages of either sort are present. What other factors, then, make this shift of residence desirable from the woman's point of view? We must look at two things, the attributes of the roles of sister and wife, as these are affected by increasing age, and the residence of a woman's children and grandchildren.

It is, I believe, significant that none of the five women I knew who held chiefly titles, the *Ewuritche*, lived with husbands, although all still had ex-husbands living in the same village. Damba Yiri Wuritche was a partial exception to this. She had not yet passed the age of childbearing and considered herself married. However, although she was nominally a wife, she cooked for and slept with her husband irregularly, and lived not in his compound but in that of her brother. This is the only instance of non-resident marriage which came to my attention, and in fact more closely resembles the Hausa 'marriage of taking up the stick' as described by M. G. Smith (1955: 52-3). It seems quite clear that women who hold formal positions of prestige prefer to maximize this by withdrawing at least in part from the role of wife. This finds an echo in the Gonja saying that 'two chiefs cannot stay in the same house' (*Bawura banyɔ, ba minan tchina laŋkonle*). For a husband is the 'chief' in his own house so far as his wife is concerned. When a wife becomes a chief indeed, she no longer is content to remain under the jurisdiction of a husband.

I cite the case of the Ewuritches to stress the point that authority and prestige are important in determining choice of residence for older women. This factor affects the women of each estate somewhat differently. In Table 1 data was presented to show that men and women of all three estates intermarry freely. These figures indicate that women of the Ruling estate more frequently marry either Commoners or Muslims than they do men of their own group. And indeed, men of the Ruling estate say that women from their own group make difficult wives and it appears that either they marry accordingly, or that these women themselves prefer to marry out. When a woman of the Ruling estate marries out and returns to kin in old age, she is not only maximizing her status by activating her role as sister, but she is associating herself with 'brothers' who are likely to hold major chiefships and thus borrowing from their glory. The present paramount chief has moved, as custom demands, from his own Division of Daboya to the capital at Damongo, and his household there includes, in addition to his wives and children, several 'sisters' who have chosen to leave not only their husbands but also their natal Division in order to participate in the life at court. There are tangible rewards for so doing. On the occasion of the enrobing of the new chief of Kusawgu Division I met two of the YagbumWura's 'sisters' who had been sent to represent him at the ceremony and who were treated throughout with the greatest respect. At the capital each has her own compound and attends her 'brother's' audience daily.

Another trend observed in Table 1 was the somewhat higher degree of estate endogamy which characterized the marriages of Muslim women than would have been predicted on the basis of the average for the population as a whole. This almost certainly has to do with their religion. For while Muslim men who marry pagans can and do insist that their wives learn to pray and to prepare food in the prescribed ways, Muslim women have no such control. Those who marry out tend, it is recognized, to lapse in piety. In many villages there is no mosque nor a Mallam to lead prayers. And while it is possible for a woman to continue to avoid pork and all meat which is not ritually killed, this can be a real hardship in a household where these prohibitions are not otherwise observed. These same considerations would seem to apply to the very high (in Buipe, total) rate of return of Muslim women to their kin in old age. For them, to the factors which affect all women alike is added the wish to die in the faith and among believers.

Terminal separation for those women of the Ruling estate who marry out, serves to maximize status by reassociating them with kin in positions of power. For Muslim women this may also be a consideration, but in addition there is the factor of returning to the religion of their fathers. That neither of these forces operate where Commoner women are concerned is reflected in the fact that although they also return to kin in old age, they do so less consistently than women of other estates. Commoner women who exchange the role of wife for that of sister better their status in the domestic domain but not in the community as a whole.

The status accorded an elderly woman approaches that of a male elder. She possesses the wisdom and ritual knowledge associated with age, and is accorded commensurate respect. The Gonja are very conscious of seniority of age as the basis of respect and deference. Siblings, and all degrees of cousin are designated by two terms, *nda* and *nsupo*, meaning respectively older and younger relative of the same generation, regardless of sex. An older sibling may reprove or physically chastise a younger, but never the reverse. This principle operates jointly with that of deference of the junior generation to that directly above it. By the time a woman reaches late middle age there are apt to be few members left of her parents' generation. Her surviving kin tend to be mostly younger 'siblings' and 'children', her own and those of her siblings and cousins. She is thus, when living among kin, in a genealogically superior position. In her husband's house, however, she is not only subordinate to him, as is every wife, but she is surrounded by his kin, with whom, unless she has married a kinsman, considerations of birth order are secondary to the constraints of affinity. The role of wife is defined as subordinate, while that of sister is not.

An obvious limiting factor in an older woman's choice of residence is the residence of her children. In a society where the domestic family is based on the localized patrilineage, a wife who remains with her husband in old age is assured continual residence with her sons and their children. As her daughters disperse on marriage the older woman who returned to her own patrikin would, except where patrilateral cross-cousin marriage is commonly practised, be separated from both sons and daughters and all her grandchildren. In the case of the typically matrilineal Ashanti, the tendency of adult sons to reside with their maternal kin means that the wife who separates from her husband to live with her lineage kin is at the same time likely to be living with her sons, as well as with any daughters who are living with uncles rather than husbands. And although sons' sons will eventually leave to join their matrikin, this will be compensated for by the arrival of daughters' sons.

Table 10. *Residence and source of support of elderly unmarried women in Buipe*

Woman resident with her:	Woman supported by:			
	Son, living neo-locally	Son with his maternal kin	Her natal kin only	Husband of foster child
Maternal kin	.	3	2	.
Paternal kin	.	3	5	.
Chief	1	.	.	1
Total	1	6	7	1

The Gonja situation falls between these two ideal types as might be expected in the absence of lineages of either sort. The headship of a compound traditionally passes in the agnatic line, usually from father to son or to a dead brother's son, should he be the elder. Exceptions do occur, and Commoner compound heads are somewhat more likely than others to be uterine kin of their predecessors. Yet it is very rare to find a woman living as the dependant of a son who is resident in her dead husband's house. As Table 10 shows, in Buipe, of the 15 elderly women living with kin [24] none was supported by a son living in his dead father's house, and one only by a son living neo-locally, that is, not resident with either his paternal or his maternal kin. Of the remaining 14, one half were supported by kin of the same or ascendent generations only, 'brothers' or 'mother's brothers', and slightly less than half by a son living with his maternal kin. Of the women living with sons, half were living with their maternal kin and half with paternal kin. The women without sons tended to live with paternal kin rather than with their mother's people.

Now it might seem that the gains from such an arrangement were not sufficient to balance the losses accruing from leaving a husband's house if sons are likely to remain behind. But the picture is more complex than this for several reasons. First, if a woman has married more than once and has borne children in each marriage, then the home of her natal kin provides a neutral ground where the children of each union may visit her and where she may equally well rear any foster children entrusted to her. For as noted earlier, the termination of a marriage by death or divorce often results in the dispersal of the children. Although infant sons may accompany the mother when she remarries, they are unlikely to remain there under the control of a step-father. Reluctance to do so is expressed in the formalized refusal to farm for a step-father. This does not have the status of a prohibition, but the refusal of a step-child to farm is accepted as justified. Hence the adolescent and adult sons of a woman's previous marriages are most unlikely to be living with her and her present husband when in late middle age she begins to consider a terminal separation.

Secondly, one or possibly two sons may have been sent to their maternal kin as foster children. They may in this case have married there and settled down to farm with a mother's brother. Although it is usually the case, as the Gonja insist, that a man who has grown up with his maternal kin will eventually return to the house of his father, this is frequently delayed until after the death of the foster parent. Where this pattern is followed, a woman who leaves her husband to join her brothers is going also to the village or compound where her son's young family currently resides. Six of the 15 cases in Table 10 follow this pattern.

Then again, youths of the Ruling estate if they have grown up in their father's house, frequently spend the years of early adulthood 'walking about' (ba ji kalembo). This may take the form of going south to seek work, or of becoming a day labourer with one of the departments or firms in Northern Ghana which hire casual labour. Or it may involve extended visits to kin in other villages or Divisions. Protracted dry season hunting activities may take small parties off to temporary bush camps. Mobility at this age is a response to three sorts of pressures. On the one hand, there is the reluctance of adult sons, particularly eldest sons, to live under the daily constraints of paternal authority. And secondly, the pattern of succession to office, which goes strictly by seniority of birth order among those eligible, means that a young man who has older brothers must look forward to a waiting period of perhaps several years or even decades before he can expect to enter even the lower ranks of chiefship. For he will not be given a title until his older brothers, paternal half-brothers, and patrilateral parallel cousins have themselves succeeded to one. It is possible for a man to succeed to a junior title while his father is still alive, but in practice this usually happens only to the sons of very elderly men, themselves approaching middle age.

Finally there is the fear that witchcraft may be used against them by fellow villagers. The Gonja are confident that no one is subject to witchcraft when he is among strangers, although this has its own dangers. But witchcraft, in the sense of premeditated injury through mystical agencies, is only a threat where people know one. 'Chiefs' sons', that is, members of the Ruling estate, are in particular danger, not only from their own rivals for office, but especially from attempts to injure their senior titled kinsmen through them. For one of the axioms of witchcraft in Gonja is that when a witch finds the victim's defences impenetrable, the original victim will be attacked by harming someone close to him who is less able to protect himself. Fear of witchcraft in their father's village was several times given by young men of the Ruling estate as the reason why they had temporarily left home.

For these reasons the mother of young men of the Ruling estate cannot count on her sons' continuous residence with their father. That these sons will almost certainly return after his death has little bearing on their mother's decision to leave him, because unless at that time a son is present who is in a position to support her, she would in any case almost certainly return to her kin. There is no instance in my records of three villages with a total population of around 1000 in which a widow is living with kin of a deceased husband other than her own son. Of the three instances in which a widow lived as a dependant of an adult son in his father's house, two of the sons occupied senior chiefships and thus presumably were in a better position to support her than her natal kin. Also, both women were very elderly and no longer had even classificatory siblings still alive. Their choice then fell between living with their own children or with siblings' children, and, understandably, both preferred the former. The third instance was a case of marriage to a kinsman where the widow was living at the same time with kin and with affines.

Whereas sons may be an undependable source of support for their mother, adult daughters are equally unpredictable in their movements. To begin with they are living in virilocal marriage. This may be in their natal village, but is equally likely to be in another village of the Division or even in another Division. Furthermore, the consistently high rate of divorce both before and after the birth of children means that whatever their residence at a given time, this is apt to change. In any case, there was in these three villages only one case where an elderly woman was living as a dependant of her married daughter and her husband, and she was considered insane. Married daughters eagerly look forward to visiting their mothers and do so daily if they are in the same village, several times a year if in nearby villages and every two or three years, often for several weeks at a time, if they live in villages many miles apart. The period immediately following the birth of a first child is always an occasion for such a visit which often lasts for many months. This may be repeated at the birth of subsequent children if for any reason the daughter has particular need of her mother's help, as for instance after the birth of twins. And it is, for preference, to the mother that a young woman goes when she separates from her husband, for, I have been told: 'Your father will be trying to make you go back to your husband, but your mother will let you sit quietly there until you marry.'

If a woman has married in her natal village, there is virtually no change in her relations with her children when she leaves the house of her husband for that of her brothers. So long as they remain in the same village all her children will come to wish her good morning and good evening and gossip, and will continue to defer to her wishes.

To summarize then, a woman does not greatly prejudice her close relationship to her own children and to her grandchildren by leaving her husband in old age to reside with kin. Her daughters will in any case be living in virilocal marriage and will continue to visit her wherever she is. In fact, they will do so more freely and for longer periods if she is living with her kin than would be the case if she were with a step-father. In early adulthood men of the Ruling estate are apt to be away from their father's village for long stretches of time. And in all three estates one or more sons may in any case be living with maternal kin. If their mother has remarried, sons too are likely to feel constrained in visiting the house of a step-father, whereas they are welcomed by their mother's kin.

In discussing the residence of a woman's children, we must, in order to do justice to Gonja custom, consider also the children of siblings. For these are, in a very real sense, felt to be one's own. This was stated and reaffirmed again and again, and is reinforced by the institution of fostering and by the lines of inheritance of property which tends to pass between 'siblings' including first and second cousins, in order of birth. Hence the body of kin for whom wealth is held in trust is composed of siblings and their children. The obligations which are associated with such a kin group include economic support, succour in illness or trouble and contributions to the costs of litigation and funerals. A woman who leaves a husband to reside with a sibling is reasserting her position in this kin group, especially the rights of herself and her children *vis-à-vis* its property and its personnel. Rights in the personnel include the right to a sibling's daughter or granddaughter as a foster child, upon whose help a woman is particularly dependent as her own strength fails.

There is one final aspect of the social organization which is relevant to women's residence in old age. This has to do with the personal shrine (*akalibi*). A woman's shrine is established on her first marriage and thereafter follows her, wherever she may live. She always bears the major burden of finding money for sacrificial animals, and although a husband usually performs the sacrifices for a young wife, her brother may do so equally well. And so may the woman herself, especially in maturity and old age. Not only is she independent of a husband for spiritual ease in this respect, but the latter has no role to play in her rapport with her forefathers. These she may sacrifice to (*nyina*) wherever she is living, but if she is with siblings she may, by contributing to joint offerings, do so more frequently and at less personal expense. Thus a woman's spiritual well-being is, if anything, enhanced by her residence with kin. [25]

In discussing the roles available to elderly women, the residence of their children and grandchildren, and the relative independence of women in their relations with their personal shrines and with ancestors, we have again been dealing partially within the actor's frame of reference. For such factors enter into a woman's assessment of what is for her the best course of action. However, they are analytically relevant on another level, for at the same time they are the 'givens', the constant features, of the social system within which Gonja women live. That is, this system is one in which marriage to the kinsman of a deceased spouse is prohibited and in which there is a positive obligation on men to support their full and classificatory sisters when the latter choose to live with them; it is one in which full and half-siblings and cousins share the same set of obligations and are apt to be scattered throughout several villages and even two or three political Divisions. Among the duties and concomitant rights which these 'siblings' share, are, in addition to the obligation to support one another, the right to inherit from one another and rights over each other's children. And it is as characteristics of the social structure that these factors are reflected in patterns of residence, both of children and of their parents.

Finally there is the problem of the sort of effects which the institution of terminal separation may be expected to have on the social structure in its turn. In other words, what happens when women regularly return to live with kin in old age rather than remaining with their husbands in the latters' villages and compounds? The results are far reaching and must not be considered solely as chronic disruption of marriage. For as Turner stressed with regard to divorce among the Ndembu (1957: 69) the return of women to their kin on divorce or widowhood may in fact constitute a functional prerequisite for a given type of social system. [26]

The functions of terminal separation among the Gonja are in some ways similar to those of a high incidence of divorce at other periods of a woman's life and to the return of a woman to her kin on being widowed, and cannot be considered separately from these. However, the particular significance of terminal separation rests in part in its relative inevitability: many women remain with a single husband for all of their married lives, but however happy their marriage it appears to be almost inevitable that if they live to old age they will spend their last years with kin. And in part the special significance of terminal separation lies in the fact that it represents a final and permanent identification of a woman with her kin rather than a temporary sojourn between marriages.

Divorce, a widow's return to kin, and terminal separation, all serve to limit the generation span of the domestic family. A man and his wife, or wives, do not live in old age surrounded by all their sons or all their daughters and *their* families. There may indeed be, living with a man, a married son, an adolescent son, a sister's son, a divorced daughter and her young children. But his wife is elsewhere, perhaps being supported by a son who is living with his maternal kin. And some of the paternal and maternal half-siblings of the generation of young adults in the compound (and indeed of the generation below them) are in other compounds, villages and other Divisions. There is no single, clear-cut, group which stays together over time.

The termination of marriage, by whatever cause, not only is consistent with this dispersal, but makes it inevitable in the Gonja system. For, as has been shown, the rights of both parents in children persist after conjugal ties are severed, and consequently the children tend to be dispersed when a marriage breaks up. As indicated in Table 2, while approximately one-quarter of the men in the Buipe census married women whose natal village was also Buipe, another quarter married outside of the village and about one-half outside of Buipe Division. The average distance between spouses' natal villages for those marrying outside of Buipe Division was 43 miles. Thus dispersal here refers to the return of a woman and her children, either temporarily during youth or middle age, or permanently for the woman in old age, to kin who are living in three cases out of four in other villages and in about half the cases in other Divisions which may be many miles away.

This situation has certain clear similarities to Ndembu, Bemba and other Central African groups. It must be remembered, however, that these moves occur, not within a framework of small, temporary villages but rather between permanent villages of fixed political allegiance and with populations of from 60 to several hundred people. These permanent villages serve as fixed points of reference between which people move. And when these moves are made, links are maintained with each village. Thus a woman who leaves to marry will return in old age, and meanwhile she and her natal kin exchange visits, whatever the distance which separates them. If a woman takes young children with her at divorce, the boys will almost certainly return eventually to their paternal home. And girls, although they may marry from their mother's village, must seek the consent of their father and his kin to the match, and may later return to his village to live with a kinsman either temporarily on divorce or permanently in old age. Where boys have remained with their agnatic kin, both in adolescence and as adults they will visit their mother, occasionally in the village of a subsequent husband, but most frequently in her own village [27]. These visits may or may not be connected with future expectations of inheritance. This is determined by seniority of age among a group of classificatory siblings and not by the closeness of particular relationships, as for instance that between a man and the sister's son he fostered. But the maintaining of contact by one member of a sibling group serves to reassert the rights of the group as a whole. In the same way, children who disperse at the termination of their parents' marriage continue to visit and keep in touch. It is between full and maternal half-siblings, wherever these may be living, that the closest ties in adulthood lie.

The fact that people who are united by these strong primary bonds of siblingship and parenthood are often living in widely separated villages, and that such ties tend to be maintained regardless of intervening distances is among the most important and characteristic features of Gonja social structure. The dispersion is rendered inevitable by the combination of marriage between natives of different villages and Divisions, and the subsequent break-up of the families created by these marriages. Once initiated, the system is self-perpetuating, in that further marriages tend to occur between two villages, when, as a result of the links growing out of one union, their people start visiting back and forth. And as we have seen, marriage in turn results in dispersal of those who are close relatives.

On the level of the total social system, two things appear to follow from frequent divorce, widow return, and terminal separation in Gonja. First, it would appear to be instrumental in maintaining the balance between maternal and paternal kin which is, in spite of virilocal residence and marriage across large distances, so marked throughout the system. For by the very act of a woman leaving her husband, their children are forcibly reminded that the parents do not form a permanent unit, either as the basis of a domestic group or as a couple whose interests are indissolubly identified. The parents' separation means the disbanding of the family of orientation. Father and mother are each identified more closely with their natal kin and village; the children must now relate to these directly and no longer through the domestic family based on their parents' marriage.

The second function has to do with the very fact that these links are maintained over such considerable distances. And it must be remembered that they are not links between groups, but particularistic, kinship, links between individuals. Further, they are links between individuals who are often members of different social estates (Table 1). It seems likely that the relatively egalitarian character of the links between the three estates, and the very persistence of the union of the various Divisions as a federation is related to these mechanisms by which individual links between members of different villages, Divisions and estates are maintained over space and through time.

It must be stressed that this is not the equivalent of saying that without such mechanisms the Gonja state would not exist. The point is, rather, that it would take a different form. This is more than a tautology, for a particular kind of developmental cycle and the concomitant pattern of divorce, which are features of the domestic organization, are seen as related, on the political level, to the nature of social stratification and the integration of the state.

Finally, in stressing the need to describe not only the frequency but also the *pattern* of divorce which characterize a given society, it is not intended to imply that this is an original approach [28], nor that the variables suggested are necessarily the only ōnes likely to be worth while. It does seem the case that the frequency with which women of various ages change marital partners will always be worth considering. This is mainly so because (with respect to differences between early divorce and divorce during the years of active childbearing) childbearing for successive unrelated husbands leads inevitably to dispersed groups of maternal siblings; also ties of parenthood are less likely to be completely·severed at divorce than are ties pertaining solely to the conjugal relationship. The importance of distinguishing divorce in old age from that which occurs earlier lies in the fact that where divorce, or terminal separation, is a regular feature of women's old age, this must have direct repercussions on the definition of roles available to adult women, the composition of residential groups, and the territorial distribution and definition of role obligations of the members of kin groups.

APPENDIX: A NOTE ON THE DEFINITION OF DIVORCE

The Gonja material raises problems to do with marriage 'stability' and the definitions of marriage and divorce which have been skirted in this paper. For instance, I have treated marriages following on a period of conjugal separation as fully legitimate unions (as do the Gonja). It might be maintained that in the absence of a formal divorce they more closely resemble either cicisbeism or secondary marriage. Since a man has no rights over the wife who has married again, nor in any children she bears to subsequent husbands, the Gonja situation clearly differs from cicisbeism as defined by Meek. [29] I have not treated Gonja marriage as including secondary marriage although it appears to have many similarities to the forms of secondary marriage described by M. G. Smith (1953). I hope in a later paper to explore the similarities and differences between the Gonja institution and those discussed in this extremely interesting Northern Nigerian material.

For present purposes it should be made clear that for the Gonja, prolonged conjugal separation has been treated as the equivalent of *de facto* divorce. While there exist in Gonja mechanisms of jural divorce, there are also recognized patterns— a wife's departure, her husband's failure to seek her return, or her repeated refusal of his pleas—by which *de facto* divorce is accomplished. Subsequent marriages are held to be valid and former husbands do not in fact make claims against their successors for recompense, return of courting expenses, or for children born of the latters' unions.

The concept of *de facto* divorce has the merit of covering the practice of terminal separation. Were it not for this custom, divorce might be defined as conjugal separation followed by remarriage. But remarriage for women past the menopause is extremely rare, if it occurs at all, [30] and terminal separation very frequent. In several cases in which both former spouses still lived in the same village, while they were in some instances still united by bonds of common parenthood, there was no persisting sexual or economic tie between them.[31] They were for all practical purposes as effectively divorced as if the wife had married again.

It should be noted that this use of *de facto* divorce differs from Stenning's (1959: 173 ff.).[32] Among the pastoral Wodaabe Fulani *de facto* divorce seems to occur only when the two husbands do not recognize a common clan or religious authority who is able to reach and enforce a settlement. Further, marriages following on *de facto* divorce alone are mainly of a sort (*deetuki*) which Stenning defines as cicisbean unions.

Among the Gonja, the prolonged conjugal separation which I have treated as the equivalent of a *de facto* divorce renders equally legitimate a subsequent marriage whether with a member of the same or a different community as the former spouse, and such a marriage is no different from, or less valid than, any previous one.

NOTES

[1] My two periods of field work in Central Gonja, from June 1956 to March 1957 and from July 1957 to December 1957, were supported by a Ford Foundation Fellowship. The Bartle Frere Fund of Cambridge University also contributed towards the expenses of the first trip. I am most grateful for this assistance, without which the work could not have been carried out.

[2] *The Gold Coast Census of Population, 1948.*

[3] The Gonja kinship terminology is strongly classificatory, and in order to approximate this usage I have placed the literal translation of a kinship term in inverted commas when it applies to a classificatory kinsman, e.g. 'brother' = first or second (and occasionally more distant) cousin.

[4] Fieldwork was carried out in Central Gonja for a total of 15 months, during which time I lived in three villages. Strictly speaking statements apply to these villages although generalization to the rest of Central Gonja appears warranted. Commoner groups in both east and west are not sufficiently well known to allow an estimate of the effects on these institutions there. Visits to Salaga in the east and Bole in the west lead me to suspect that differences on the domestic level are small.

[5] Because shifts in residence occur throughout an individual's lifetime, it is necessary to specify what is meant by ego's village or ego's wife's village. Here both men and their wives have been identified with their fathers' villages. This is not necessarily that in which they were reared, or that in which they were living when courting.

[6] In 1956–57 West African currency was exchangeable at par with British. No part of this payment is reclaimable on divorce.

[7] In 1956–57 the amount of adultery fines varied for Commoners from £1 to £5 and for chiefs and other office-holders might be as high as £15–£25.

[8] See J. Goody (1962) for distinction between masculine and other categories of property.

[9] A similar distinction must be made for girls with respect to genetrix and socializing agent.

[10] This situation is rather complicated and merits study on its own. If the *genitor* has contributed to a child's upkeep by sending food and money with fair regularity it may be said that he has reared the child, although the foster parent will also claim to have reared a boy or girl whom he has trained and ministered to during childhood and adolescence.

[11] This differs from the fostering described by Forde for the Yakö (1941) in that it is explicitly defined as a right of the parents' siblings while the parents' marriage is intact, and that a step-parent is infrequently a foster parent. Djamour (1959)

describes one form of adoption for the Singapore Malay as fostering. This again appears to differ from the Gonja institution in that among the latter there is a *right* of parents' kin to claim foster children, and also in that [among the Malays the child returns to the parents' home in late childhood or adolescence, the points at which the Gonja foster child is most likely to be sent away. Malay foster parents appear always to be women while this is specifically not the case in Gonja.

[12] This may seem a small point, but it does show that a distinction is made; it may be that every society informally penalizes, that is, ridicules, the child born out of wedlock, though he may not be otherwise handicapped.

[13] The question arises as to whether in the absence of any particular stress on the legitimacy of children there is some form of puberty ceremony which serves to identify the reproductive powers of a nubile girl with her kin and to separate these from her sexuality, which must then be alienated to a consort outside the group. This appears to me one function of girls' puberty ceremonies among the Ashanti (Rattray 1927: 69ff.) and the Nayar (Gough 1955, 1959). There are no puberty rites for members of either sex in Gonja, which seems linked to the absence of corporate descent groups in which rights *in genetricem* may be vested.

[14] I am indebted to Fortes's 'Time and Social Structure' (1949b), for the idea that divorce in old age might have particular significance.

[15] 'Treatment' consisted mainly of aspirin and pleas that the sick be taken to the nearest hospital, some 25 miles away.

[16] That is, including marriages of barren women.

[17] Except where there are mitigating circumstances such as the husband's impotence or sterility.

[18] With the occasional exception of ritual services in the propitiation of the husband's and their children's ancestors.

[19] I neglected to ascertain whether this applies only to the first husband, or whether a woman is never fully widowed in this sense so long as any previous husband outlives a more recent spouse who dies first. My impression is that survival of any previous spouse implies this very limited continuation of 'ownership' rights.

[20] The Fulani practice (Stenning 1959) of an elderly woman and her husband being supported by different sons, each in a separate kraal, is rather similar. However the Fulani wife does not usually rejoin her natal kin, either alone or with a son who supports her, as is the Gonja pattern.

[21] Relevant information is lacking on one of the fifteen women.

[22] This 'cultural blind-spot' is so marked that it is unlikely to be acccidental. It seems likely that for even minimal stability of marriage the actors must assume that, at least in *their* case, it will last.

[23] These women varied between 70 and 30 years of age. If cooking had really been his major concern one or two of the younger wives would have sufficed to fill his needs and he could have released the other ones. But the number of his wives was a matter of great pride to him and he could not bear to reduce this by even one.

[24] This includes two women who are dependants of chiefs. Neither has natal kin in the village, nor elsewhere that I was able to discover. Both are almost certainly of slave descent although no mention was ever made of this. Such people are referred to as belonging to the kin of those who originally owned them—'they are our family (*kana*)' is the expression. They are treated as dependants only because no direct kinship connexion can be traced. In another generation or two this will no longer be the case and they will become kin indeed.

[25] This should not be too strongly emphasized, as the Gonja are not greatly concerned with their forefathers. It is very rarely, for instance, that a sacrifice is made to those more remote than the immediately previous generation. Dead parents are asked to inform *their* forefathers, but names of the latter are seldom specified.

[26] A similar point was also made by Forde (1941) and Gluckman (1950) in pointing out that in some societies the family is a transitional unit, while the continuity and stability necessary for the persistence of the system are provided by groups based on other organizing principles, that is, descent, locality, etc.

[27] This, again, may be the village of either parent.

[28] Any sufficiently detailed ethnographical account will probably include information on relevant points. See especially Gluckman (1950), Djamour (1959), Stenning (1959) and R. T. Smith (1956). For a specifically numerical approach see Forde (1941), Turner (1957) and Fortes (1949 b) who distinguish explicitly the marital status of women at different ages. Mitchell and Barnes (1950) present data broken down by age, but do not discuss the implications in any detail.

[29] '...cicisbeism ...is the counterpart of concubinage, i.e. the woman has a male partner in sex relations, but if children are born to this union, the cicisbeo is not the legal father', (1925, 1: 197).

[30] I did come across one elderly couple, Commoners, who probably married when the wife was in late middle age.

[31] Ritual ties do persist, see above.

[32] In Stenning's usage *de facto* divorce consists '...solely of a rupture of conjugal relations' and *de jure* divorce consists 'of a formal adjudication as well as a rupture of conjugal relations...' (1959: 179).

TAITA BRIDEWEALTH AND AFFINAL RELATIONSHIPS

By GRACE HARRIS

The purpose of this essay is to describe and analyse the nature of affinal roles and relationships among the Taita of Kenya as seen through the institution of bridewealth. There is an attempt to seek out the interconnexions between the form of affinal relationships on the one hand and, on the other, the distribution of affinal ties—between the *how* and the *who* of affinity. The forms of specific affinal relations, more particularly those of a man and his close male affines, are related to certain broad structural features of Taita society. This last project, especially, requires the inclusion of a general introduction to Taita life.

INTRODUCTION

The Taita Hills rise from the plain of southern Kenya about 100 miles inland from Mombasa. The largest massif, Dabida, is inhabited by the major portion of the Taita people who numbered in 1948 about 53,000. Restricted largely to the hills by the aridity of the surrounding country, the Taita cultivate a variety of subsistence crops and a few others for small-scale export. Relatively small herds of cattle, goats and sheep graze on upland and plains pastures. Most of the work of subsistence agriculture is done by women and adolescent girls while men, in addition to doing the heavy farming tasks, tend cash-crops and herds. Men also go out to work in the townships and in Mombasa.

Over most of the hills, and especially in the middle altitudes (2500 to 4500 feet), homesteads are grouped in scattered small hamlets and villages set close to or in the midst of cultivated tracts. These areas of dispersed settlement tend to be relatively well endowed with arable land and water, with the inhabitants dependent largely on their upland fields and only secondarily on plains gardens at the foot of the hills; pasture is scarce. Where there are large, compact settlements of up to several hundred households there is heavy dependence on plains cultivation, since upland soil and water resources are poor although pasture land is plentiful.

Those parts of the hills with a relatively good supply of arable land have served as refuge areas during times of food shortage when other parts of the hills have suffered severe famines. People in areas with plenty of pasturage offer indirect access to their resources through the practice called *vuturi*, in which the owner of a beast gives it into the keeping of another man, who has the right to its products. Numerous other *vuturi* arrangements are made between men of the same community or different communities (see below) whatever the relative resources, for purposes of insurance and concealment, while small-scale barter and sale of food-stuffs provide further economic links within and between different parts of the hills. [1]

Descent groups called *vichuku vibaha* (sing. *kichuku kibaha*) or 'large lineages' are composed of the descendants in the male line of a common male ancestor usually four to six generations removed from today's elders. The males of this unit maintain dominance over a tract of upland territory and often a section of plains as well. Since the large lineage is *not* exogamous, the localized group is not composed simply of a core of adult males living with their wives and children, all of the women having married in. On the contrary, a substantial proportion of the female population of a large lineage also remains part of the localized group.

Between some large lineages the existence of more or less remote agnatic links is recognized without their exact nature being of much interest. Though the amount of association continued between related lineages varies greatly, separation in time and space lead ultimately to the extinction of ties. The absence of an exogamic bond leaves no basis for remembering links indefinitely.

A large lineage functions as a corporate group in limited respects. Every male has a right to live somewhere within the territory and to build a permanent herd-enclosure or herder's shelter on the grazing lands; non-members require permission for either. A shrine centre and a repository for the skulls of the dead are ritual foci. Apart from a few ritual observances, however, mobilization of an entire lineage or its body of elders occurs rarely, when there is the threat of large-scale encroachment on the territory or when rights are to be granted to outsiders.

Otherwise, the large lineage operates as a group within which individually held rights in land and livestock are transmitted by inheritance and within which there is a certain amount of control over the disposition of inherited land by pawn, loan or sale. Therefore rights in inherited property depend on *specific* agnatic ties, especially on close ones. As one would expect, then, segments of a low order are functionally important.

While his father is still alive a married man acquires rights in that land belonging to his father but cultivated by his mother. After the father's death the other land belonging to him is divided by birth order among the sons who, together, form his *nyumba* or house. Each should get a portion of land of the various types (moist valley-bottom, irrigated, dry hillside, plains) suited to different crops. As with land, so with livestock, there is some apportionment by matri-segments, each of which is called a *munyango*, door, during the lifetime of the father. But the latter remains in direct control. After the father's death and when all sons have taken brides, the final distribution of remaining animals follows birth order. With both kinds of property, the eldest gets the largest of the shares, which descend in size until that of the youngest, who receives certain perquisites as the comfort of the parents' old age. [2]

Final settlement of an estate waits upon the settlement of various loans. These include a customary loan of land to sons-in-law. Such land, cultivated by the daughters of a man, cannot be taken away from them so long as they live. It is reclaimed by the heirs of the brothers, i.e. the grandsons of the original owner, who thus form the *ifwa* or inheritance group (literally death or funeral) within which the original estate is settled. These close agnates have a common interest in conserving land-rights within the group, and it is they who exert pressure on a man not to sell valuable land except to some one among themselves.

Inequities (as against inequalities) in the division of livestock among a man's sons occur for many reasons and loans between brothers further complicate matters. Therefore the *ifwa* group also has to settle livestock accounts. Furthermore, should one of their number die without legal male issue, an heir is chosen from among the heirs of the other *ifwa* members. Since incest regulations forbid cohabitation of persons who have a common grandparent, there cannot be marriages linking members of an *ifwa*.

Members of an *ifwa* constitute the third generation of the *kinyumba* (pl. *vinyumba*) or room founded by their grandfather, and the heirs to all the *vinyumba* founded by the sons of one man make up a *kichuku kitini* (pl. *vichuku vitini*) or small lineage. Search for an heir to the property of a man without legal sons rarely has to go outside this four-generation segment. It is not surprising, then, that genealogical rearrangement occurs beyond this level, with the various small lineages fitted into wider segments, the founders of which usually are treated as the sons of the large lineage progenitor by various wives.

The basic rule governing choice of a spouse has been mentioned—that prohibiting marriage between persons with a common grandparent. Ordinarily, descent being patrilineal, it would be necessary only to be certain that prospective spouses do not have the same grandfather. It sometimes happens, however, that a woman bears children to successive husbands, the children of each man being reckoned his legal offspring. The woman's grandchildren cannot marry among themselves.

Persons who have a common great-grandparent can marry, but it is considered preferable that the spouses be descended from different wives of their common ancestor. Marriage between kin of this degree is called sorcery marriage (*kulovua kwa vusavi*) and requires the ritual killing of kinship (*kubwaga kichuku*). Beyond this degree any marriage with consanguineal kin is permitted with the proviso that spouses ought not to reckon each other as classificatory parent and child. However, if the relationship is well beyond the range of sorcery marriage membership in adjacent generations is overlooked.

Other rules forbid marriage with certain affines. Two brothers cannot marry two sisters and one brother–sister pair cannot marry another such pair. Stated another way, a man cannot marry the sister of either his brother's wife or his sister's husband; a woman cannot marry the brother of either her sister's husband or her brother's wife. Marriage with a spouse's parent's sibling or sibling's child is also forbidden.

While the sororate and sororal polygyny are not allowed, the levirate is practised. The preferred husband-surrogate is the deceased's own brother, younger or older; but a more remote agnate, a father's sister's son, or even a matrilateral cousin of the dead man can be chosen. Such choices are actually practicable because of the high degree of local endogamy.

Typically, two or three (sometimes more) large lineages form a local community which we call a neighbourhood, after the Taita term *izanga*, meaning country or locality. The association of lineages forming a neighbourhood has two major features. First, over and above lineage endogamy, there is heavy intermarriage among the member lineages so that most marriages are intra-neighbourhood. Secondly, it is virtually impossible for a man to live in one neighbourhood and to buy or even borrow land elsewhere, but within a single neighbourhood a large number of transactions are effected.

As men seek to fulfil their needs for land of particular kinds, to replace exhausted gardens left fallow, to put additional land under cultivation, they must borrow, buy, or take in pawn land belonging to men who are members of their own lineages or of the associated lineages. Sometimes a change of residence is desirable in order to be at a convenient distance from current cultivations. Therefore households are moved from time to time, either to another plot of land owned by the head or to a piece of borrowed land, on which non-permanent buildings may be erected.

At any time, then, the householders resident in the territory dominated by one lineage include a scattering of men of the associated lineages. Many of these ultimately move back to the parts of the neighbourhood dominated by their own lineages, but others stay on (especially if they live on purchased land) and their sons may eventually return to the original sites. Thus each lineage has less than completely exclusive occupation of its territory. The neighbourhood is itself highly exclusive but within it there is much exchange of land as well as movement. In a very real sense the neighbourhood can be looked on as a land-use unit.

The neighbourhood is not wholly closed, for migration from one locality to another occurs and there are customary ways of integrating 'foreigners'. [3] Neither are the configurations completely stable, for the marriage patterns shift and population changes bring about realignments. Usually, changing marriage patterns and population movements are interrelated. None the less, residents of a neighbourhood act on the assumption that theirs is a long-term association. The large amount of intra-neighbourhood marriage means that everyone is related to everyone else by some tie of consanguineal or affinal kinship. One expression of this state of affairs is the description of co-residents as 'people who understand one another' or 'people who have reached an agreement'.

Given its tendency towards exclusiveness, the neighbourhood obviously is a political unit. Within it the age-status system which cuts across lineage and local boundaries is manifested concretely in the controls exercised by *ad hoc* councils of elders which settle disputes and decide the course of local affairs. Nowadays some, but by no means all, neighbourhoods are roughly co-extensive with some of the modern administrative units called sub-locations. Sub-locations are grouped into locations under Government-appointed chiefs who, like sub-location headmen, are salaried civil servants. Elders, the highest indigenous authorities, continue to exercise much control and influence, however.

A young married man remains under the domination of his father, who controls the property used by members of his domestic group and family. [4] Even livestock earned by the young man is jointly housed and herded with his father's beasts. In any case, he is forbidden to compete openly or extensively for wealth in herds lest he be guilty of attempting to 'surpass' his father.

The father's death and the final division of the estate make a man an independent householder, free to compete. If the years bring material prosperity and a flourishing domestic group, the acquisition of ritual pre-rogatives follows. Shrines of his own and participation in the lineage shrine-centre both validate and enhance the status of a rich man: they make him an elder. As an elder he takes part in community affairs, helping to settle disputes, reach decisions and carry out the many ritual activities which bring together neighbourhood residents in various combinations. [5] Livestock transactions, including *vuturi*, link him to men of other neighbourhoods. So do blood-pacts which also perform a 'national' political function. [6]

The ritual system of the Taita flourishes despite almost three-quarters of a century's mission activity. It includes a variety of private and public sacrifices, offerings and counter-sorcery. [7] However, there are today no national rites or any single ritual official or leader with adherents throughout the hills. Their language and traditions, common way of life, the knowledge that formerly they joined in raids into other tribal territories and today's adminis-trative unity in a single sub-District provide their sense of oneness. Con-tainment in their little knot of hills underlies it.

TYPES OF BRIDEWEALTH ARRANGEMENTS

In many situations in Taita various services are performed by men for their fathers-in-law and the latters' sons. Dunning for debts; serving out beer at a beer-drink; acting as agent in bridewealth affairs; sweeping the homestead clearing on each morning of the mortuary observances following a death: all these tasks, and others, may be given to the husbands of daughters and sisters. Taita sum up the relationship of most men to their close male affines by saying that 'honour' is due to the wife's father and brother. They imply general deference as well as the performance of specific duties. Typically, Taita explain the deference which most men show to their close affines by pointing out that they have been 'given' wives. A woman is said to be the most precious of the world's goods. Yet reference to Taita 'values' or to a supposedly fixed scale of valued goods does not help our understanding very much. Ascertaining the position of a good in the scale does not tell us how that good will be employed socially or how it enters the exchange system. Women, like other goods, may be gathered in as tribute in some social systems and distributed as largesse in others. In the first case bridewealth is a donation from a social superior; in the second it is an inferior return.

A third possibility is a relationship of equivalence, with bridewealth considered complete and adequate return for rights in a woman. Certain instances of affinal relationships in Taita are of this sort. In these, there is mutual deference and the duties listed above are not imposed on the son- or brother-in-law. In all such cases the son- or brother-in-law is an elder at the time of marriage.[8] Not only do these departures require explanation, but the dominant pattern cannot itself be understood without taking them into account.

It must be noted that with the passage of time a man who married as a youth also finds relations with his male affines less formal and, as he ages, he is released from menial tasks, especially when there are younger kinsmen available. Perhaps we are dealing only with natural consideration for advancing years.

To see that more than this is involved we must examine bridewealth arrangements, asking whether men who marry as elders ever enter into contracts which differ from those of non-elders. Not only amounts and kind of bridewealth must be considered, but what might be called the terms of credit, in relation to the removal of the bride from her parental home, must also be dealt with. Taking these into account, five main varieties of bridewealth arrangements can be distinguished. Although the distinctions do not yield a series of co-ordinate types, they are the significant ones.

Exposition can begin with the arrangement which will be called *completed betrothal*, according to which many or most, but not all. payments are made during a betrothal period lasting two years or more. The betrothal is terminated when the bride's parents give their permission for her removal to the groom's homestead. The remaining payments are left outstanding for some time. Total amounts of the various items asked and paid are fairly well standardized within each of the areas corresponding roughly to the modern locations.

Description of completed betrothal provides the opportunity to consider the nature of Taita bridewealth and its more important jural aspects. Other kinds of arrangement can be considered briefly before turning to the implications of the differences among them.

COMPLETED BETROTHAL

Kind and order of payments

Bridewealth is known as *vupe*, a word which also means 'affinity'; it is, besides, the term for the permitted removal of the bride to her new home. *Vupe* in the sense of bridewealth now consists of live-stock and numerous other items of various kinds. The items and amounts referred to below are those current in the years 1950–52, and attention is given only to such shifts in emphasis as were observed during the time. The use of the present tense, then, refers to that period. [9]

Payment of the livestock portion of bridewealth gives a man (and his agnates) rights in the woman's reproductive capacities. Henceforth any children born to her belong to his large lineage. His property rights will pass to the male offspring and the bridewealth of daughters is his due.

Of the livestock payments, the most important single animal is *kifu*, 'womb'. Bridewealth *kifu* is a special instance of a more general type of transaction with this name in which one party contracts for a heifer calf as yet unborn. In order for the transaction to be complete, the heifer calf must itself reach maturity and bear a calf of either sex. If it dies before doing so, another heifer must be supplied or payments (usually in small stock or money) are not completed. Therefore the *kifu* transaction is by its nature not regarded as closed when the heifer calf is born.

In the case of bridewealth *kifu*, even the transfer of the *kifu*-bearing cow to the stock enclosure of the girl's father promotes the union's development. It is evidence of the *intent* to secure final rights over the woman's child-bearing capacities. The man becomes *pater*-elect. As such he acquires the tacit approval of the bride's parents for the sexual relations which will lead to the realization of her reproductive powers. Therefore, should a betrothed woman conceive while still under her father's roof, the usual fine for impregnating an unmarried girl is not due and no shame attaches to the couple, at least among Pagans. [10] An extra beast is required, however, 'for having made her a woman before her time'.

The other livestock payments include (in all but Bura location) one bull called *mlisha*, 'the herder'. This, as well as a number of small stock, go to the bride's father. [11] The only other person who regularly receives any portion of the livestock payments is the bride's mother's brother. A bull called *kivavuye*, 'thing of the mother's brother' is owing to him provided he contributed a goat or its equivalent to the girl's initiation festivities. One other live beast may be due: the bull called *vulela*, 'nurture', paid to whoever raised the bride if her own *pater* did not do so.

Other beasts are required for slaughtering. One is a bull called *horo* (or *oro*) which is divided between the two fathers, each of whom distributes meat to his close kin. Sometimes a large male goat (not castrated) is furnished instead. Another beast, either a castrated goat or a bull, [12] goes to the bride's parents to share among their kin, the man's side receiving only the usual 'herder's portion' of ribs. Other animals are required by Pagans for haruspication in order to be certain that the match is auspicious. If the couple share a common great-grandparent, a goat or bull is killed and divided between the two sides 'to kill kinship'. Finally, one other animal, a castrated goat or a bull, ought ultimately to be supplied, when the wife is past menopause. Called *gilale* or *gulale*, it is supposed to mark the completion of the union. [13]

The order in which these animals are transferred or supplied is highly variable. Quite commonly all the live beasts due to the bride's father are demanded before removal of the bride is allowed. On the other hand, the mother's brother may be given his bull while some payments to the father are deferred. It is usual to wait until after co-residence is established to furnish the animals for ceremonial division; indeed, some maintain that *horo* is properly supplied only when the couple have a child old enough to share in the meal of titbits which, as on all ritual occasions, takes place before the main portions are shared out and carried home. Occasionally, though, *horo* or the beast supplied for the woman's kin alone are asked while the bride is still at home. In no case of prolonged betrothal are all the livestock payments complete when the bride goes to her new home.

Throughout the betrothal period the rest of *vupe* is presented in numerous lots, either as the accompaniment of or the occasion for many visits and conferences. Named portions of sugar cane beer are furnished for the couple's close male kinsmen at various stages of the match; other special beer-drinks honour the bride's father and her mother's brother, [14] and one is the occasion for a visit by the bride's kin to the village where she will go to live. Participation in a bridewealth beer-drink makes a man witness to the proceedings and entails the duty of testifying should a case concerning them arise. At the same time, the beer is reckoned as a prestation due from the groom's side. Christians substitute tea with large quantities of sugar and tinned milk.

Small amounts of foodstuffs may be demanded as accompaniments to the transfer of livestock or of the main food prestations. The latter include a large amount of plantains nominally given to the bride's mother by the groom's mother, but distributed by the former to her close female kin. These women are thereby obligated to contribute labour and food when eventually a house

is built for the bride. Amounts of cooked porridge vary; in the more prosperous locations, large amounts are furnished for a crowd of the bride's
female kin to take home after feasting the groom's womenfolk in return. The
traditional female obligation to grind maize for the bride's mother is often
commuted to a large payment of maize, requiring a heavy cash outlay. Among
Christians, quantities of sugar are demanded as a substitute for the sugar cane
beer which the serving of tea does not equal in cost.

Cash expenditures dominate the remainder of the prestations. Actual cash
payments go to the girl to secure her agreement to the betrothal, and to her
parents and mother's brother to bind them to the match; the latter payments
are *malasi*. A bride's sisters, her parents' sisters and her mother's brothers'
wives may receive small amounts of cash or goods, but in most areas this is
regarded as an unnecessary innovation. The parents often demand small cash
payments to accompany major prestations and to replace certain goods formerly given. Other traditional items are now replaced by purchased goods
such as blankets, clothing and farming tools. Numerous items of clothing,
cheap jewellery and cosmetics are sent to the girl throughout the betrothal
period.

Finally, there is labour service. The groom is required to furnish his own
and his male kinsmen's labour in the bride's mother's fields for a set number of
days or in a fixed number of garden plots. In most parts of the hills the groom
is also required to provide labour to build a new livestock enclosure for his
father-in-law if one is needed. A few people still require the services of the
groom's female kin to grind maize. However, as this service is now so often
commuted to payment in maize, so also the tendency is for money to take the
place of the other labour services.

Of the *vupe* items other than livestock, it is common for most to be paid
during the course of a long betrothal. Indeed, one of the main features of a
betrothal is the continuous demand by the bride and her parents for more
food, money and goods even though the limits on what is considered proper are
known. Clothing and implements for the parents often are not given until after
months of co-residence. The prestation to the mother-in-law initiates the use
of a reciprocal gift-name. [15] Instead of making optional money payments to
other female kin of the bride these may be given (also optionally) blankets or
cloths after co-residence is established. Gift names also come into effect with
them. The cash payments may be deferred as well, but if this is done the
amounts are agreed on during the betrothal period. In this case demands and
promises then serve to carry proceedings toward their end.

Jural obligations

All the prestations mentioned constitute one entity in so far as the girl's
father is liable for their return should the match be broken off before

co-residence is established. Given co-residence without the birth of a child, he is liable for everything except the personal gifts to the girl and her kin and the girl's engagement money. Should the union be broken after the birth of children, the husband has the right to keep his rights in them, relinquishing claim to everything paid until then and paying any livestock debts. Or he can give up the offspring to the wife's father or brother and demand the return of the bridewealth or its equivalent in money. Ordinarily restitution for non-livestock payments, other than *malasi*, particularly foodstuffs, should not be demanded or made if the union has lasted for some years with or without the birth of children. This is so even though the payments described are to be distinguished from the many *douceurs* of foodstuffs which initiate the betrothal, the wedding garments for the bride if there is a church wedding, the small sums of money given the bride and her companions to persuade them to proceed to the groom's homestead, and the animals slaughtered for the celebration following the bride's removal. None of these is counted as *vupe* and their return is not even considered.

Responsibility for and distribution of the various portions of *vupe* sheds further light on their significance. It is notable that a very narrow range of male kinsmen is involved. A man's father is responsible for livestock payments, even though the resources he employs may be those on which the son has primary claim. The latter include the animals paid in at the marriage of his linked sister. [16] Also, the cow which bears the *kifu* calf in the father-in-law's enclosure ought to be left there if possible, to bear calves forming the nucleus of the young man's own herd. One or more of these can be promised as further bridewealth payment. Cash earnings of the son are increasingly important as fathers have come to feel that their sons can now afford to save towards the purchase of bridewealth animals.

If a man's own father is dead, his father's brother is responsible for arranging a marriage for him in consultation with his mother. The resources come from the dead man's estate. After that estate is divided the son becomes solely responsible for his outstanding bridewealth debts. While the father lives, the father's brother has only a moral obligation to make contributions which count as long-term loans payable to his heirs. Besides the father only the mother's linked brother has a specific obligation, to supply one bull which he can reclaim should the wife prove barren. For beer, foodstuffs and other items the father is again jurally responsible. The resources on which he draws may come from others as donations from kinsmen to be returned in the course of mutual aid, or as formal loans.

As to distribution, only the bride's father and her mother's brother receive livestock and, as we have seen, the latter's claim is conditional. Aside from what the bride herself receives, major money payments go to the mother and father who also receive labour services or substitutes for them. Goods other than foodstuffs go to the father, mother and mother's brother, and the last also receives a money payment. Thus the 'three parents', to use a Taita phrase, are the chief recipients.

Shares of meat from the specially slaughtered animals are distributed to the siblings of the parents and, through them, to their spouses and children; if there are grandparents alive they receive shares. This distribution marks out the bride's circle of close kin. Among them, only those *female* kin may sometimes receive special prestations with whom the bride and her mother customarily exchange help with domestic and agricultural work. No comparable prestations ever go to male kinsmen, even optionally; the limitations on their concern with the bridewealth is not obscured.

More remote female kin receive shares of cooked food. Except as they partake of these, male kin otherwise share only in the beer-drinks. On such occasions one or two close agnates, preferably brothers, are present because they may have to be involved directly if the bride's father dies; the mother's brother of the bride, when he is present, is there as an honoured guest who should take an interest in the affairs of his sister's child; a son-in-law or a sister's husband comes along as retainer; a matrikinsman or two may come as witnesses who have no possible self-interest to tempt them from honesty. All act as witnesses and in this capacity alone they would have to share in the beer.

The limited obligations of male kinsmen on the groom's side contrast in some respects with the rights extended to them. In theory, at least, agnates other than brothers and even matrikinsmen have the right of sexual access to a man's wife in his absence, provided that none tries to form a lasting liaison with her. Of more immediate significance is the limited involvement of male kin of *both* parties to a union. This means that it is legitimate to focus attention on the relationships of a man and his immediate affines.

Developments after co-residence

When the bride's parents give their permission, the couple take up residence together either at the homestead of the husband's parents or, if he has been married before, at his own place. Christian parents delay longest and demand the most nearly complete payment before granting permission, because once the church wedding has taken place the state of bridewealth payments has no bearing on the union's validity in Kenya law. Even so, something is always left unpaid.

As we have seen, transfer of livestock, specifically the *kifu* heifer, means that even before co-residence is established the groom is already 'husband' in having a tentative claim over the woman's reproductive capacities, and he exercises sexual rights. The acquisition of these rights, however, is the result of proceedings in which his father has taken the most active part. Replacement of the *kifu* heifer should it die without reproducing, and payment of outstanding debts, ought in theory to be met by the husband's father also. But he may be involved in the betrothal of another son, or he may lack the means. Whatever the circumstances, the position of bridewealth debtor is assumed more and more by the husband after he has entered into enjoyment of domestic rights as well. [17] Paternal responsibility may become a fiction.

During the first few years after co-residence is established the wife's parents demand, and usually manage to extract, money and goods still owed to them. However, the demand for and evasion of final livestock payments often tends to become a formality the primary consequence of which is to keep the issue alive. From the point of view of the father-in-law it is well not to press quickly for replacement of the *kifu* heifer or for any other live animals due. By leaving debts uncollected he can avoid paying livestock debts of his own and maintain a source on which to draw in an emergency. This is one way of saving for a time when his own son has to make his first bridewealth payments. Furthermore, replacement twice-over is the limit of the claim. Loss of the third heifer falls on the father-in-law, but if he does not press for replacement he can avoid some of the risk by collecting only when he must soon disburse. He has, in effect, an insured savings-account.

Both sides have reason to 'wait and see' how the domestic union fares, lest they become involved in problems of divorce and repayment. Children are crucial. Though barrenness cannot be cited as grounds for divorce, other reasons are not hard to find. Therefore the father of a woman who has borne no children is in no position to press for payment, and there is no reason why the husband should be eager to complete payment for rights which he may never realize.

Extending the completion of bridewealth over a long time follows the pattern of most transactions in Taita. On the creditor's side the desire to press claims must be balanced against the advantages of retaining the other party as a debtor. On the other side, the desirability of being debt-free must be weighed against the assurance of receiving what is paid for. Sooner or later the remaining *vupe* payments are demanded in earnest, and if they are not forthcoming the woman may be persuaded to return to her parental home. Faced with loss of her services the husband goes to plead for her return. Actually, the father-in-law's jural position is weak, for having permitted co-residence and allowed the couple to live undisturbed for some time, he will be told that 'he has given his daughter to that man'. Non-completion of payments does not alter this fact and the husband has the right to charge his wife with desertion should she remain in her parental home for a long time. The father-in-law can threaten to come to an agreement with some other man more ready to pay, and to return the bridewealth already given. Usually the outcome is a promise to pay, the return of the wife, and actual payment in part or whole some time later.

This situation points to the importance for the affinal relationship of the fact that the exercise of conjugal rights is in part independent of the strict jural significance of particular bridewealth prestations. Initial payment of *kifu* makes a man *pater*-elect to a woman's children. Though the *kifu* payment may be 'incomplete' long after co-residence is established, the initial payment safeguards his position. Sexual rights have been enjoyed since the betrothal period and domestic rights since the removal of the bride—all with the agreement of the father-in-law. The man has behaved as husband and son-in-law and he has been treated as such by others.

In this manner final validation of the conjugal union lags behind its *de facto* development. The affinal relationship between a man and his father-in-law is that of debtor and creditor, but the creditor is in effect bound by his previous recognition of the union to extend credit further, unless he wishes to put an end to the marriage. [18] Temporarily 'repossessing' his daughter has little more than nuisance value. Litigation is not a popular alternative in Taita since it is regarded as poor taste or worse to hale a son-in-law into court. The relationship is by definition that of a magnanimous and long-suffering creditor and a grateful debtor; litigation alters it beyond all recognition.

It is not surprising, therefore, to find that the threat of supernatural sanctions becomes more and more important if with the passing years children have been born and are growing up. As part of the pattern of supernatural threats, 'injured hearts' of a man's close affines endanger the well-being of his herds and his children. In the event of illness or death among the children or in the herd, haruspication may reveal the father-in-law's concealed anger. Then payment (or a firm promise of it) should speed recovery or ensure future safety.

Hence in their middle years many men complete payments, including those of the beasts to be slaughtered for special meat distribution. Sometimes, however, a man evades final payment, spending the rest of his life in debt, after his father-in-law's death, to his wife's linked brother whose 'heart' may be 'injured' if payment is too long delayed. In the most extreme cases, a union begun with a formal betrothal is not fully validated until after the deaths of the partners, when their son completes the bridewealth payments.

Curtailed betrothal

Wearying of a lengthy betrothal and knowing that he cannot meet the demands of the bride's parents for some time, a man may take his bride away without permission. Sometimes the couple plan the escapade themselves, but usually a girl must be persuaded at an opportune time and place to go away with the man. Night-time dances are a favourite occasion, but girls also abscond during the day from their work in the gardens: hence the term *arusi ya mchugunyi*: 'bean-field wedding'. Another method is that of pseudo-abduction. A man and a few friends surprise the girl and carry her off, kicking and screaming. If the couple are known to be betrothed no one but very close kin are bound to interfere. [19] It appears that acceptance of the betrothal money obliges the girl to elope should she be asked to do so.

The couple spend the night at the man's homestead, where the other residents 'discover' the bride next morning. This is a feature present in all modern arrangements except church weddings. Removal of the bride with her parents' permission also takes place at night and most of the community are supposed to know nothing about it until the next day. So far as the general public is concerned, the important fact is that the couple behave as spouses. The next question is whether those concerned with validating the union with bridewealth will allow them to live as spouses.

It is rare for a man's parents to risk accusations of 'haughtiness' by turning the girl away. On the other side, the bride's parents are sure to be troublesome. If her father is determined to force payment he commands his daughter to come home. [20] Not having granted permission to remove the bride, he is on firmer ground than if he had done so. Nevertheless, when a couple have gone off together once they are likely to do so again. The girl's parents are therefore under pressure to grant permission unless they are prepared to keep her under constant surveillance. In most such cases the bride's parents fight a losing battle. Often they do not attempt to win it but, after a display of anger for form's sake, they accept promises for the remaining bridewealth.

After this happens the course of affairs is much the same as in cases of completed betrothal. The difference lies in the fact that, depending on how greatly the betrothal has been curtailed, the husband has won more favourable terms of credit in relation to the achievement of co-residence. *Kifu* and some of the other livestock payments must be made fairly soon (within six months or a year) or the father-in-law may try again to take back the woman. Even these payments can often be delayed successfully when the woman's parents have resigned themselves to the union. As when permission is granted after only some payments, the father-in-law often has reasons of his own for not pressing his demands.

Curtailed betrothals are of course greatly embarrassing to Christian parents. They are forced to choose between countenancing what they regard as a sinful liaison until more of the bridewealth is paid and holding a church wedding before they are safely in possession of most of the bridewealth. [21]

Elopement

Many couples elope without any betrothal and, therefore, without any previous payment of any sort. In this event a woman's father, unbound by any agreement even to a betrothal, has several choices. First, if he really objects to the man he can refuse to undertake bridewealth discussions, force his daughter to return, and try to arrange a betrothal with someone of his own choice. Repeated elopements may force the father to abandon these efforts and should this happen, the status of the union remains undecided. If the couple remain together for some years, the woman's father usually breaks down and accepts bridewealth. Until this happens relations between him and his would-be son-in-law are likely to be very strained and even afterwards they may well be something less than amicable.

A second possible course is to conduct a campaign for early payment of at least some of the bridewealth, using the same techniques as in cases of curtailed betrothal, but adding the threat of accepting bridewealth from someone else. Thirdly, he may be willing to accept token payments and promises for a considerable time, especially if he likes the man personally. The same factors which operate in cases of completed and curtailed betrothal help to make it possible for him to tolerate deferring payments. When this happens, the husband is indeed a debtor to his father-in-law and his deference is far more than an empty show.

Uxorilocal labour-service

Co-residence can be established without a long betrothal by going to live at the homestead of the father-in-law. This procedure entails the postponement of most or all payments. Formerly, the son-in-law would 'work off' all the payments by doing herding or agricultural work for the wife's father. Nowadays he can also go out to work for wages with which to purchase *vupe* goods.

If work is to be substituted for bridewealth payments, a rough schedule of equivalents must be worked out. Actually, it is possible for men to receive very favourable terms from their fathers-in-law, though most Taita regard such subservience with a distaste which detracts from the practical advantages. Besides the service counted towards bridewealth, uxorilocal residence implies and involves the more regular performance of all manner of services for the father-in-law than when residence is virilocal.

Debt-free marriage

Arranging a match for his daughter or sister, a man may agree to the immediate payment of bridewealth, or at least to the rapid completion of payments. Some betrothal period may be observed, but the procedure is greatly simplified. Most or all of the payments are commuted to livestock and money or entirely to livestock; in some cases it is even commuted entirely to small stock, eliminating the *kifu* payment with its element of tentativeness. Labour-service is omitted. Furthermore, it is acceptable for the husband-to-be to offer more than the customary local amount. The whole transaction is arranged as an affair pleasing to both sides. The son- or brother-in-law (sister's husband) in this case is not subject to demands for services or deference. The relationship is supposed to be one of mutual regard and co-operation.

Of the arrangements described, all are available to non-elders except the last: only elders can have initially debt-free marriages. Non-elders are always involved in some kind of long-term indebtedness. Some completed betrothals manifest the minimum of indebtedness, but even then some debts are always left outstanding. Curtailed betrothal, elopement and uxorilocal labour-service involve a man in greater indebtedness to his father-in-law and, should the latter die, to his wife's brother. Elders, on the other hand, can contract marriages without long-term indebtedness. Equally important, elders can offer more than the local customary amount, while for a non-elder to do so would be to risk being accused of an attempt to 'surpass' his father-in-law.

Clearly wealth differences are important. When a man and his father have substantial resources, it is feasible to make most of the major payments during a betrothal period of two years. Poverty spurs men to curtail their betrothals, elope, or enter uxorilocal labour-service. Elders are by definition men of means who can afford to make large payments all at once or over a short period.

However, the means and wishes of husbands-to-be are only one side of the story. The other side is the willingness or unwillingness of women's fathers to accept the terms. It is, in fact, *unacceptable* for a non-elder to complete all payments quickly, and offers to exceed the customary local amounts would be intolerable. As against these restraints on payment, curtailed betrothal and elopement frequently prove quite acceptable in spite of the show of angry threats. Far from being rare departures from the form of completed betrothal, these two practices are very common, [22] although uxorilocal labour-service is rare. The practical advantages to the father-in-law of leaving debts outstanding may be recalled. But then the question arises whether there would not be just as many advantages in keeping an elder son-in-law in debt.

It is obvious that whether or not the affinal relationship must be one of long-term indebtedness is determined, in part at least, by other than narrowly practical considerations. Bridewealth arrangements clearly are a manifestation also of other elements in the social situation, in particular the positions of the parties in the age-status system. This is quite a different question from that raised in the beginning.

In the age-status system, a man who has not yet established a household of his own is by definition lower than one who is the head of his own domestic group. A young man is therefore lower in status than his father-in-law. The kind of bridewealth arrangement which implies equivalence would contradict their inequality in the age-status hierarchy. Therefore he cannot have an arrangement without some long-term indebtedness. If he is prosperous, he can minimize the indebtedness aspect by having a completed betrothal; if he is poor, curtailed betrothal, elopement or uxorilocal labour-service are open to him.

In the case of a man marrying in early adulthood, the developmental aspect of relations with his affines also reflect age-status. As the years go by, he and his wife occupy a house of their own, their household affairs gradually become more and more independent of those of his father, and children are born and grow up, adding to his responsibilities. All this results in a somewhat higher status in the community at large, as a 'man of maturity' (*mundu wa henga*). The gap in status between him and his father-in-law certainly has not closed. The father-in-law's status has also been changing and he may even by this time have become an elder. But the son-in-law is a householder and, if he has come into his inheritance, a man of property as well. As such, he is worthy of more consideration.

With respect to the relationship between a man and his wife's brother, their initial equivalence or near-equivalence in the age-status system becomes increasingly important as the years pass. After they have both become householders and therefore more independent of their respective fathers, they can engage in co-operative activities on their own, helping with each other's work and perhaps embarking on a joint trading venture. If both become elders, they are likely to co-operate in ritual activities. A man calls upon his sister's husband (his *mlamu*) to help him carry out a rite and to witness the correctness of his ritual acts, but the reverse occurs as well when a man asks his wife's brother (also *mlamu*) to help him with his ritual affairs.

When an elder marries he does not have to wait for this kind of development. He enters the affinal relationship as equal or even superior to his father-in-law in the age-status system, and almost certainly as the superior of his wife's brother. In keeping with his position, then, he can be allowed a bridewealth arrangement free of the implications of long-term indebtedness. Just as completion of payments in later years is, for a man who marries young, consonant with his rise in status, so prompt payment and even payment in excess of the usual amount is suitable for an elder.

Yet the importance of age-status *as such* cannot be pushed too far. In the first place, developmental changes are not so sweeping as wholly to redefine affinal roles and relationships. A man is still deferential to his father-in-law and his wife's brother in later years; he *owes* them help, they *honour* him with theirs. In the second place, all is well only when we confine ourselves to bridegrooms occupying positions at the extremes of the age-status hierarchy: youths who are clearly inferior to their fathers-in-law and elders who are their equals or superiors. In order for the Taita to be consistent, it should be found that the arrangements entered into by men marrying in their middle years (whether because they are widowed, divorced, or polygamous) vary depending on whether the wife's father is an elder, and therefore superior in status, or just another middle-aged householder.

This is not the case. With respect to bridewealth indebtedness, the primary distinction is simply between elders on the one hand, and the non-elders who constitute the great majority on the other. It is necessary to ask, therefore, what other characteristics all non-elders have in common which bear upon their bridewealth arrangements and which distinguish them from elders. There is, of course, the distribution of their marriage ties: most non-elders marry locally, within their own lineages and neighbourhoods, while extra-neighbourhood marriages are most usually entered by elders. This difference between elders and non-elders is related to the different expectations which they and their close affines have of one another regarding property other than bridewealth. We can examine these expectations and then return to the question of their bearing on bridewealth arrangements.

PROPERTY AND AFFINAL EXPECTATIONS

We have seen that membership in a large lineage gives a man the right to reside in the territory it dominates and to pasture his livestock on the common land. Rights in specific pieces of land are acquired primarily by inheritance from the *pater*, but also by other means. The ways in which inherited rights are supplemented by those acquired in other ways is significant for affinal relationships. If a man is one of a number of sons, his inherited land [23] may be too meagre for his needs. Even if the amount is considerable, it may not include the kinds of land he requires. Since every householder aims at exploiting land of the various kinds in order to obtain a variety of foodstuffs (as well as to insure against total crop loss), it may be necessary to acquire land of the desired kind or to effect exchanges. The inheritance system results in the distribution to each son of scattered parcels of land and, if these are too small to be worth while, reconsolidation is called for. Finally, and of considerable importance, the inherited parcels may be inconveniently distributed from the point of view of those who work the land, especially the women who raise the subsistence crops.

These needs are not equally pressing at all times. Their importance to a man varies as the domestic groups of which he is successively a member pass through their developmental cycle. When a young man brings his bride home, this event marks a new stage in the development of his parental household, for the new couple form part of it. The domestic obligations of the spouses to one another are not fully developed. Neither are the economic ones, including the husband's obligation to supply his wife with sufficient land and the wife's to supply him with food. On the production side, the young wife is part of her mother-in-law's work team, cultivating under her direction and in company with her and any unmarried girls of the household. When the husband is at home he is part of his father's work group, occasionally performing heavy agricultural tasks, building, herding, and nowadays growing cash crops. After a time, the husband's mother begins to set aside pieces of 'her' fields for her daughter-in-law to cultivate; these form the core of the son's inheritance in land. Even then the daughter-in-law is at her service. All farm produce is stored by the mother-in-law and rationed out by her, day by day. Women cook together and all the adults of one sex eat together. Only money creates a serious division when the young people's desire to spend it on themselves, or to save for their future, conflicts with the young man's duty to contribute to his parents.

During this stage, then, a man is really a dependent member of his parental household and his wife has been added as another dependant. The stage corresponds with the period during which his father is still immediately concerned in his bridewealth affairs, while he himself is called on to perform various tasks for his affines. There is no question of his being involved with them in land matters yet.

If a child born to the couple survives and especially if there is a second, they can move towards the establishment of their own household. [24] Preparation for the marriage of a younger brother of the husband further stimulates what is the initial step in the break-up of the parental household. Both sets of parents co-operate to build a house and the husband's mother supervises the building of the storage shelf, for the young wife is now to maintain and supervise her own food supply. Indeed, initiation of a separate household is usually phrased in terms of the wife's right to an establishment for herself and her children. The man's right to independence from his parents is then made a derivative of his duty to care for and support his own wife and offspring.

There is not a complete break with the parental household, to which the offshoot remains attached in various ways. However, three interrelated changes occur: (1) The relationship of the spouses alters, for now each owes domestic and economic services primarily to the other, whatever the other obligations. (2) The husband begins his progress towards complete independence from his father. (3) The husband begins to turn to kin other than his parents for help in meeting the needs of a growing family.

One of the most pressing needs is likely to be land. Unless he is an only son, a man can count on receiving only part of the land cultivated by his mother, and in any case she must be left with enough for herself for as long as she lives. Land retained by the father is a possible source of additional supplies. But while the father cannot impoverish his heirs by disposing of all his land, and although he has a moral obligation to help each son acquire fields, he has considerable freedom to dispose of unassigned fields, especially if they have been acquired through his own efforts. Such land he may choose to retain or to dispose of to others, leaving the son to seek land elsewhere. 'Elsewhere' does not mean 'anywhere' for, as has been pointed out, a man finds it difficult, albeit not always impossible, to acquire land outside the neighbourhood in which he resides.

For our purposes there are two relevant aspects of the intra-neighbourhood system of land transactions. First, the pattern of transferrers (those who sell, pawn or loan) and recipients of land manifests the differences between householders whose domestic groups are at different developmental stages, that is, the differences which are fundamental to the age-status system. Young men are recipients of land but not transferrers: as heads of domestic groups in the expanding phase of their cycle they seek land from older men. Elders whose households have diminished needs are transferrers of land but not recipients. Middle-aged men are either transferrers or recipients and very often the same individual is both. These men are engaged in consolidating their holdings, acquiring land of some kinds while disposing of other varieties, enlarging their holdings of land suitable for cash-crops, and so on. Their household needs are likely to be at their maximum. (This is so even if, in later years, polygamous unions postpone the ultimate decline of their households, for polygamy on a large scale is not found in Taita today. [25]) Like young men they are seekers of land but, like elders, they also have land to disburse.

Besides age-status, kinship relationships play a part in land transactions, but relationships of different kinds are of varying importance in the overall pattern. Close agnates are not, by and large, involved in loans of land because of the danger that the borrower might try later to claim that the field was part of his inheritance. Some sales occur between close and remote agnates, however, and remote agnates lend land to one another as well. Affinal ties are utilized very frequently. The relationship most often involved is that of father-in-law and son-in-law. A loan of land from the former to the latter is, indeed, the only land transaction (other than agnatic inheritance) which is viewed as customary and morally desirable. The loan is phrased as being made to the transferrer's daughter 'for the sake of the grandchildren', but since only men participate in the actual transactions it is in effect a loan to the son-in-law. However, land so loaned is cultivated by the transferrer's daughter, whose claim to its continued use supersedes her brothers' claims to inherit it for the duration of her life. Therefore land which a man receives on loan from his father-in-law is often retained for many years after the latter's death. The transaction becomes essentially an obligatory loan from the wife's brother(s).

Loans made initially by the wife's brother also occur 'so that the sister will not be without food'. But whether the original transferrer is wife's father or wife's brother, the latter's heirs must reclaim the land. The result is that, as loans between close affines are common, so loans to a man from his close matrikinsmen are concomitantly infrequent. [26] A man is not likely to receive a long-term loan of land from his mother's brother or from the mother's brother's sons who, on the contrary, demand the return of land loaned by their father or father's father. Short-term loans from close matrikinsmen are sometimes converted into sales, but there is a danger in these reciprocal to that inhering in loans between close agnates. That is, the purchase of land from the mother's brother may later be denied by the mother's brother's son arguing that the transaction was merely a loan and he has the right to demand return of the land. In this case the danger lies on the recipient's rather than on the transferrer's side.

Remote kin of all kinds enter into all the varieties of transactions, but the nature of the ties and even their existence is commonly ignored. Instead, the bonds of neighbourliness are called upon. Since, given the nature of the neighbourhood, virtually everyone in it is related to everyone else in some way, almost all transactions are in fact between affinal or consanguineous kin; but it is the relationship of 'people who understand one another' which is made the basis for particular transactions.

Having considered age-status and kinship in relation to land transactions, we can return now to the matter of the place of land in the mutual expectations of affines. The young householder seeks additional land within his own neighbourhood. Of the specific and close kinship ties which he can call upon, the affinal is most promising—provided his affines are members of the same local community. At the time when his own household has expanding needs, his father-in-law is likely to be in a position to dispense land. The latter's own sons may well be seeking land themselves but, as we have seen, a father has considerable freedom to dispose of at least part of his land, he can choose to distribute some to sons-in-law, and it is right that he do so 'for the sake of the grand-children'. The period during which a man is likely to become a land debtor to his father-in-law is also the time when he undertakes more and more responsibility for the completion of his bridewealth arrangements. Thus land indebtedness is added to his other debts to his father-in-law.

Arrival at the status of middle-aged householder finds a man in a different situation with respect to land, as described above. Relevant to affinal relations is the fact that he is likely to have retained the land borrowed from his father-in-law. When the latter has died, then, the indebtedness is transferred to the wife's brother, who is himself probably the head of a mature household. Any bridewealth debts still outstanding are also, of course, owed to him. Therefore this period, which may see a man engaged in many co-operative activities with his wife's brother, may also be one of double indebtedness.

In these days when good land for cash crops is more widely sought by middle-aged as well as young men, the land loaned by the father-in-law may be a source of friction between a man and his wife's brother. During 1950-52 a few cases were brought against men who tried to reclaim land loaned by their fathers to the husbands of sisters during the sisters' life-times. During those years, at least, the decisions went against the women's brothers and in favour of their husbands. At the same time, the attempts of a few men to claim that portions of their fathers-in-law's land *must* be lent to them were denied. This modern development has exacerbated the rivalry between a woman's husband and her brother for land originally belonging to her father, but the element is inherent in the system of land-holding and land transactions.

With this kind of land indebtedness to his affines a man marrying as an elder has nothing to do. He has accumulated land resources in the past years, while the needs of his household, even with its lifetime prolonged by the new marriage, are unlikely to be great. [27] Instead of borrowing land, he may himself act as transferrer, lending or selling land to his wife's father or her brother.

With respect to livestock, which we may consider much more briefly, elders and non-elders are also in very different positions *vis-à-vis* their affines. A young man must leave animals which he has acquired by his own efforts in the keeping of his father, mixed in with the latter's herd. Though, as we have seen, he may use these animals as bridewealth payments, he is not free to use them in other kinds of transactions of his own choosing and without his father's advice lest he risk accusations of trying to 'surpass' his father. Even after the death of his father, the actual partition of the latter's estate may have to await the marriages of younger brothers, further delaying his entry into the field of competition for livestock.

During the years when he is most likely to become indebted to his affines for land loans, then, a man has only one way of becoming involved with his affines in livestock transactions aside from bridewealth. This is by leaving in his father-in-law's keeping the cow which produced the heifer calf (always providing that his father's resources allow him to retain this animal and its other offspring). Like other *vuturi* arrangements this one honours the keeper by demonstrating the trust which the animal's owner has in him, in addition to conferring material benefits in the right to use milk. However, the honour and the practical gains certainly are not sufficient to put the father-in-law in the son-in-law's debt to an extent which greatly modifies the form of their relationship.

During the years following the death of his father and partition of the estate, a man tries to enlarge his holdings by careful husbandry and by means of various kinds of transactions, in particular by converting small stock or money into heifers acquired through non-bridewealth *kifu* transactions. At the same time he may be using bearing cows of his own to provide *kifu* heifers for other men, thereby enlarging his own holdings of small stock—

76

with which to acquire more heifers, and so on. Thus a middle-aged man may be engaged in many livestock transactions, sometimes as transferrer and sometimes as recipient, as he may be involved in numerous land transactions.

Of course there is the possibility that his resources will always be meagre and that therefore he will be only a minor participant in the competition for wealth in livestock. Real success in the acquisition of large herds is an achievement of very few Taita men. For most, their middle and later years bring added responsibilities but their resources, even augmented by the bridewealth of daughters, do not always suffice. There are the initial bridewealth payments to be made for sons; the frequent necessity to use small stock for sacrifices on behalf of himself, his wife, or children instead of converting it to cattle; nowadays, there is even occasional need to sell stock to pay school fees. Even if he has finished paying his own bridewealth, he has little scope for other kinds of livestock involvements with his affines. Should such a man lose his wife by death or divorce and choose to keep his children, he is not in a much better position than an unmarried youth. Having sole responsibility for his own initial payments, he may find it necessary to borrow in order to give *kifu*, and to become involved in long-term indebtedness to his new affines.

Elderhood, on the other hand, by definition implies at least moderate wealth in livestock: elders possess not only the freedom to enter into any transactions they wish, but the means of doing so. They are sought as transferrers of *kifu*. Other men also go to them for long-term loans of stock, thereby becoming their debtors and owing them deference. They have many *vuturi* arrangements, putting their own stock out while keeping that of other men. Elders enter mutual-aid partnerships whereby they furnish each other with animals for sacrifices and debt payments in order not to kill beasts from their own herds or disturb a *vuturi* arrangement with someone else.

Every elder enters into some of these arrangements with men in his own neighbourhood, but unlike land transactions, those in livestock need not be so confined. One elder is likely to have livestock debtors, *vuturi*-partners and mutual-aid partners scattered about the hills. Indeed, one of the objectives pursued by an elder is the establishment of a network of relationships beyond the bounds of his own local community. Access to outside grazing land and protection against spying are important advantages of *vuturi* arrangements with non-local men. Especially when they follow on or lead to the establishment of blood-pacts, extra-neighbourhood livestock transactions give an elder entrée into other communities and provide him with ties which supplement those based on kinship and propinquity. At the same time, transactions within the neighbourhood reinforce and modify existing ties in that kinsmen and neighbours become livestock debtors or partners also. But however he distributes his livestock transactions within and beyond his own neighbourhood, an elder, by virtue of his wealth, is in an advantageous position relative to others, including affines and potential affines. Far from having of necessity to remain in debt to others he can have others in debt to him. He can offer livestock loans or the advantages of a partnership to other men, including his prospective affines.

To sum up the expectations of affines with respect to property: though the payment of bridewealth is the only property transaction which affines *must* effect, other transactions may mould their relationships. We have seen that many young men searching for land utilize the moral claim to a parcel of land from the father-in-law; middle-aged non-elders may retain such land borrowed earlier (or, if they marry again, they may obtain more land in the same way). Thus many non-elders do in fact add land indebtedness to bridewealth indebtedness, while elders do not usually borrow land from anyone, including affines. Non-elders, as well as accumulating land, are in process of trying to build up their livestock holdings and they are not in a position to offer many loans or partnerships to affines or others; elders, with their wealth, can promise many such advantages.

'Promise' is a key word. For in trying to see the bearing on bridewealth arrangements of other expectations with respect to property, we have to ask whether the mere *possibility* that other transactions will take place is really that important. Does the fact that a young prospective son-in-law is *likely* to become a land-debtor or that an elder *may* in future engage in non-bridewealth livestock transactions with his affines affect bridewealth arrangements?

The problem is illuminated by considering an aspect of Taita affinity which so far has been taken as given: the distribution of affinal ties.

AFFINAL RELATIONSHIPS AND THE DISTRIBUTION OF AFFINAL TIES

It has been said that there is a high degree of local endogamy in Taita although there are no *prescriptive* marriage rules. To be somewhat more precise, it is found that of the wives of men belonging to a neighbourhood, roughly 30% have married within their own lineages, while about another 50% have married within the neighbourhood: thus (allowing for variation between neighbourhoods) some 80% of the wives have been taken from within their husbands' own local community. Of the non-local wives, half or more come from neighbourhoods which are not adjacent to the one in which they are married but rather from communities which, in Taita terms, are 'rather distant'. This leaves only a small percentage who have come in from adjacent neighbourhoods.

The relation between this pattern and the elder : non-elder dichotomy is important. The overwhelming proportion of the women from within the neighbourhood and from adjacent neighbourhoods are the wives of men who are non-elders or who were not yet elders at the time of the marriage. This in itself would hardly be surprising, since most men are non-elders. More significantly, marriages involving women from 'distant' communities are almost wholly confined to elders, with most of the current few exceptions resulting from the tendency of a few prominent Christian families to form alliances which cut across neighbourhood lines. Most non-elders, marrying within the neighbourhood, have as their affines members of the same local community. Elders, having in youth or middle years married within the neighbourhood, tend to take wives from outside it, mostly from non-adjacent communities. Therefore those more recently established affinal ties of elders tend to be with people of 'distant' localities.

This being so, the expectations which an elder's affines or prospective affines have of him are more than a mere possibility. Elders' extra-neighbourhood marriages are an integral part of their network of economic and political alliances. The establishment of these requires that an elder first make use of the chains of personal friendships and alliances already established by kinsmen and friends belonging to his own neighbourhood. Through accompanying others on their trips, or by visiting a 'distant' area under the aegis of a kinsman's blood-pact, an elder locates men of other communities who are themselves interested in forming extra-neighbourhood ties. The results are mutual-aid partnerships with other elders, long-term relationships with poorer men who borrow stock, and those *vuturi* arrangements which Taita prize so much. Co-operation in livestock-buying ventures in Pare, or some other kind of joint enterprise, may develop. Exchanges of powerful 'medicines' are important.

A marriage may result from these alliances, adding the affinal tie to the economic and other bonds and ensuring their continuance. There are other possibilities, too. The establishment of economic relations with some men in a distant neighbourhood can lead, if an elder conducts himself with discretion, to his being on a footing of familiarity with other men there. A marriage with a daughter or sister of one of these strengthens his position as an acceptable 'foreigner'. It is highly likely that livestock arrangements other than bridewealth will be established with such affines, for they will want to take advantage of the opportunity to extend their own extra-neighbourhood projects, and the elder himself can thereby become less dependent on his original alliances. When an elder marries 'abroad', then, his affines have quite definite economic expectations: they are certain either of continuing the arrangements already made or of establishing new ones.

There are political considerations as well. Within a neighbourhood there is constant and close involvement of elders with one another in the management of community affairs. Extra-neighbourhood alliances break into the exclusiveness of a local community. Blood-pacts are the most spectacular from the political point of view since they include kin of the partners in the oath of non-violence and protection. Blood-pacts often arise directly or indirectly from involvement in extra-neighbourhood livestock ventures and are utilized to establish others. In any case, the scheme of enterprises which includes both extra-neighbourhood livestock transactions and extra-neighbourhood marriages is obviously of political significance.

Through individual ties of kinship and neighbourliness, one set of 'foreign' ties tends to beget others. The result is the development of ties between pairs and sets of non-adjacent neighbourhoods which are numerous *relative* to the ties which usually obtain between adjacent communities, though very slight by comparison with intra-neighbourhood ties. In the past, these relationships were valuable in creating alliances against adjacent communities with which feuds sometimes developed. Today they are still important, partly in a negative way. The elders of a neighbourhood are furnished with extra-neighbourhood ties without having to become involved with the residents of adjacent neighbourhoods who might try to take advantage of the opportunity to encroach upon land. [28]

From the point of view of individuals, extra-neighbourhood ties furnish them with a field of operations where they are *relatively* independent of their local peers. Blood-pacts, which formerly made it possible for men to move about safely, today still ensure a reception free of that wholehearted suspicion and hostility with which Taita greet complete 'strangers' from other neighbourhoods. Their importance for a man's local relationships lies in the fact that his pacts oblige him to protect his pact-partner against his own kinsmen and neighbours should he discover a plot among them. A pact thus drives a wedge between a man and his fellow residents.

An affinal tie has something of the same effect (hence, according to Taita, the undesirability of marriages between communities whose residents 'have not come to understand one another'). But whereas a non-elder marrying 'abroad' is looked at askance, an elder is in a more secure position because, having married earlier from within the neighbourhood, he is already bound to local people in a variety of ways. Still, the effects of extra-neighbourhood marriages of elders may be compared with those of blood-pacts, and not merely because these marriages are often with women related to pact-partners of the elder or his kinsmen. The extra-neighbourhood affinal ties of an elder provide him, as his livestock transactions do, with a field of operations beyond his circle of kin and neighbours and they remove him from complete involvement with them. His affines are provided with entrée into his neighbourhood in so far as friendly visits are possible under his protection for, as an elder, he carries political weight in his own community.

In every respect, then, an elder is the equal or superior of his affines or prospective affines in more meaningful terms than those of a simple statement of his position in the age-status hierarchy. The latter has to be seen in the framework of the economic and political practices and prerogatives which operate in relations within and between local communities. Looked at in this way, it can be seen that as a son-in-law or brother-in-law an elder offers positive advantages to his affines. His right to an initially debt-free marriage is congruent with this fact.

The bridewealth arrangements of non-elders marrying locally are also in keeping with the actual, and not merely the possible, economic and political relations of affines. We have seen that non-elders are recipients of land but that, although a loan of land to a son- or brother-in-law is morally desirable and customary, such a loan is not always effected. There are, however, other, though more indirect ways in which a non-elder may be said to be indebted to his affines when he marries locally. Marriage within the neighbourhood further links a man to people with whom he already has many and varied ties. His status is maintained as one of the community of persons 'who have come to understand one another'; he is not 'an eater in two places' (*mʒa kuvi*). Therefore he retains his claim to consideration for land loans even from people with whom he has no very close kinship tie.

Equally important, a wife from within the neighbourhood is herself instrumental in forwarding a man's acquisition of land. As the primary cultivators, Taita women have a great deal of freedom to organize their agricultural work, and this extends to making arrangements for the temporary exchange of plots for the sake of convenience and to the arranging of loans and even sales. The actual transactions must be carried out by the men concerned, but the fact remains that women are often instrumental in bringing them about. A woman who marries within her neighbourhood can therefore make use of her ties with female kin and neighbours to arrange transactions which her husband will carry out. One might say that a local wife brings her husband something like the 'good-will' of a business firm, though here the valued connexion is with potential creditors rather than customers. Turning to another simile, we might call the bridewealth given for a local wife a sort of 'key money'. By its payment a man obtains not only rights to sexual and domestic services and rights in the woman's reproductive capacities, but access to the neighbourhood pool of land resources. His indebtedness to her agnates for this asset cannot, by its very nature, cease. As we shall see, this interpretation cannot be accepted without some qualification.

Politically, a non-elder son-in-law or brother-in-law is unlikely to be of much importance individually. Young men, still to some degree dependent on their fathers and in the role of land-debtors-at-large, are pawns in the game in which older men acquire each other's sons as debtors, usually only can-celling out one another's efforts to build up bodies of junior followers. An older man has more weight in community affairs and, as we have seen, he may have some land-debtors of his own. Without having achieved elderhood through wealth and ritual prerogatives he offers no special political advantages as a son- or brother-in-law. It is politically advantageous to the non-elder marrying locally to be able to call upon the tie with his father-in-law should he be party to a dispute in the neighbourhood: he is furnished with a potential ally even against his own agnates. As between brothers-in-law this kind of advantage is a mutual one, when in later years they are active participants in community affairs.

We might conclude, therefore, that the economic and political subordination of non-elders marrying locally is great enough to account for their having to make bridewealth arrangements which entail some degree of long-term indebtedness. This kind of arrangement does seem to be congruent with their position, within the context of the local community. For this to be an entirely satisfactory conclusion, however, we ought to find that in the small proportion of cases in which non-elders marry non-locally, the bridewealth arrangements reflect the *absence* of this subordination which stems from the close involvement with affines who are also neighbours.

What we find, however, is that *all* non-elders, from wherever they take their spouses, always have arrangements with *some* long-term indebtedness, but the *distribution of the types* of arrangements varies with the locality from which the wife is taken. The completed betrothal arrangement occurs for both local and non-local marriages of non-elders. In the non-local marriages, completed betrothal is in fact the most common form. In contrast, curtailed betrothals are rare in non-local marriages, while both they and elopements are very common in local unions. Elopements involving couples who are members of different neighbourhoods are extremely rare and when they do occur the couple usually abscond to one of the towns or cities. With uxorilocal labour service we find the opposite distribution: it is an uncommon arrangement in any event, but when it occurs it is almost always (if not always) in cases of non-local marriage. In terms of the relative indebtedness of the various arrangements, most non-local marriages involve the minimal indebtedness permitted to non-elders and a few the maximal indebtedness—that of uxorilocal labour-service.

Why should the non-local marriages of non-elders entail any indebtedness? We might possibly see an answer in special features of some non-local marriages. It is sometimes found that the non-local wives of non-elders come chiefly from one lineage in an adjacent neighbourhood. Other features of this kind of situation make it clear that such a clustering of marriages is a prelude either to: (a) realignment of lineages, that is, alteration in neighbourhood boundaries; or (b) the gradual withdrawal of the border lineage to another area with the possibility of its members leaving their lands to others. Therefore we might say that some of the affinal expectations involved approximate those characteristic of intra-neighbourhood marriages. But this still leaves those cases of non-local marriages (of non-elders) which occur in the absence of such special conditions. It is impossible to argue, in the face of what has gone before, that all local and non-local ties are somehow equivalent in terms of the interaction and expectations of affines—*except* in so far as the common feature of *all* non-elders' marriages is the inability of the husband to offer economic and political advantages. We come back to the fact that the status of non-elders makes unsuitable an arrangement which implies his equivalence with or superiority to the wife's father and brother.

Given the above, we should now phrase the inquiry in terms of the *choices* open to non-elders marrying locally as against those taking wives from other neighbourhoods. After all, not all men even wish to contract a debt-free marriage.

The limitation of uxorilocal labour-service to non-local marriages is easily understandable. In this case the man moves out of his own residential unit and, at least in part, cuts his ties with his home group. There would be objections to a man's living with his affines in one neighbourhood and cultivating land in his old one. Although he may eventually take his wife away from her natal community and return to his own, during his stay in the former place he is completely dependent on his affines for everything, including land. In short, there is total involvement in a 'foreign' neighbourhood which is the counterpart of total involvement in the natal one. Hence the mutual exclusiveness of uxorilocal labour-service and elopement. The latter is a choice open to men marrying locally precisely because of their total involvement in the local community.

The fact that a non-elder marrying locally can choose elopement—or curtailed betrothal—obviously has to do with the nature of the local community as a continuing (albeit not static) endogamous unit. The frequent occurrence of elopements and curtailed betrothals as *acceptable* modes of establishing co-residence, securing extension of bridewealth credit, assumes the maintenance of the pattern. The local groom who carries off his betrothed without permission is one of the people 'who have come to understand one another'. His affines are certain to be bound to him already by some ties of kinship, but even if these are remote, there is the expectation that their relationship as neighbours will endure, that they will continue to be involved together from time to time in a variety of economic, political and ritual affairs. [29] This provides the basis for permitting—and even encouraging— the extension of indebtedness in curtailed betrothals and elopements, absent in cases of non-local marriages of non-elders.

Actually, there are three aspects. First, as seen from the jural point of view, the pattern of intra-neighbourhood expectations allows the co-residence of the couple, even when no payments are made, to be treated as a union to some degree already validated: promises stand temporarily for payments where people known to one another are concerned. Next, from the individual's point of view, a local man is under the affinal eye—he can be kept under observation and can therefore be trusted as a non-local man might not be. There are so many occasions for contact other than the special visits incumbent upon affines. Finally, in terms of the status system, heavy indebtedness is in keeping with the groom's indirect indebtedness with respect to land.

We can see, too, that the particular form which the whole of the bride-wealth transaction has come to have is in keeping with the dominant pattern of marriage choices. [30] The long drawn-out series of payments is feasible since the persons required for their collection, transport and distribution live near enough to one another for the organizational aspects not to be burdensome. The distances to be travelled usually are short and easy, making it possible for the immediate parties to use young girls, sometimes mere children, as go-betweens and carriers of small items. The importance of foodstuffs and of women's participation are appropriate if only because it is expected that the bride will continue to engage in domestic and agricultural co-operation with her former work-mates.

As with elders, then, so with non-elders: treatment of their relationships with their close affines requires reference to the structure of relations in and between neighbourhoods. It is in terms of these economic and political ties that age-status is meaningful generally and specifically with respect to affinity.

TAITA AFFINITY AND SOCIAL STRUCTURE

I shall conclude by summarizing the interconnexions between the dominant forms of affinal relationships as related to the age-status system on the one hand and other features of the social structure on the other.

There is slight development of the large lineage as a corporate group and a correspondingly high degree of independence of household heads from their agnates. Inherently bound up with a property system which provides other means for transferring property besides inheritance, this independence allows men to look to non-agnates as transferrers or recipients of land. Given the importance of land as a resource under the indigenous rules of use and tenure, the process of search and dispersal follows the changing needs of a householder; hence it becomes an aspect of the age-status system as the latter is tied, in Taita, to household position. Given, further, the relatively closed nature of Taita neighbourhoods as land-use units, a premium is placed on maintaining potential access to as much land as possible within the residential unit. The combination of independence from agnates (and the corresponding impossibility of relying solely on them for material assistance) with the dependence on *seniors* for additional land within the neighbourhood, enhances the value for a non-elder of marrying within the local community. The result is, broadly, that affinal ties are magnified and become complementary to those of agnation, and the dominant marriage pattern is maintained.

With respect to livestock, independence of agnates from one another is also important, as is the existence of modes of transfer additional to inheritance. But livestock is less important as a resource than as wealth. Its ownership is tied to the age-status system in a different way in that competition for wealth is limited to older men whose fathers have died, and who can therefore try to become elders. Indirect access to extra-neighbourhood grazing land is desirable and is implemented by the fact that the scope of livestock transactions, including *vuturi*, is not confined to neighbourhoods. Since the latter do encompass the persons with whom elders have the most immediately important ties (agnates and affines acquired by early marriages, persons involved in land transactions, community politics and ritual affairs), the use of livestock in transactions tends to be a matter of individually established special ties. Again, given the relatively closed nature of the local community, together with the absence of tribal political authorities and the absence of ranking among descent groups, these ties are politically important. When elders marry 'abroad' as part of the process of extending and strengthening their external ties, the resulting affinal relationships take on a political hue. In terms of the linkages between communities, 'foreign' affinal ties do not complement agnation in the same way as they do in societies with exogamous descent groups. Here, instead, they form one element in a network of largely particularistic ties which link together members of various communities without drawing them into extensive interaction.

The nature of Taita local communities as land-use units which are highly endogamous and interconnected by particularistic ties calls to mind certain societies elsewhere. The Kalinga of northern Luzon might be likened to the Taita even though they have a system of kindreds with bilateral inheritance of land rights. There is a sense in which, though land passes patrilineally in Taita, the affinal loan plus the use made of the wife's ability to arrange transactions is equivalent to the land which a locally married Kalinga woman adds to that of her husband. As in Taita, the relatively closed local communities are linked by special ties, in this case by 'pact-holders'. Also as in Taita, there is an intimate connexion between the local affiliation of spouses and the maintenance of or access to land rights.

All this is in accord with the fact, long recognized by many social anthropologists, that in practice systems which differ in rule of descent may function in much the same way with respect to local group organization because of the operation of rules concerning residence and land rights. This paper, organized around the special problems of bridewealth and affinity, should contribute also to the much-needed comparison of systems of endogamous communities operating with different rules of descent. It is clear that an understanding of local community structure must in any event underlie the comparative treatment of bridewealth.

NOTES

[1] The general political importance of these relations, especially those linking arable-rich with pasture-rich areas, has been dealt with by A. Harris, in 'The social organization of the Wataita', unpublished Ph.D. dissertation, Cambridge University, 1958: 143–51.

[2] In a few areas final distribution also follows matrisegment and then birth order within it.

[3] Migration out of Taita as a whole has taken place also. The plains limit outward expansion, but there has been some emigration beyond the confines of the subDistrict to Pare, Chagga, Giriama, and Kamba country.

[4] Not only wives, married sons and unmarried children within the domestic group, but also married daughters who are members of other domestic groups but who may be cultivating some of their fathers' land.

[5] I have sketched the ritual aspects of the age-status system in 'Possession "Hysteria" in a Kenya Tribe', *American Anthropologist*, 1957: 56, no. 6, 1046–66.

[6] Compare A. Harris 'The political role of blood pacts in Taita', a paper read at the Fifty-eighth Annual Meeting of the American Anthropological Association, Mexico City, December 1959.

[7] Details are given in G. Harris, 'The ritual system of the Wataita', unpublished Ph.D. dissertation, Cambridge University, 1955.

[8] It is not implied that the marriage in question is the elder's first. It is unlikely to be that, since very few Taita men remain unmarried past the age of forty. Today most men marry in their early or middle twenties—somewhat earlier, it is said, than in former generations.

[9] Some Taita allege that over many generations bridewealth payments have undergone changes from payment in honey and labour to the use of goods of various kinds, through the addition of livestock in varying numbers, and on to the increasing commutation to money. Like today's differences between locations, the past variations do not point to alterations in the marriage system. Certainly there have been changes in amounts depending on conditions of scarcity or plenty. More recently Government has taken steps towards standardizing and stabilizing bridewealth, but with such changes as may have come about since 1952 we cannot be concerned.

[10] The attitude of Christian parents is quite otherwise, though Christian sons-in-law do not so readily forsake the old way.

[11] Total numbers of small stock vary from eight to fifteen depending on the location. There are also differences as to the inclusion of one or more male goats and the substitution of an ewe for one of the female goats. Bulls may be substituted for small stock at the rate of one bull per five head of small stock.

[12] The types of animals have special names but this prestation has itself no other name so far as I am aware.

[13] The name may stand for *malago gilale*, 'may the affair rest', or *vupe gulale*, 'may bridewealth affairs rest'.

[14] Whenever beer is furnished, unfermented cane juice is supplied for the women of the household.

[15] The giver and the recipient of a gift call each other by one of a set of special names: giver and recipient of a knife = *aruvu*; of a virgin beast = *atago*: of money =

apesa. Though other gifts may pass between the parties later, the name derived from the original gift is retained.

[16] Brothers and sisters closest to one another in age are linked. As a man has rights in his linked sister's bridewealth, and a beast is due to him when each of her daughters marries, so each daughter's initiation requires that he slaughter a goat.

[17] If he already has one or more wives, he has had the sole responsibility since the beginning of the betrothal, for a man's father is responsible only for helping him to obtain one wife.

[18] Needless to say, many fathers get no co-operation from their daughters at such times.

[19] Real abductions occur from time to time but these do not lead to marriage since the girl is rescued by kinsmen, or she runs away or threatens to commit suicide.

[20] Usually by means of her mother, who appears first to denounce the man as a scoundrel and to take away her wayward daughter.

[21] English-speaking Taita Christians have been known to refer to 'rape' in such cases. It may be imagined what alarms can be spread by this confusion.

[22] I do not consider my census material adequate for a statistical analysis of bridewealth arrangements, but I estimate that no more than half of non-elders marry with completed betrothals.

[23] From this point on, land (rather than rights in land) is spoken of as being owned, borrowed, inherited, etc., in order to avoid some cumbersome constructions.

[24] If the husband is an only or youngest son he has a moral obligation to remain close to the parents and ought not to move outside the village or hamlet; in many cases such a man never acquires his own house but remains in the parental homestead.

[25] A very few genealogies include men with up to twelve wives, but four wives were the maximum for most polygamists in the past as it is today. It is not always possible to tell how many of the wives of the rare large-scale polygamists of the past were actually leviratic spouses, due to the Taita tendency to condense genealogies in the lateral dimension at higher levels.

[26] A. Harris has discussed the distribution of land transactions with respect to age-status and kinship (A. Harris, 'The social organization of the Wataita', chapter IX) and he intends to publish a separate and detailed discussion.

[27] His married sons by earlier wives may well suffer, however, for they must see land which might come to them and their wives go instead to the father's new wife.

[28] This danger is not so great in neighbourhoods of the dry uplands the residents of which concentrate on plains cultivation; there, according to A. Harris, we find a somewhat greater development of ties between adjacent communities than elsewhere. (See A. Harris, *ibid*. pp. 168–70.)

[29] It is not surprising, therefore, that one young man who had had a curtailed betrothal assured another who had eloped that he need not be concerned about his affines' display of anger 'because those people can't cut your throat'. How different this statement is from those recorded in so many other parts of Africa that 'we marry those whom we fight', and how appropriate it is to the Taita system.

[30] This is not to say that this form of bridewealth is unsuitable for all other marriage systems. It must be expected that a given cultural form will 'fit' more than one structural situation, a fact that enormously complicates the theoretical assessment of anthropological interpretations.

[31] Field-work underlying this paper was done from July 1950 to August 1952 under a grant from the Colonial Social Science Research Council, whom I thank.

GISU MARRIAGE AND
AFFINAL RELATIONS

By JEAN LA FONTAINE

INTRODUCTION

The subject of this article is the choice of a wife in a society which has no rules of preferential or prescribed marriage. [1] Anthropologists have paid a great deal of attention to marriage as an institution and to the significance of marriage payments. It has long been recognized that the affinal ties created by a marriage produce links between distinct and often antagonistic groups and as such are part of the social organization. Rules of preferential or pre-scribed marriage have been demonstrated to be important principles of social structure. Societies which have these rules have been closely analysed to discover the degree of conformity to the rule and the motives for deviation from it. But few comparable studies have been made in societies where rules of this sort are absent. [2] There appears to be an assumption that in these societies choice is random and hence of no direct structural significance.

Obviously, in any society, even one which has no sanctioned directives of choice, the field of possible mates is not entirely 'free'. Incest prohibitions debar certain categories of persons from being chosen as spouses; political, economic and geographical considerations may make some choices undesirable or impracticable. The distinctive feature of societies with a rule of marriage, prescribed or preferential, is that the range within which a man may choose is marked out by a rule of kinship. Affinity and kinship are directly linked in these societies; in others, of which the Gisu are an example, there is no such explicit association. None the less, I wish to show that marriage choices in a society of the latter type do conform to a discernible norm and that this norm is a feature of the social organization.

In order to understand why Gisu men follow a pattern in choosing their wives, it is necessary to set out the considerations involved in the choice. Those with which we are concerned are the considerations which are common to all individuals because they derive from the way in which Gisu society is organized. The nature of Gisu marriage and the payments by which it is con-tracted are of primary significance and features of the economical and political systems are also relevant. The norm is the result of the way in which individ-uals seek to combine these elements in the situation to their own advantage. An examination of changes in some of the issues at stake shows that the norm (the solutions arrived at by most men) is also changing. The direction of this

88

change emphasizes the distinction that has always been implicit in the Gisu notion of marriage: that between acquiring a wife and acquiring affines.

The Gisu are a Bantu-speaking people living on the south-western slopes of Mount Elgon, an extinct volcano which lies across the Kenya–Uganda border, some fifty miles north of Lake Victoria. [3] Their closest affinities, linguistically and culturally, are with the tribes of the Nyanza region of Kenya rather than the Interlacustrine Bantu to the west. In general terms, they can be classed as the westernmost extension of the north-eastern Bantu, although they lack the elaborate age-set system which characterizes many of the tribes in this group. North of the Gisu lie the Nilo-Hamites, [4] Sebei, Turkana and Karamojong and farther to the west, the Iteso, who once raided the plains to the west of Mount Elgon. An impressionistic view of Gisu culture would depict it as the area of overlap of three main types of social organization: the acephalous societies, Bantu and Nilo-Hamite, in which the political framework is provided by groups recruited on the basis of (social) age; the northern group, where lineage organization becomes increasingly important; and the Bantu kingdoms of the west whose major characteristics are a feudal type of political organization with a distinct ruling caste in most of the tribes. In these societies the patron–client relationship is a salient feature of the social organization. [5]

The Gisu are settled densely throughout their territory and there is little uncultivated land. Their settlements are not compact villages; the homesteads are scattered through the millet fields and plantain groves from which they obtain their staple foods. The terms 'village' and 'village-cluster', which will be used in this paper, refer to areas of occupation with clearly marked boundaries, rather than purely residential units. The men living in a locality of this sort, belong, ideally, to one lineage and Gisu add a prefix of locality to the lineage name to indicate defined and inhabited areas.

The framework of Gisu social structure is a series of patrilineal localized lineages. A genealogy, varying between eleven and thirteen generations in depth from the oldest living generation, traces the descent of all Gisu from the apical ancestor and charts a succession of ever more inclusive lineage segments. With the exception of the minimal lineage, lineage segments are associated with a tract of territory over which they claim exclusive rights of cultivation and settlement. The basic tenet of the system is that a defined local group is a lineage and the genealogical charter may be adjusted to accommodate movements of groups from one area to another. Movement was usually the result of inter-village fighting for land, but the Gisu were also expanding northwards at the expense of their neighbours, the pastoral Sebei.

The basic unit in the traditional political system was the village, settled by a minor lineage. The head of the village was the lineage head. Political unity under an acknowledged head was sometimes, but not invariably, the attribute of a whole village-cluster (major lineage), but rivalry between the segments and boundary disputes between its component villages militated against its emergence as a stable political entity. The lineage ties between the segments of a village-cluster might induce them to act together against a common enemy, but on occasion they collected allies from other villages to fight against one another or joined in disputes on opposite sides. Above the village-cluster there was no political unity, [6] although the people of a district (members of one maximal lineage) felt themselves, and were considered by outsiders, to be set off from members of other maximal lineages by usages of speech and distinctive ritual practices.

Lineage heads were elected by the men of the lineage concerned, meeting in council at the end-of-mourning ceremonies for the previous head. They were chosen for qualities which marked them out as already powerful enough to carry out the duties expected of them. This was essential since the office of lineage head was not endowed with special power or any control of force to implement his orders. The components of a leader's power were prestige, influence and connexions useful to the group. The total of these represented any man's *position* in his village. Prestige accrued to a man who was wealthy, possessed a good reputation, was punctilious in fulfilling his obligations and generous to others less fortunate. I use *prestige* to refer to the characteristics which earn a man the esteem of others and their deference to his opinions and advice. A leader also had *influence*; that is, he was able to prevail on others to accept his decisions by virtue of his relations with them. Influence was usually acquired by economic help: loans or gifts of land or cattle, but it might also be acquired through force of personality and sagacity. Finally, a man whose kinship and affinal ties were of such a kind that they provided his group with a means of conducting their external relations [7] was almost invariably of importance within it. Here we are concerned primarily with affinal ties and they are crucial in that they can be chosen. But kinship ties were also important. A judicious marriage might provide a man's sons with important and useful maternal kin so that provided the obligations of kinship were generously fulfilled, a man could profit from his father's choice of a wife.

The ways in which leadership was attained in traditional Gisu society depended largely on wealth. Leaders were (and are still today) rich men. The lineage head was endowed with legitimate authority by his election to office but he was usually only *primus inter pares*. In former times there were no great differences in wealth; the rich man was one who could marry several wives and still find a surplus of the goods which all men possessed to use in gaining influence. While the sons of rich men started with an advantage over their fellows, there was no hereditary class of rich families and it was possible for men to improve their economic position. It was essentially an egalitarian society in which disputes, either between individuals or groups, were settled by arbitration. Any man might perform the function of go-between but unless he had influence and important connexions he would be unlikely to succeed.

MARRIAGE

The exogamous unit is the minimal lineage, whose members trace their descent patrilineally from an ancestor three to five generations removed from the oldest living generation. Gisu often speak as though a lineage were composed only of men, since women are always under the jural authority of some man; in the case of a minimal lineage the male members number between thirty and fifty. It is this unit which exercises rights of guardianship over the land which its members own. The consent of the minimal lineage is required if a man wishes to lend, lease or sell his land to a non-member and inheritance disputes are referred to it. Unlike segments of a higher order, the minimal lineage is not associated with a continuous tract of land; its members live anywhere in the village (minor lineage area) where they own plots. Mutual help and loyalty at all times are enjoined on members of the same minimal lineage and it is to this group that a man's primary allegiance is owed. In the following discussion the term lineage, unless qualified by a specific term denoting its span, refers to the minimal lineage.

There are rules, consistent with the total social structure, prohibiting marriage between certain categories of relatives but, compared with other similar societies, Gisu restrictions do not cover a wide range of persons. No Gisu may marry a member of his own, his mother's or paternal grandmother's lineage. Two people who can trace descent from a common ancestor or ancestress three generations removed from themselves, through any genealogical connexion, may not marry. The children of men circumcised at the same homestead may not marry, nor may the children of blood-brothers. These prohibitions emphasize the ties of kinship and underline the primary importance of the minimal lineage. Outside this group agnates may become affines. Marriage prohibitions mark out those people with whom ties are a matter of descent and filiation; these ties are acquired at birth and cannot normally be broken. [8] Affinal ties, by contrast, are a matter of choice and result from a contract which can be rescinded.

A Gisu marriage is established by the payment of bridewealth to the woman's father. The amount varies in a manner that will be discussed in detail below, but certain items are essential. They are: a heifer, a bull (or the equivalent number of goats), a large he-goat, a spear and a hoe. They symbolize, severally, the rights over the woman which are transferred to her husband. Once the marriage has been legally established by the payment of these articles, the husband has exclusive rights over his wife's domestic and sexual services and her labour. He represents her in any disputes outside his

91

domestic group and is held responsible for her actions. Should she commit adultery, her husband can claim damages against her lover. Her lineage hand over responsibility for her, retaining only the right to see that she is not ill-treated, which includes the right to avenge her if she is killed.

A man's rights over his wife are heritable property. At his death his widow is normally inherited by a brother or classificatory brother, subject to the woman's consent. If she does not wish to marry the designated heir she may choose any agnate of her husband's (of the right generation) or failing that may choose to return to her father. In the latter case an adjustment is made in regard to the bridewealth if the woman is still of child-bearing age. The children of an inherited wife are the children of their begetter although it is considered a duty to name the first child after the dead man, particularly if it is a boy.

Divorce is possible if either spouse fails to fulfil his or her duties or if the wife is barren or commits adultery. The contract is rescinded by the repayment of the bridewealth less certain gifts which are only presented by the bridegroom if it is the girl's first marriage. Divorce is not uncommon and the marital histories of most men include one or two marriages that ended in divorce. Gisu men complain that their wives always hold their fathers' interests at heart and that disputes with one's affines often cause conjugal ruptures. If disharmony is clearly the husband's fault he cannot recover his bridewealth so that men have an incentive to fulfil their obligations. A man should consult his first wife when he proposes to take a second; she cannot refuse to allow this but it is said that it is a common cause of divorce. A first wife has no jural precedence over subsequent wives and women often complain that their husband's resources are not sufficient to support two families, or to fulfil the duties they owe to their affines. If a man's first wife comes from an influential family he may listen to her and wait before taking a second wife; if not, he will usually ignore her objections..

The ceremonies which establish a marriage demonstrate clearly the interest of the two lineages concerned and of the extra-lineage kin of bride and bridegroom. The initial approach is made by the man's kin. Usually his father's brother and sister are sent as messengers to the girl's father. There is a series of visits back and forth, designed to give each party a chance of assessing the circumstances of the family and minimal lineage into which their kinsman or kinswoman is about to marry. If the initial visits satisfy both parties, then a discussion is held at the bridegroom's home to determine the amount of the bridewealth. After some of the items have been paid, preparations are made for the ceremony by which the bride is transferred to her new home. [9] The rites follow the pattern of a *rite de passage*, the girl being separated from her status as a daughter and transferred to that of married woman, with an intervening period of transition during which she lives in her husband's home as a guest. Elements in the ritual parallel the ceremonies of initiation which mark the passage of a Gisu man from boyhood to full adult status.

While marriage is primarily the concern of the two lineages, whose responsibility is demonstrated by their attendance at feasts given by the parents of the couple, each in their own home, the bride's mother's brother also has a significant part to play. This extra-lineage relative performs special duties which, together with the duties he fulfils at a youth's initiation, demonstrate the continuing links between individuals in different lineages. These links result from the marriage of women who retain certain rights in their natal lineages, while bearing children for the lineage of their husbands.

CHOICE OF WIFE

Gisu say that in pre-European times a man's father had a large share in the choice of his wife, particularly the first wife. A man might even insist on his son's marrying a particular girl. Today this is uncommon and it seems to have been usual, even in former times, for a man to choose a wife from among a number of girls of whom his father had indicated approval and then to inform his father of the choice. In any case, Gisu speak as if a man chooses his wife, but in the discussion that follows it must be remembered that his father is consulted and that his advice carries considerable weight. Women cannot be said to choose their husbands in the same way, although today many Gisu girls are able to marry men of their own choosing. A Gisu girl might always refuse to marry the man of her father's choice if he displeased her; in fact Gisu women show a strong sense of filial duty and often identify their own interests with their father's. [10] However, a marriage is a contract between men in Gisu society and in speaking of the choice of a spouse we are really talking of the selection of wives on the one hand and of sons-in-law on the other.

Besides prohibiting the choice of certain classes of women, the structure of Gisu society also defines the issues at stake for an individual who wishes to marry. The choice of a wife is not a selection purely on the basis of personal attributes, although they have their importance. The acquisition of a wife means, for a Gisu man, the balancing of various considerations. Some of them derive from the social structure, others from the economic system and others from the nature of political leadership. In order to understand why there should be similarity in the way a large number of men solve the problem we must analyse the motives of both parties to the marriage contract. The two most important facts in the situation are: first, that marriage is legitimized by the payment of bridewealth, the amount of which varies and is subject to negotiation; and secondly, that affinal ties have potential political value. Since affinal relations are themselves influenced by bridewealth payments, it is convenient to set them out in some detail first.

AFFINAL RELATIONS

The rights and duties existing between affines pertain primarily to the men most concerned: a man and his father and brothers, and his wife's father and brothers. These are the persons between whom relations are crucial, but a marriage also involves the whole of two minimal lineages. The degree to which obligations are considered morally binding varies according to the degree of connexion. It is least between two men who are merely classificatory brothers or fathers of two spouses, most binding between a man and his wife's true father. This fact should be borne in mind during the following discussion.

Since it is only the minimal lineage which is exogamous, affines may be, and often are, agnates. But they are affines first and then agnates. Gisu say: *I busoni ke bulimu bulebi da*—'in affinity there is no kinship', and an affinal tie generally takes precedence over an agnatic one in determining relations between two men. If two men are close agnates, i.e. of the same minimal lineage, they cannot be affines; therefore, Gisu argue, if they are affines they are merely distant agnates and the ties between affines must be considered stronger. In marginal cases a man may appeal to either an agnatic or an affinal tie according to the situation, but in general an agnate ceases to be treated as such when he becomes an affine.

The way in which affinal terminology is used shows clearly that a marriage is the concern of two corporate groups. Affinal terms are used for all members of the spouse's (minimal) lineage and may also be used to members of the natal lineage of any agnate's spouse. This extension of affinal terminology is accompanied by expectations of loyalty and help, though to a lesser degree than obtains between 'true' affines. Each exogamous group therefore has a 'field' of affinal relations, consisting of the affinal ties of its individual members. Some of these may be more important politically than others and emphasis may be laid on different connexions at different times and for different purposes.

The duties entailed in affinal relations are based on an ideal of strong solidarity with certain obligatory modes of expression. Political help was never a binding duty; the political usefulness of affines depended, as it still does, on good relations with them. However, affines are expected to offer support in any crisis; attendance at funerals is a particularly binding duty. Affines were not committed to giving help in war, although they might be asked to do so. On the other hand they were, and are, obliged to attend work-parties, to give assistance by lending and leasing land to one another and, today, by lending money. These transactions are still considered business arrangements in that loans must be repaid, but an affine should not refuse to help in this way. It is not uncommon to find brothers-in-law as partners in a trading concern. Attendance at a funeral has its practical value, for each mourner is obliged to make some contribution towards mortuary expenses. Some of the total will be spent on providing a beast and beer for the end-of-mourning rites, to which all mourners must be invited. Finally an affine is frequently chosen as a go-between in disputes, and, in former, less peaceful times, as a surety in villages other than one's own.

The agnatic ties between members of the same minor or major lineage may be strengthened by a marriage which establishes them as affines. Affinal ties may also provide a refuge from internal disputes in the village. An individual's position within his lineage may be considerably enhanced by the nature of his affinal connexions. A man's political standing depends on the acquisition of a following within his own village. A common means of gaining support outside the minimal lineage segment, which is a part of the village, is to marry into another segment of the same minor lineage. In doing this a man acquires support from a group which is normally in competition with his own. If his affines are influential in their own minimal lineage his claims on their support will make him a valuable member of his own lineage. A lineage head, whether of a minimal or minor lineage, must be able to unite his lineage behind him; he must also be able to negotiate with other similar groups on their behalf. Affinal ties are most importa..t in this respect. A man who has a wife from a neighbouring village is an obvious choice for negotiator in the event of a dispute between the two villages. His affines may be persuaded to induce their agnates to accept a settlement. Formerly affines were approached when a village needed allies in wars. In short, affines can be of great value in Gisu society; the degree to which their usefulness can be exploited however depends on the maintenance of cordial relations with them (discussed below in the analysis of bridewealth payments).

The behaviour expected from affines is determined by the sex and generation of the persons concerned. As in kinship relations, great emphasis is laid on the separation between generations. In affinal relations this separation is not bridged by the unity of common descent or genealogical connexions (see above). Hence parents-in-law and children-in-law are obliged to treat one another with exaggerated respect to a degree not found in any other cross-generational relationship. The general term for affines (*umusoni* pl. *basoni*) is a derivative of the word for shame (*busoni*) which also means affinity. The term for in-laws of a different generation adds *umusoni* to the appropriate kinship term, e.g. father-in-law *baba umusoni*; son-in-law *umwaana umusoni*. The terms may only be used in reference; the junior addresses his senior by a term of respect and the senior uses the kinship term alone or, occasionally, a personal name.

Where there is also a distinction in sex between affines of different generations, the relationship is one of avoidance. A man must avoid his mother-in-law and daughter-in-law, a woman her father-in-law and son-in-law. The degree to which the avoidance is thought obligatory varies in different parts of Bugisu, but nowhere may they address one another directly, eat together, or sleep in the same hut. The birth of children to the younger couple does not alter the behaviour thought proper between affines, although in some areas informants said that there used to be a ceremony performed 'to allow a man to see his mother-in-law'. Informants stressed that its performance depended on the good relations obtaining between the individuals concerned; it was never an automatic stage in the development of a marriage.

By contrast, affines of the same generation are essentially equal; they address one another by reciprocal terms: *mukwasi* = brother-in-law, *umulamu* = sister-in-law (woman speaking), *masagwa* = parent of my child's spouse. Such affines may address one another by personal names, although brothers-in-law and parents of spouses tend to use the affinal term. The term for brother-in-law is also used by persons who are not so related but have an easy friendship or partnership. In this sense it can be translated by the English 'mate' or 'chum'; schoolboys commonly use it to one another, as do men who are working together on some joint enterprise. This use of the term points to the essential nature of affinal relations, as opposed to the ties of kinship. They are ties derived from a voluntary association, not imposed on an individual by the fact of his birth. There is perhaps less tension in the relations between brothers-in-law than between brothers, although the latter are expected to show more affection and are bound to offer help. Debts to affines should be repaid; those owing to an agnate may be allowed to lapse until the creditor has need of something when he will ask for an equivalent favour, not the repayment of the debt.

THE ECONOMIC ASPECT OF AFFINAL RELATIONS: BRIDEWEALTH

The structure of affinal relations lays down the broad outlines of the relations between affines but its importance and strength derive from other considerations as well. The contract by which these relations are established is an economic transaction, the payment of bridewealth and the amount and mode of its payment have an important effect on the relationships which ensue.

Bridewealth for a man's first wife should be paid by his father and he may call on his brothers and close agnates to help. In return they will expect similar help when they need it. Although the total amount may be contributed by the bridegroom's father in this way, Gisu always talk as if it is the bridegroom himself who pays bridewealth. Today, many young men do pay a substantial share of the bridewealth even for a first wife and even in former times subsequent wives were most often paid for by the husband. The bridewealth is paid to the bride's father and becomes his property, apart from one beast, a large he-goat, which he must give to the girl's mother's brother. The goat, known as *imbuzi ye gamezi*, is an essential item of the bridewealth and Gisu say it is paid in recognition of the mother's part in bearing and rearing the girl. The bride's father does not share the bridewealth among his agnates and they have no jurally recognized claim on it. It should be kept in trust to provide the bridewealth for her brothers, although if she has none approaching marriageable age, it is considered permissible for her father to marry another wife with the beasts. It is a heinous breach of paternal duties to marry another wife with a daughter's bridewealth if, in doing so, a son is deprived of his chance to set up his own household.

Bridewealth is paid in instalments so that, for the first few years of his married life, a man is his father-in-law's debtor. Gisu bridewealth is high, compared with the wealth of most men. Over the last forty years it is said to have risen considerably and now the cash value of the goods handed over rarely falls below 600 shillings and may reach as high as 1600–2000 shillings. It is difficult to estimate the economic position of Gisu for they will not allow measurement of their fields, nor an estimate of their harvest. However, most men grow some cash crop, which they market through a co-operative society.[11] From the books of these societies a rough estimate of the cash earnings of an average farmer may be computed. By this reckoning, [12] the average annual income from coffee was 387 shillings, and from cotton slightly less. Thus the amount that is paid in bridewealth is more than a year's cash income and it is therefore understandable why the economic aspect of marriage looms large for both parties.

The negotiations which fix the amount of bridewealth to be paid are vital, particularly for the payer, since bargaining is possible. The stipulated items which have already been described do not form a fixed proportion of the total. Both the quality and size of the stipulated items and the number and kind of items additional to them are subject to agreement between the parties to the transaction. A considerable amount of haggling goes on. The means by which each party assesses its bargaining position will be described in detail below, but first it must be made clear that although this is an economic transaction, similar to others which Gisu transact, it is a transaction of a particular type.

Gisu recognize that marriage entails an economic transaction and that the bonds it creates between giver and receiver of bridewealth are similar to, though more lasting than, those created by other economic transactions. They use the word *khugula* = to buy, of obtaining a wife and the bride's agnates open the proceedings with a formal statement of their demands, couched in these terms: *Nikhugulisa umukaana wefe zikafu...*, 'we are selling you our daughter for...cows.' Nevertheless, the transaction belongs to a specific set of exchanges that are set apart from ordinary market transactions. [13] The exchange of a woman for cattle and other items of bridewealth is the most important of a type of exchanges in which items of higher intrinsic worth are acquired by exchanging objects of lower worth for them.

The objects involved in this type of exchange are all living things: rats, [14] hens, goats, cattle, women; they are ranked in order of value. But each object has also a particular intrinsic value, apart from its value in numbers of other objects. The possession of a cow is in this sense worth more than the possession of six goats, even though the exchange value of a cow is about six goats. (There is no exact equivalent since each exchange involves agreement between the parties.) There is greater public esteem to be obtained from owning the objects of higher prestige value. These objects can be exchanged (and Gisu use the word *khubugula*, to obtain, rather than the simple *khugula*, to buy) only for objects immediately above or below them on the scale of value. Rats cannot be exchanged directly for goats, or hens for women. The Gisu speak as if these exchanges form a closed system and illustrate it by saying: 'A boy traps rats, exchanges them for a hen. When the hen has enough chicks and they have grown, he exchanges them for a goat; when he has enough goats he exchanges them for a cow. When he has enough cows he marries and begets a son who starts to trap rats.' In fact the whole series of exchanges is rarely carried out by any one individual and the items can be exchanged ordinarily but the ideal serves to mark off these transactions from normal sales.

A feature of the type of exchange we are discussing is that the parties to it are thought to have a more than merely transient relationship. There is an element of conferring a favour in the act of the man who parts with the object of higher social value. As in any economic transaction the value of objects exchanged must be equal; both parties must be satisfied with their side of the bargain. But the man who acquires a goat for hens is, in Gisu eyes, obliged to his partner in the exchange for enabling him to acquire a goat which carries the potentiality of becoming a cow and eventually a wife. The higher on the scale the transaction takes place the greater is the sense of obligation. Often such exchanges take place between kinsmen and the sense of obligation for a particular favour is assimilated to the general obligations that kinsmen should feel, but they may be between unrelated men. In the latter case the benefactor is entitled to expect loyalty and occasional small services from his beneficiary. [15] At the top of the scale comes the transaction which establishes a marriage and here the sense of indebtedness is great. Gisu say that the payment of bridewealth in full can never entirely wipe out what is owed to a father-in-law; in exchange for cattle and other objects he has given the means by which a household will be established and a line of sons and grandsons founded to perpetuate his son-in-law's name. Even though the bridewealth represented fairly the 'value' of the girl her father is still her husband's benefactor. A woman's father and brothers are thus in a position to demand favours and help from her husband which he will find it hard to refuse, without the risk of being labelled an unworthy affine and one who shirks his social obligations. This is a reputation no Gisu wishes to acquire.

BRIDEWEALTH AS A MEASURE OF VALUE

The degree to which a man will be his wife's father's debtor, as distinct from his beneficiary in the sense we have been discussing, is determined by the total amount of bridewealth that is paid. In many marriages the jurally necessary items may form only half the bridewealth; in others this minimum is all that is paid. These variations reflect, in part, the worth of the particular girl. An assessment of her value is determined by the qualities of physical appearance, character and social standing which she possesses.

Gisu are admirers of womanly beauty and will readily discuss the attributes of colouring, features and figure which define their feminine ideal. A girl who is light-skinned, tall, well-rounded but neither fat nor thin, who is strong and well proportioned, is a beauty. No less important are qualities of character. The ideal wife should be neither vain nor a flirt (the Gisu expression for a girl who is too conscious of her charms for the opposite sex is *ali ni zimoni zindehi*, 'she has long (wide) eyes'). She should be industrious, thrifty, and obedient, courteous to guests, loyal and not addicted to gossip. The girl who possesses the admired qualities of appearance and character may expect that an extra cow or goats should be demanded for her in bridewealth. The agnates of an ugly, idle or unruly young woman will be careful to moderate their demands to an amount which is not far above the minimum. Today there is an additional criterion of value which is used to assess a girl's 'worth'. Educated girls have a higher price than uneducated ones. The reason for this is explained, by fathers, as the necessity to recover the money spent on education; by husbands, as reflecting favourably on the successful suitor. It is considered that it takes greater strength of character (*bunyali*) to manage an educated wife. Besides the prestige that marriage to an educated woman will bring, her learning brings an economic advantage. An educated woman may find work in a village school or dispensary. As her earnings belong legally to her husband, her value as a producer is enhanced above that of an uneducated woman. [16]

While personal characteristics, such as have been mentioned above, are taken into account in estimating the amount of bridewealth that is to be demanded for a particular girl, a most important criterion for assessing the value of a woman as wife is what her family [17] connexions are. The fact that, by acquiring a wife, a man becomes the son-in-law of her father and the brother-in-law of her brothers is a consideration which carries great weight with both parties. Today there are fewer marriages which are arranged by the elder agnates of the pair, as Gisu claim was the custom in former times. Less emphasis is placed on the importance of the alliance between lineages as such, but the position and wealth of the prospective affines are still important factors and influence the choice of a spouse. Many young men, when asked how they would choose a wife, specified a well-established and influential father or brothers as desirable. Affinal ties create bonds between men that entail not only specific obligations but a general solidarity that may prove useful in varying spheres of life. Namondo's father-in-law asked him to bicycle 17 miles to the local town for nails for the house he was building; Wodero obtained his post as a clerk through the good offices of a brother-in-law of his father. Musole cultivates a plot of land in another maximal lineage which has been lent him by a brother-in-law and in 1954 Makanya, a parish chief, settled a dispute between his own village and another village of his parish by appealing to his brother-in-law, the most important man in the other village and Makanya's direct superior. So useful are affinal ties that one Christian chief declared that it was virtually impossible for a chief to live up to the Christian ideal of monogamy: 'he should marry several wives, then he has friends and can rule the people'. The more influential a woman's father and brothers are the more desirable they are as affines. Hence the higher bridewealth that is paid for the daughter of a chief or wealthy man is a recognition of the value of links with her kin as well as of her higher social standing. Conversely, a man hopes to acquire a useful son-in-law and values his daughter's suitors according to their economic and social standing.

The final factor affecting the amount of bridewealth paid in a marriage which must be mentioned here, is the distance, spatial and social, between the natal homes of the bride and groom. Gisu bridewealth is paid in instalments, and during the period in which the payments have not been completed, the son-in-law will be subject to requests for small services, assistance and loans from his wife's fathers and brothers. In order to prevent the demands becoming too burdensome, for he cannot refuse without offence being given, a man prefers to live not too near his wife's natal home. As one man put it: 'If my wife's home is near, then her father and brothers are always visiting me, or they are always asking her to go home and help them. In each case this means presenting them with a fowl. I can't afford it.' For the same reasons, a man would like his daughter to marry in a village near his own so as to be able to take advantage of the hold he has over her husband. If she marries a man from a considerable distance, the bridewealth is normally increased, in order to compensate the woman's family for their inability to benefit in this way. Gisu call it 'paying for the loss of the girl' but neither party is in any doubt as to the real meaning of the phrase. Thus to marry a girl from a distant village, or from a genealogically unconnected village which has little social contact with her own village, is more expensive.

We are now in a position to see the objectives of both parties to the marriage contract. The prospective groom wants a wife who is attractive and who will be a good worker and mother of his children. He wants influential in-laws who may be able to help him rise in standing, but he wants them not to be in a position, for any reason, to impose their demands on him continually. The bride's father wishes to increase his wealth by his daughter's marriage, to exploit any assets that she may have, both in her own right and as his daughter, in order to acquire not only the goods he will receive for her but also a son-in-law who will be useful as an ally and able to render him the occasional services he may require. The contradictions in this situation are expressed in the haggling over the terms of the bridewealth.

BRIDEWEALTH BARGAINING

Bridewealth negotiations are carried out by two groups of men, acting on behalf of the parties concerned and representing the interest of their respective lineages. Such a group is know as *lihe*, a term also used for the war-party of a lineage. There is no hard and fast rule to determine who these men shall be. In one typical case the bride's group consisted of: her full brother, her half-brother, her father's father's brother's son and an influential elder of the lineage, classificatory brother of her father. The groom's party comprised: the groom, his full brother and his father's full and half-brothers. The only requirement is that neither father should be present. Gisu social structure enjoins a strict separation between the conjugal roles of proximate generations which is particularly stringent in the case of parent and child, so that neither of these two persons who are closely concerned in the outcome of the discussion may take part in it. If it is the young man's first marriage his father will be expected to pay the bridewealth for him; the girl's father is the person to whom it is paid. The two principals are represented at the discussion by the agnates whom they choose to form the *lihe*; detailed instructions are given them and for their efforts they are rewarded with a gift. The brothers of bride and groom, who almost always take part in bridewealth discussions, have their own interest in procuring a good bargain. The bride's brothers will claim beasts from her bridewealth to help pay for their own wives; the groom's brothers will be more likely to obtain parental assistance for their marriages in future if they see to it that not too much of the paternal capital is expended on their brother's wife. The older agnates lend their skill in discussion to the proceedings and act as the representatives of the minimal lineages concerned, whose care is always to see that members of the lineage do not dissipate their wealth unwisely. Bridewealth is not corporate lineage property as such but members of a minimal lineage are potential heirs to one another[18] and Gisu believe that the prosperity of any member is the good fortune of the whole lineage.

The relative bargaining strength of the two groups is affected by the events which had led to the discussion. Gisu distinguish between a marriage in which the girl is taken from her father's home after the correct negotiations and payments have been made and with full ceremonial and a marriage which is legitimized after the girl has left her father's control. The former is called *khuira umukaasi hango* 'to take a woman from home' (i.e. her father's home); the latter is known as *khubesa umukaana*, 'to seduce a girl'. Seduction is considered morally wrong, but certain procedures are recognized as being the only course of action when the disapproval of either, or both, sets of agnates have prevented a couple having their own way. The most admired of these is elopement. The young man waits, with some of his age-mates or agnates of his own generation by a spring or river. When the girl comes to fetch water, the young men leap out and carry her off. Propriety demands that she should struggle and make a show of resistance, but unless she is genuinely surprised, which seems to be rare, she will not make herself heard. She is taken to the house of a senior maternal relative of her captors, usually his mother's brother, and placed under his care. This relative must then send messengers to both fathers and arrange for bridewealth discussions to take place. Since the young man's intentions are 'honourable', he does not normally sleep with the girl until the formalities of marriage have been carried out.

A young man may make his sweetheart pregnant to force her father to allow them to marry, since the scandal of bearing an illegitimate child will damage the reputation of the family in which it occurs. Finally, if it is the disapproval of the young man's father and father's brothers which is the obstacle to a marriage, a suitor may steal the necessary beasts from his father. This course of action is likely if the man's father declares that he is too young to marry or that the cattle are needed for something else; an objection may also be raised to the particular girl. In any of these circumstances, the young man may take cattle from the herd belonging to his father, father's brothers, or agnatic cousins; he then drives them over to his sweetheart's father and asks for her in marriage. If his request is granted, the cattle are accepted and a message sent to the young man's senior agnates to inform them of the marriage. The girl's father may make additional demands, in which case a discussion is arranged, but whatever the outcome, the marriage is jurally established once the cattle have been accepted.

In all these cases of irregular procedure, the position of the two groups of agnates towards one another is altered. In a case of elopement, the groom and his agnates are in a much better position to bargain than they would be if the marriage had proceeded according to the rules. To carry off a girl reflects favourably on them, because it is a source of pride that one of their lineage was strong enough to flout the girl's guardians openly. On the other hand, to make a girl pregnant is considered reprehensible conduct, since it is morally wrong and ritually dangerous for a woman to become pregnant while living in her father's household. Moreover, there is a taboo on bridewealth discussion being carried out or payments made until the child is born, so that the first child of the marriage is born out of wedlock, which casts a slur on both lineages. In such a case, relations between the affines are likely to be strained; they can be rendered cordial after an elopement, although the girl's father is considered to have 'lost face' and will be unable to exert much authority over the son-in-law he has acquired in this irregular manner.

In the third type of irregular courtship, where cattle are taken from a man's senior agnates without their permission, affinal solidarity suffers most. The young man's father is unable to recover his beasts and annul the marriage. It is his duty to provide for his son's marriage and public opinion usually concludes that it was his neglect of that duty which led to the drastic action. If his son has taken beasts from his father's brothers or agnatic cousins, then the father must see that they are recompensed from his own herd. The bride's father is in a somewhat ambiguous position. In that he has received cattle for his daughter he can be said to have the normal standing of a father-in-law. In order to obtain his consent he will have been given more than he would normally get as a first payment or even *in toto*. But he has ceded his rights over his daughter in a highly irregular manner and without agreement with his peers (*bachewe*)—his brothers and other agnates and the young man's senior agnates. He can expect little deference from his son-in-law and only the minimum of affinal assistance from his son-in-law's agnates.

In the normal situation, the bridewealth discussion takes place after a series of visits which have revealed to each group the social standing, reputation and economic resources of the other. They meet with a clear idea of what is likely to be demanded of them. The groom and his agnates are concerned to resist the demands of the bride's agnates and pay as little as possible above the minimum. They will be asked a price that reflects the assessment of the bride's worth reached by her agnates and their estimate of her suitor's capacity to pay. If the groom's party cannot reduce this figure, they will commit him, or his father, to paying a sum which he cannot afford. Payments will not be completed for an unusual length of time and during those years the groom will be in an inferior position, liable to all sorts of demands on his time and resources. His agnates will also suffer, for he will be obliged to apply to them for help in maintaining good relations with his father-in-law. The latter has the stronger jural position; Gisu law allows him to sue for payment of the balance of the bridewealth at any time. The defendant can only plead guilty and hope that his father-in-law will not press the matter to extremes. For a father-in-law, like any creditor, may, with the permission of his debtor's lineage, seize as security or in lieu of payment, land or cattle belonging to his debtor or his debtor's close agnates. He should not do this, particularly if by this action he jeopardizes the future inheritance of his grandchildren, but he holds the right to sue for payment as a sanction for his son-in-law's good behaviour. On the other hand, if relations between them are good, the father-in-law may waive some of the later payments, but such a possibility cannot be depended upon. It is therefore of great importance for the groom and his agnates to keep the bridewealth down to a point which does not overstrain their resources, both existing and expected.

The groom's agnates cannot haggle over the payments in such a way as to indicate that they cannot afford to meet them, lest their prestige suffer. Even if such an admission lowered the price they were asked, they would leave their agnate in a difficult position. His father-in-law would be likely to impose on him to a greater extent, knowing that his economic position would not support a sudden demand for complete payment. In a situation in which the girl's father is clearly the poorer, the greater equality in standing between the two groups is plain in their demeanour during the bridewealth discussions. If the prospective groom and his supporters show their confidence in being able to meet any demands made on them, they will ensure a position of co-operation on equal terms for the groom in future dealings with his affines. The bridegroom's position as beneficiary of his father-in-law is balanced by his membership of a richer family or lineage. At the outset of a marriage such a situation is rare because the girl's father is careful to investigate the resources of her suitor and phrase his demands accordingly. One can see it though, in the later stages of a marriage, when there are few or no payments outstanding on the bridewealth and the relationship between father- and son-in-law is one of mutual profit.

THE CYCLE OF AFFINAL RELATIONS

A man who is about to marry, or his father for him, must allocate his existing resources to his best advantage. This implies that he must take thought for the future since the obligations that he undertakes at his marriage will involve him in expenditure for several years at least. There is an expected course which relations with his affines will normally take; the points at which demands will be heavy can be anticipated to a certain extent. The cycle of affinal relations depends on the normal career of the average Gisu man. As a young man in his early twenties, a few years past initiation, most of his energies and wealth will be directed towards the establishment of himself as the head of a stable and flourishing household. Once this is done, he can turn his attention to building up his position in the village. Such resources as he can spare he will direct towards the increase of his prestige and influence. He will assist his agnates and kin and begin to achieve a circle of people who support him. If his affairs prosper he will take a second wife. The peak of a man's career is generally reached by the time his sons are about to be initiated and enter the world of adults. He must then provide the expenses of establishing them: he must pay for their initiation, hand over some of his property to them and provide them with wives. His economic resources must support a heavy burden, and in order to maintain the position he has built up in the village he must press his creditors, among whom his sons-in-law are important, for fulfilment of their obligations. When all his sons are established as householders, a man's political power begins to decline, although his prestige (as opposed to his control of others) may remain high enough for him to play an influential part in his village's affairs. In Bugisu, the effective political leaders are only rarely men with grown grandsons. Normally they are middle-aged men.

The development of the careers of two men who are father-in-law and son-in-law to one another affects the relations between them. It is this that produces the course of affairs that can be predicted and which the younger man must take into account when he marries. The period of increased demands on him will come sooner or later according to whether his wife has many brothers and sisters and whether they are older or younger. If she is the eldest sibling, then her husband may expect that demands on him will not be heavy for some years, until her brothers are pressing their father to pay for wives for them. If she is the youngest, with one or two brothers as yet unmarried, then his obligations as a son-in-law will be heavy immediately, but he can look forward to a period of decreased demands and increased support later, when he is beginning his own upward climb. It is not unusual, however, for pressure to be put on a man to pay further instalments of bridewealth at a time when he is beginning to use his surplus goods to further his political career. Good relations with his affines are desirable and in order to avoid having to choose between them he will have to counter his father-in-law's demands with tactful resistance and procrastination. Ideally he should arrange matters so that he can cope with having to pay instalments of the bridewealth without impairing his accumulation of goods for use in other ways. It is here that the amount of bridewealth that has been agreed on becomes relevant. A man who agrees to a heavy bridewealth in order to marry the girl who attracts him or in order to acquire influential affines may involve himself in difficulties later.

The son-in-law derives his greatest benefit from his affinal ties if he can weather the period of heavy demands, without depreciating his resources or alienating his affines' good-will. As his father-in-law withdraws from an active part in political life, relations with his son-in-law become more equable. The affinal ties become mutually profitable. In return for having fulfilled his economic obligations, the younger man will be able to ask his father-in-law to use his prestige and influence to help him. The smooth development of a profitable alliance continues after the death of his wife's father. No one of her brothers inherits the father's standing as benefactor and creditor, although they may sue jointly for arrears of bridewealth. They are, to some extent, believed to be indebted in their turn to their sister's husband, whose payments have been used to provide them with wives. From this point on, if there have been no serious disputes affinal relations become largely independent of domestic harmony between the pair whose marriage gave rise to them. Separation may occur but it does not usually entail divorce, particularly if the woman is past the age of childbearing. She may be living with another man or in a separate household near an adult son, but her brothers and her husband will continue to enjoy as cordial relations as if she were still in her husband's homestead. The households of many elderly men may contain one or two of the women they have married, but they continue to enjoy the good-will and support of all the men with whom they have affinal links.

LIMITATIONS ON CHOICE

We have been examining certain aspects of Gisu social structure which affect the situation in which a man chooses his wife. The variable amounts paid as bridewealth reflect the value of different women as wives and the value of affinal connexions that will be set up by the marriage; the nature of affinal ties themselves and the fact that a man must not deplete the economic resources with which he may achieve political eminence; all these facts, taken in conjunction, define a course of action which offers the best solution of the problem. This is to marry a woman from a family similar to one's own in social standing and wealth. In this way a man may be reasonably sure of paying a bridewealth that will not be a constant burden. There is a Gisu saying which reflects this notion: *Umudambi ka'ira umukaana wo'mugasya da* 'the poor man does not marry the daughter of a lineage head'. If a man marries such a girl, the advantages of having powerful affines will be offset by the higher bridewealth that he will have to pay. If, on the other hand, he marries a woman from a family poorer or less influential than his own, he will not acquire useful affines. A wife of equivalent standing will come from a family whose men will not be people of greatly superior political standing, although her father will have the greater influence of an older man. Their activities will not make demands on him that are greater than he can anticipate. Formerly, it is said, a man was more influenced by the wishes of his father and other senior agnates when he chose a wife; she might even be chosen for him. Similarity of social and economic circumstances was the major guide then as it is now. The modern schoolboy writing an essay, in English, on Gisu marriage lays great emphasis on the priority of these considerations.

Given the traditional system of solving both individual and group dispute by negotiation, affinal ties provided an important source of political influence. Other ties were also made use of but affinal ties could be chosen, and hence a man could, by a judicious marriage, advance his own career. The most advantageous places to have affines were in villages bordering on one's own or in other minimal lineages within it. Thus, although a Gisu might choose a girl from any of those not prohibited to him by ties of kinship, he had a positive advantage in restricting the field of possible wives to girls from families with a standing similar to his own, in either his own or neighbouring villages. Further considerations, which will be described now, might narrow the field even further.

Marriage prohibitions prevent a Gisu from marrying a girl from three lineages: his own, his mother's and his paternal grandmother's. The range of forbidden kin effectively include all but a few girls of his maternal grandmother's lineage, unless a ceremony of cutting kinship is performed. The exchange of sisters between two men is forbidden, so that a man may not marry the sisters or agnatic cousins of the men his own sisters or agnatic cousins have married. In fact it is considered better not to marry any girl of the lineage into which a sister, own or classificatory, has married. Gisu practise widow inheritance and since sororal polygyny is prohibited, it is considered inadvisable to marry into the same lineage as a brother or agnatic cousin from whom a wife may be inherited, lest having a wife from the same minimal lineage as the widow should prevent a man from performing his duty towards his dead kinsman. Nor should a man marry into the same lineage as his father. These limitations narrow the range of possibilities within which a man may choose still further, although they do not have the force of the prohibitions on marriage with blood relatives.

As an example of how Gisu social structure marks out a class of women as possible wives for any one man let us consider the case of Labalesio. Labalesio comes from a family of moderate wealth and influence; his father has two wives and Labalesio has two brothers and two sisters who are already married. He also has three male agnatic cousins who are married. The women of the lineages of his two grandmothers are also prohibited to him. Of the nearby minimal lineages, there are only seven (out of eighteen) from which he can choose a wife. Of these seven, one, a minimal lineage of his own village, has no unmarried girls of the right age. He may choose from the girls of six lineages (about 250 families), of whom at least half will be from poorer families and thus not a 'good' choice. If he goes beyond the immediately neighbouring villages, as he probably will do, he will have to pay a higher bridewealth. (His father is very active politically and is paying school fees for several younger children, so that Labalesio's choice of a wife will be carefully scrutinized by his father.) This case is not unusual; the restrictions are obviously greater for the sons of men who have more than two wives. But all Gisu men, whether rich or poor, choose from among a far smaller number of women than appears at first sight.

AFFINAL TIES AND VILLAGE ORGANIZATION

The following section is concerned with the implications of what has been established for the society, rather than for individuals. The exogamous unit is the minimal lineage, which is not an independent political or territorial unit. It is an integral part of the village upon which political activity, both as regards leadership and inter-group disputes, is based. Men are disposed, as we have seen, to choose wives from their own or neighbouring villages, since in this way they make affinal ties which are useful to them politically. The village then contains exogamous segments linked by affinal ties as well as the ties of common descent. It is linked to neighbouring villages in a similar way. The nature of the linkage can be shown by an examination of the affinal ties of Bulwala village, in relation to the wider system of which it is a part.

There are five component minimal lineages of Lwala minor lineage, on which Bulwala village is based. One of these, Mamalo, has recently split off from Namahe lineage and is considered, by some villagers, to be still a part of it as far as marriage is concerned. The village consists of 137 households, of which seventeen are composed of either a widow and her unmarried son or an elderly widow living alone or with a young grandchild. As we are interested in the range from which Lwala men choose their wives, widows are counted as representing a marriage. Also included are forty-three women, who were married to Lwala men but have since either died or been divorced since subsequent events do not affect the fact that the choice of a wife was made. As the survey from which the following data are taken was primarily aimed at obtaining information about household composition, complete data on the marriages of women born in the village is lacking, so that our view of Lwala's affinal ties is restricted to those resulting from the marriage of its men.

The total number of marriages ever made, of which one spouse still lives in the village, is 150. Of these nineteen were with Lwala women. If we examine these marriages in detail it appears that each of the minimal segments of Lwala minor lineage gave and received a roughly equivalent number of women. The exception is Mamalo which, as has been pointed out, is still considered part of Namahe. In the course of time the affinal ties which bridge the cleavage between exogamous segments in the village become ties of extra-lineage kinship; for the children of these marriages have mother's brothers and maternal grandparents in their own village. Men who have no such kinship ties outside their own minimal segment contract marriages which give them another kind of ally in brother segments. Thus the intricate network of ties which counteract the divisions produced by the descent system is continually renewed. We can see this if we consider the ages of the men who have contracted the nineteen intra-village marriages: five are over 61, eight are between 41 and 60, four are under 40. There are two widows who are Lwala women.

However, marriages within the village form only just over 11% of the total number of marriages. The remainder comprises marriages with women from outside Bulwala. Where these women come from is determined, to a large extent, by the position of the village in the wider lineage and territorial framework: sixteen marriages are with women of Faka village and fifteen with women of Namahande. Both of these villages belong to the village-cluster of which Lwala is a part. Marriage with women from them is thus marriage with agnates, for they are fellow-members of the major lineage of which Lwala minor lineage is a segment. In all, one-third (50 out of 150) marriages are marriages with agnates and the affinal ties created by them strengthen the association between groups recruited on the basis of unilineal descent.

Outside the village-cluster, the pattern of spouse choice follows a different principle. It is not influenced as much by the structure of the descent system. Distance is still an important consideration: the farther away a village, the fewer marriages have taken place between its women and Lwala men. But here distance is a matter of geographical not genealogical separation. Mugwedi village of the neighbouring maximal lineage, which has a common boundary with Lwala village, provides more wives than either Nagami or Masobo village, although both the latter belong to the same maximal lineage as Lwala. This fact is directly related to the way in which the traditional political system worked. The largest group that ever combined for political action was the village-cluster, that is, the men of one major lineage. Beyond this, relations were at least potentially hostile, and it made little difference if the groups concerned were of the same maximal lineage or not. The cultural and ritual symbols of the maximal lineage's identity were not supported by any mechanism that could make for political unity. Moreover, the traditional system provided an incentive to marriage with geographically close villages rather than villages which were related on the basis of common membership of a lineage but which were not neighbours. Territorial contiguity involved villages in relations which were more continuous and more productive of disputes than relations with distant but genealogically related villages. The need for ties to bridge the cleavages between neighbouring villages was stronger than the impulse towards closer unity within the whole maximal lineage. Thus more wives are chosen from neighbouring villages in other maximal lineage areas than from villages in more distant village-clusters of the maximal lineage of which Lwala is a part.

Fig. 1 shows the total range of Lwala's affinal relations. The marriages contracted by Lwala men and the kinship ties which result from them for children of the marriage serve to draw the village together and embed it more

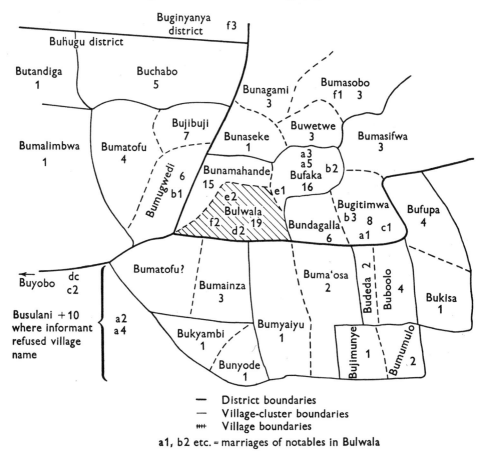

Fig. 1. Affinal ties of men of Lwala minor lineage.

firmly in the political setting. Outside the range of the largest group of political importance affinal ties do not strengthen the ties of unilineal descent but serve to offset the divergent and often conflicting territorial interests of villages which are geographically close, regardless of their lineage affiliations. The need for a basis to conduct affairs with neighbouring villages and greater knowledge of their inhabitants than the men of the village possessed encouraged them to seek their wives there rather than among the more distant agnates of another village-cluster. Ties between contiguous villages might even be stronger than the ties of common descent. It is not uncommon for accounts of wars to reveal that a village joined with a neighbouring unrelated village to fight villages of its own maximal lineage or even of its own village-cluster.

One further aspect of the norm of wife-choosing has relevance for the wider social system. The tendency to choose a wife from a family of similar social standing and wealth results in a wider than average spread of the affinal ties of rich men. First, rich men, and their sons, are able to pay the higher bridewealth that marriage with a girl from a distant village will entail. Secondly, the group within which rich men choose their wives is drawn from a larger area. Within his own and neighbouring villages there are few families whose position makes them particularly desirable affines for a man of more than average wealth. Some of them will be already related to him in the forbidden degrees of kinship since it is from this group that his father and brothers have taken wives. He is therefore forced to consider a wider range of villages in order to obtain the sort of advantages that a poorer man can find in neighbouring villages. Rich men do marry girls of poorer families but since they are able to afford more than one wife they can also marry with an affinal alliance in mind. The marriages of leaders in a village usually show a balance between marriages which strengthen the ties with other segments of their village and village-cluster and marriages which provide ties further afield (see below).

Rich men are more often polygynists. Of fifty-three chiefs the percentage of polygynists was: higher chiefs (county and subcounty chiefs 87 %; lower chiefs (parish chiefs and village headmen) 66 %). [19] The percentage for Bulwala as a whole, excluding its notables and chiefs, was just under 15 %. Polygyny is a source of prestige and of greater influence since the polygynist has a larger number of affines on whom to call for support. The marriages of the six most influential men in Bulwala illustrate what has been said. Between them these six men have seventeen wives. Each man, with one exception, has at least one wife from outside the circle of villages where most Lwala men get their wives. (The exception is a young man and may marry again.) Three wives come from Lwala village, four from villages in the same village-cluster (a slightly higher proportion than that for the village as whole). Five wives come from other villages in the same maximal lineage area, but outside the village-cluster, and five from villages in other maximal lineage areas. Of these latter, all but one come from villages which do not border directly on Bulwala. These men therefore command a position which makes them valuable negotiators for the village, since their affines are numerous and widely distributed in the villages within Lwala's orbit of political activity.

In the Gisu political system, leadership is acquired by men who have two assets: the ability to weld together segments of a lineage, whose tendency is to maintain their separateness by supporting only their own members and also the ability to act on behalf of a group (of whatever size) in its external relations. Affinal ties provide one means by which both these assets may be acquired. They enable a man to acquire supporters through whom he can wield influence in a group with which he has no other connexions and from which he is excluded by virtue of his lineage membership. In 1954 I attended the funeral of a pregnant woman in a village some 5 miles from where I lived. The considerable opposition to my presence there was overcome by my assistant's appealing to his father-in-law, who persuaded his agnates to allow me to attend. They also provide ties which may be utilized on behalf of the whole group. The man in Bulwala village who managed to persuade villagers of the neighbouring village to contribute towards the upkeep of a spring that sections of both villages use was a man with a brother-in-law in that village, who was chosen to act as negotiator in the dispute for that reason.

For the average villager the circle of influence he acquires at marriage is a restricted one: ordinary men like himself in his own village and village-cluster or in a few unrelated villages nearby. For a rich man it is wider and more useful. His affines are typically important men in the villages with which his own has frequent relations; he will therefore be asked on numerous occasions to intercede with them on behalf of his agnates and fellow-villagers. In so doing he increases his influence among them. It is the rich man who is able to act effectively on behalf of his lineage or village in its external relations. Moreover the rich man's scope of operations is wider. He can hope to acquire leadership within a village-cluster, by acquiring affines in its other villages and also by using his affinal ties in more distant villages to conduct the cluster's external relations.

The marital history (Fig. 2) of Musole exemplifies what we have been saying. Musole is a member of Bunagami village in the village-cluster of Bumasobo of Bumasifwa maximal lineage. He married twelve wives: three from villages in his own village-cluster, five from villages in other village-clusters of Bumasifwa and three from neighbouring maximal lineages.[20] His affines are mostly men of importance in their own villages, particularly the agnates of his non-Masifwa wives. He thus has affines strategically placed as supporters within a whole maximal lineage and is undoubtedly the most powerful man in it.

Musole is an old man now and in some ways not representative of the younger generation of leaders.[21] But they, though less likely to marry so many wives, continue a pattern of choosing which makes for a close relationship between affinal ties and positions of influence. That this relation is the result of deliberate and conscious choice is abundantly clear when the subject of marriages is discussed with chiefs and other powerful men. The opinion of one chief who considers monogamy impossible for a chief has already been quoted. It is confirmed by what young men say on the importance of choosing a wife whose father and brothers are in a position to use their influence on behalf of their affine. The tendency for chiefs to acquire ties by marrying into the groups over which they rule is one of the obstacles to be overcome before this system of rule can become rule by members of a civil service. In order to achieve this and prevent the formation of local ties which might make chiefs less impersonal in their administration, it has been the policy of the British Protectorate Government to transfer higher chiefs from post to post.

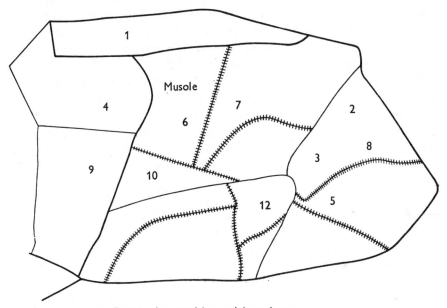

— District (maximal lineage) boundaries
— Village-cluster (major lineage) boundaries
Ⱶ Village (minor lineage) boundaries
Informant claimed not to remember affiliation of wife: 11

Fig. 2. Marriage choices of Musole.

In spite of this, chiefs often do marry local women in order to acquire a traditional type of influence which is very useful to them. One very wealthy chief has been particularly successful in this respect. The lineage affiliations of his successive (and numerous) wives form a nearly perfect record of the postings he has had during his career.

CHANGE IN THE PATTERN OF CHOICES

The preceding arguments have been designed to show that, in a society where 'individual choice is the rule', there is in effect a patterning of choices which is the logical result of the interplay of different aspects of the society in which the choices are made. The important point is that the norm which is formed is not given jural recognition in the society. Marriage to one of a particular class of women is not sanctioned in any way nor does it carry merit in itself. It depends on the assessment by each individual of the means appropriate to gain certain ends. These ends, prestige and power, are important values recognized by Gisu society. But no penalties, as such, are incurred by the man who does not pursue them but prefers to satisfy other desires. The norm may change, either when the ends to be achieved change, or when changes in the considerations involved make it possible or desirable to achieve the ends in different ways. In Bugisu, the changes have had repercussions on the institution of marriage itself, so that there are now virtually two types of Gisu marriage and for each the norm of choice is different.

The Gisu have been part of the administrative system of Uganda for nearly half a century, but the structural outline of Gisu society remains much the same. Lineage areas have become administrative units and there is political unity over a much wider area than was possible under the traditional system, but the chiefs, particularly the village and parish chiefs, rule in ways which differ little from those of the lineage heads who preceded them. The lower chiefs are usually local men, who only rarely form part of the bureaucratic *élite*, the modern educated Gisu. Land-holding and residence are still controlled by the minimal lineage and the important lineage rituals are still performed. Marriage is still legitimized by the payment of bridewealth and the traditional marriage prohibitions are still maintained.

The greatest changes have been economic and they have created a class structure which appears to be more rigid in recruitment and sharper in wealth differences than that of the traditional system. In pre-European times, membership of the upper stratum of rich and powerful men was fluid. The differential of wealth and social standing was not so great that it was impossible for the ordinary villager to become rich and powerful. The wealth of powerful men was distributed among their numerous descendants, and over the generations there was a constant reshuffle of the personnel occupying high positions. The Gisu were an expanding and disunited people; land and riches were to be had for the taking in local fighting and in wars against the Sebei. Whether a man aspired to leadership of his minimal lineage, or village, or whether he had no such ambitions, affines were a valuable source of support and every man had the incentive to consider his marriage as an alliance.

Today there is an *élite* whose members are entrenched in their superior position and likely to remain so over future generations. These people are much further removed, in terms of wealth, from the poorer members of the society than were the traditional leaders. In the early days of British administration, the men in authority used their position to acquire additional holdings of land, buying holdings cheaply from men who earned the disfavour of Government or who fled to avoid paying taxes. The fixing of permanent boundaries round Gisu territory and the enforcement of peace throughout the country has blocked the traditional avenues of expansion. Land is increasingly short, although wage-labour has provided a new means of supplementing income and acquiring wealth. The introduction of coffee and cotton as cash-crops has resulted in a general rise in the level of wealth but it has also increased the difference between the large land-holders and the ordinary peasant. The rich do not display their wealth by taking more and more wives, whether they adhere to the Christian principle of monogamy or not. Their wealth is used to educate their sons, whose inheritance is great compared with that of the peasant's son. The education they have received enables them to acquire salaried jobs which offer good pay, prestige and power, opportunities which are closed to the sons of poorer men who have had scant or no education.

As well as a rich, semi-exclusive class from which leaders are drawn, there also exists today a stratum of poor men, whose families have little chance, under the present system, [22] of improving their condition. These men have little land and must supplement their income by casual employment, often as migrant labourers. The 1948 census showed 15,000 Gisu outside Bugisu; many of these are men who leave their homes temporarily to earn cash to pay bridewealth or to build a house. Some of them settle down where they work and do not return, but it is the ambition of most men to return to their own village, buy more land and become prosperous householders. This ambition does not seem to be often realized, however, and every village has its complement of men who are intermittent residents and who take little part in the continuing life of the village. When things go wrong for them they leave, entrusting their land to the care of a wife, brother or elderly mother. For these men and for the poorer members of the village who subsist on the small amounts of land they own, political power is virtually out of reach.

Modern Gisu marriage is still legitimized by the payment of bridewealth, but the amount payable has increased rapidly with the expansion in the economy. The rise has been so fast that the African Local Government made an attempt to curb it by imposing a maximum payment of three cows and two goats, more than that being illegal with both parties to the transaction being liable to prosecution. The main effect of the ruling however has been to obscure the issue as far as the stipulated items are concerned. Some Gisu claim that the regulation established the correct payment. Marriages are still contracted by the payment of bridewealth in excess of the legal maximum and many fall considerably below it. The wider range of wealth is reflected in an ever-widening scale of bridewealth payments.

For most Gisu, marriage still involves an affinal alliance to be chosen with care. The establishment of a bureaucratic system of administration based on the old hierarchy of lineage segments has given the maximal lineage a political unity it never had and the choice of affinal alliances takes into consideration the new political situations. If one compares the marriages of men under 40 with those of older men, there appears to be a general increase in the marriages with women of other villages of the same maximal lineage outside the village-cluster. The system whereby leadership is based on wealth and personal influence is little changed. In this respect the chiefs are the successors of the lineage heads of former times. The introduction, in 1949, of elected councils has given new life to the old ways. Gisu are thoroughly versed in the art of canvassing for election; their traditional system was built on activities of this sort. In general, therefore, most villagers are faced with the same issues that were involved in marriage for their fathers and grandfathers.

There is a difference, however, for members of the educated wealthy upper class. Marriage has important connotations in the political field but politics for them is lifted out of the village and village-cluster. The wives of these men are chosen from among the sisters and daughters of colleagues and superiors in the white-collar world of government employees, teachers and senior clergy. The chiefs also maintain connexions by marrying the daughters of local notables in the areas where they are posted. The widening scope of political opportunities is a result of the establishment of the whole tribe as a political entity which in itself has facilitated the creation of a comparatively exclusive upper class. Leaders are drawn from the whole tribe, their activities require alliances which stretch beyond the boundaries of the small localities to which the lineage head was confined. An upper class drawn from all sections of the tribe can be, and is, largely self-sufficient for marriage purposes. As their increasing wealth has divided them from the bulk of the population so there has been a trend towards the crystallization of a hereditary intermarrying class whose members provide the leaders of the tribe.

For this class, bridewealth is particularly high for two reasons. The amounts involved effectively prevent non-members marrying into their ranks, for it is only rarely that a man who is not already one of this class by birth, education or profession, can pay what is demanded. In one marriage of this sort the total amount handed over in bridewealth, I was told, was over 1000 shillings, which is three times as much as the average. Secondly, bridewealth payments and the very expensive celebrations which are customary among the upper class are a form of conspicuous consumption and a demonstration of the standing of the two families involved. Members of the upper class, therefore, usually choose upper class women as their wives and pay heavily for the important connexions such a marriage will bring, to establish themselves as members of a powerful interconnected group of families and to demonstrate that their own wealth is in itself sufficient to earn themselves membership of the class.

At the other end of the scale, among the poorer sections of the community marriage is undergoing a transformation which is also related to the economic changes of the last half-century. For men with little land, who cannot spare fields from food production to grow cash-crops and for men who are often away on migrant labour, marriage is no longer considered in the light of the affinal connexions it will establish. For these men marriage often demands an expenditure which is incommensurate with their means. It is essential for a man of this sort to find a wife whose bridewealth he can afford to pay. He often cannot afford the niceties of marrying a girl 'from her father's house' and must resort to less orthodox means. Some men take the earnings of a period of migrant labour to the father of a girl as they would have taken cattle from their father's herd in former times; the subsequent contract is arranged between the man and his father-in-law, his agnates having little interest as the earnings of a man are not a lineage business.

The majority of poor men simply persuade the girl of their choice to set up house with them, trusting that they will be able to stave off her father's demands or that the *fait accompli* will force the acceptance of whatever bridewealth they may be able to offer. The father's jural powers enable him to sue for bridewealth in the court and he is usually able to exact the legal minimum but the delays involved favour the son-in-law, by giving him time to amass sufficient payments to prevent his father-in-law reclaiming the girl. Once the stipulated items have been paid the marriage is jurally established and anything over that amount must be forced from the husband by pressure on the father-in-law's part. Whether more is paid depends on the subsequent achievements of the husband and the power of his father-in-law.

For a poor man the choice of a wife is a question of obtaining the domestic and conjugal services of a woman at the least possible cost at the time or at a later date. He wishes, at all costs, to avoid placing himself in a permanent position of subjection to his father- and brothers-in-law. The daughters of wealthy and influential men are thus bad choices, for not only will their fathers expect a high bridewealth but they are in a position to force him to pay or else to give up his wife. Although no man expects to ignore his affines, the poor man counts it an advantage if his wife comes from a distant village so that her fathers and brothers are not always demanding favours of him, which is likely if they know he is poor and unable to pay more than the basic items of bridewealth. Important affinal connexions are of little value to a poor man who has neither the wealth nor the education to seek positions of power. In short, the poor man seeks a strong and healthy, industrious girl from a distant village. A woman who has been divorced often becomes the wife of a poor man since bridewealth is less for a divorcee and moreover her second husband is relieved of the duty of paying it until her father has refunded the bridewealth to her first husband. Often the marriages of poor men are founded on associations formed at markets or during periods of labour emigration, particularly in Buganda where there is a sizeable Gisu community. The negotiations usually involve only the immediate families concerned and celebrations are curtailed or non-existent. Marriage is still a contract but the subject of the contract is the transfer of the woman as wife and the legitimization of her future children. The wider issues of affinity as a political relationship are no longer relevant.

There have come to be two types of marriage in Bugisu. The distinction between them underlines the nature of bridewealth payments in this society. In order for a marriage to be jurally valid, bridewealth must be paid. The stipulated items symbolize and pay for the minimum rights of domestic and sexual services. They also legitimize the children of the union. It is important here that payments do not assure that all future progeny of the wife are legal offspring of her husband. Adulterine children are the offspring of their genitor and must be legitimized by him by payments to the woman's guardian, either her husband or her father if she is divorced for the adultery. Children born to the husband before the marriage was made legal must also be redeemed by payments. The bridewealth payments reserve the wife's sexual and procreative powers to her husband, with the presumption that her children will also be his. Thus the minimum involved in a Gisu marriage is the transfer of jurally valid claims to the labour and sexuality of a woman, to the exclusion of all other men. These rights are lineage property in that they pass to a man's heir at his death; during his lifetime they are his personal property.

In most marriages and formerly in all marriages, the stipulated items paid in bridewealth represented the core of a varying total amount. The items additional to the core are settled by negotiation and are, as we have seen, the price paid for the political value of affinity. Affinal relationships are always established by a marriage and the jural obligations entailed in them are not affected by the amount of bridewealth paid. What is at stake is the goodwill of affines and their willingness to give help and support in those situations where they have no clear-cut obligations. It is this consideration which influences individuals in their choice of a wife.

The norm of choice with which we have been concerned is the result of the actions of individuals who come to a similar decision when faced with the components of the situation in which they must choose. Formerly this situation was similar for all Gisu, and most men followed a similar course of action. Men chose a wife from among families of their own circumstances in neighbouring villages or in their own village. The affinal ties of a village embedded it more firmly in the lineage and territorial organization and provided the links on which wider groupings were built up. Today the pattern is more complicated. The tendency of members of the richest and poorest groups to marry outside the boundaries of a small group of villages (though for different reasons), is a feature of the growing unity of the tribe. Local differences and antagonisms between sections of the population which were emphasized in the traditional system are being bridged by ties which were impossible before. Yet for the middle range of Gisu, lineage exclusiveness is increasing. The greater scale of the modern political system has tended to strengthen the awareness of identity among members of lineages of a higher order than the political units on which the old system was based. The maximal lineage is now of political significance. The shortage of land has resulted in greater antagonism towards non-lineage members living and cultivating in an area to which they have no birth-right. Affines may lend land; they will lend it more readily to an affine who is also a member of the same minor, major or maximal lineage as themselves. The modern pattern of wife-choosing reflects and reinforces two opposing tendencies: the break-down of the lineage principle as the only means of identifying individuals in favour of an alignment based on hereditary wealth and influence and a contradictory trend, affecting the average villager, towards a greater emphasis on agnatic ties and lineage organization.

NOTES

[1] The field-work on which this article is based was done between 1953 and 1955 when I was a member of the East African Institute of Social Research. I am grateful to Dr A. I. Richards, then Director of the Institute, and to other Fellows for valuable advice and assistance and also to Professor M. Fortes for his helpful comments on this article.

[2] An exception is M. Fortes's analysis of the marriages of Tale men: *The Web of Kinship among the Tallensi*, 1949: 287 ff.

[3] See J. S. La Fontaine, 'The Gisu of Uganda', in the *Ethnographic Survey of Africa*.

[4] One of the Nandi-speaking tribes. See G. B. W. Huntingford, 'The Southern Nilo-Hamites', in the *Ethnographic Survey of Africa*.

[5] See L. A. Fallers, *Bantu Bureaucracy* (1956) and Audrey Richards (ed.), *East African Chiefs* (1960, p. 34).

[6] Under European administration political units have been formed from maximal lineage areas and even larger groupings along lines of division which existed in the traditional system but which had no political significance. A maximal lineage area has become a subcounty; subcounties are grouped into three counties which together make up the whole of Bugisu. The village and village-cluster have been incorporated into this system, the latter being designated a parish.

[7] Compare J. Maquet, *Le Système des relations sociales dans le Ruanda ancien* (1954) in which the author makes similar statements about leaders in the political system of the Ruanda.

[8] There is a ceremony which is used to annul the tie of kinship between a man and a woman who have a common ancestor three generations removed from themselves but who have married before it was known.

[9] For further details of the ceremony see La Fontaine, *op. cit.*

[10] The example of Elizabessi is instructive. She wished for a divorce but knew that it would be difficult for her father to refund the bridewealth. She told me that she was willing to wait until she could make out a good case that her husband had failed in his obligations towards her, when she could get a divorce without refund of bridewealth.

[11] Gisu growers are obliged to market their crops in this way; a Government regulation forbids other organizations buying the crops.

[12] The figures are not strictly comparable. The average figure for coffee was obtained as an average of the takings of 139 producers, a 1 in 10 sample from the books of three co-operatives, chosen as typical of different areas. The takings were for the season 1954–5. The figure for earnings from the sale of cotton was assessed differently since for some reason the records of the cotton co-operatives were markedly incomplete. The figure (386 shillings) was the average for 103 producers (a 1 in 10 sample) but the takings of each producer was represented by his average for several seasons. Cotton is grown in areas where coffee does not do well and it is unusual for a man to own plots of both coffee and cotton.

[13] Franz Steiner, 'Some notes on comparative economics', Brit. J. Sociology, 1954; P. J. Bohannan, 'Some principles of exchange and investment among the Tiv', American Anthropologist, 1955: 57, 1.

[14] The Gisu used to eat field-rats. Now that they no longer do so, rats do not form part of the system of progressive exchange but many informants include them when speaking about the system.

[15] This relationship is reminiscent of the patron–client tie which is so important among the Interlacustrine Bantu but it has no jural sanctions.

[16] Some men claim that an educated wife is a liability since she will not be accustomed to working in the fields, but in general education is considered to enhance a girl's value.

[17] I refer to the immediate family and close agnates of the father's. Gisu do not rank whole lineages in order of wealth. Similarly, the modern upper class of Europeanized Gisu (see below) consists of interconnected families rather than lineages.

[18] If a dead man has no sons, brothers or agnatic cousins to inherit his property an heir is chosen by the lineage. Moreover, Gisu recognize that certain lines may die out but the lineage as a corporate group persists.

[19] A survey of chiefs was done by the East African Institute. The full results are to be found in my chapter on the Gisu in East African Chiefs, ed. by Audrey Richards (1960).

[20] He claimed to have forgotten the lineage affiliation of one wife.

[21] In the early years of European administration, chiefs used their increased wealth to acquire wives on a scale hitherto unknown in Gisu society. The present generation practises a more modest degree of polygyny and buys expensive objects of consumption and display.

[22] 1953–55. I am aware that this statement might require modification in 1960. One means to advancement for men without the advantages of upper class membership is through nationalist and revolutionary organizations, such as the Uganda National Congress, which already in 1955 attracted many ambitious men of this sort.

COMPLEMENTARY FILIATION AND MARRIAGE IN THE TROBRIAND ISLANDS: A RE-EXAMINATION OF MALINOWSKI'S MATERIAL

By MARGUERITE S. ROBINSON

I. INTRODUCTION

Malinowski's data on affinity and filiation in the Trobriands are rich in scope and in detail, though widely scattered throughout his writings. This paper is an attempt to gather together the existing material on the Trobriand system of marriage and filiation and to examine the system as a whole, with particular reference to the rights and obligations derived through complementary filiation. It is characteristic of this greatest of all ethnographers that the Trobriand social system may be still further studied from his own material.

In addition to Malinowski's data, I have made use of the material collected in the Trobriands in 1950–1 by Dr H. A. Powell and presented in his Doctoral Thesis (1956). Powell's study both supplements and clarifies Malinowski's material on many important points.

It has long been recognized that filiation, in contrast with descent, is almost universally bilateral. As Radcliffe-Brown said in 1935:

The solution adopted by the great majority of human societies of the problem relating to the determination of status has been one by which a child derives certain rights and duties through the father and others of a different kind through the mother. Where the rights and duties derived through the father preponderate in social importance over those derived through the mother we have what it is usual to call a patrilineal system. Inversely a matrilineal system is one in which the rights and duties derived through the mother preponderate over those derived through the father (Radcliffe-Brown 1935: 39).

In this sense the Trobriands are, of course, a 'matrilineal' society. What will be examined in this paper is the large and important minority of the total rights and obligations derived through the father.

Complementary filiation, as Fortes says, 'provides the essential link between a sibling group and the kin of the parent who does not determine descent...a sibling group is not merely differentiated within a lineage but is further distinguished by reference to its kin ties outside the corporate unit' (Fortes 1953 *b*: 33).

Thus in a 'matrilineal' society a child has ties both with his own lineage and with his father's kin. The arrangement of these two relationships, however, may vary greatly from one 'matrilineal' society to another. Thus the rights of descent, succession, inheritance, residence, domicile and authority may be arranged and combined in many ways, producing quite different sets of relationships in different 'matrilineal' societies.

There is, nevertheless, a widespread consistency in the kinds of rights and obligations which derive through the father in 'matrilineal' societies and, as we shall see, in many respects, the Trobriands conform to this general pattern.

With regard to the question of the kinds of rights held by the father in a 'matrilineal' society, Audrey Richards said in 1934:

In a primitive society the power of the father as against the male head of the family, the maternal uncle, is manifested usually in certain well-defined ways—actual authority in the household and charge of the education of the children; the legal possession of the children in case of divorce or dissolution of the marriage; the power to arrange the marriage of the children themselves, or to share in the marriage payments made on such occasions; and in general the mutual obligations of father to son, or maternal nephew to uncle, as regards general support (Richards 1934: 272).

And as Radcliffe-Brown pointed out, in many 'matrilineal' societies there is a conception that every human being is compounded of two principles: one, called the 'blood' in Ashanti, derived from the mother, the other, the 'spirit', derived from the father (Radcliffe-Brown 1935: 40).

Fortes comments on the Ashanti conception of a child's relationship with its father as follows:

the Ashanti believe that a child cannot thrive if its father's *sunsum* ['his personality conceptualized as a personal soul'] is alienated from it; that its destiny and disposition are fixed by the *kra* ['spirit, source of life and destiny'] which is transmitted by the father; and that this puts every person into one of a limited number of named quasi-ritual categories, the *ntoro* divisions.... The *ntoro* concept...gives expression through ritual beliefs and sanctions, through etiquette and through names, to the value attached to paternity (Fortes 1950: 266–7).

There is thus a unique spiritual bond between father and child among the Ashanti and there are strong ties between them. Another example of the spiritual bond between father and child in a 'matrilineal society' is found among the Bemba. Thus Richards says:

there is in native belief an intimate magical connexion between a man and his wife and his child. The lives of the three are mysteriously entwined by the very fact of the sex act, and their common association with the fire of one hut. The sex behaviour of one partner affects the life and health of the other and the birth and safety of any children of the union.... It is for this reason that a father has a very important part to play in the ritual life of the young child. The young father...has not much power over his first children, but even he, isolated in a strange village, is hailed by the omnipotent grandmother as the *mwine*, or owner of the child, called by the child's name, and considered absolutely essential to the safety of the baby's life.... Moreover, the guardian spirits, or *mipashi*, are inherited bilaterally, and a man may go through life protected by a spirit of his father's line (Richards 1934: 277).

It is the duty of an Ashanti father to feed, clothe and educate his children, and later to set them up in life; these obligations are discharged even after divorce or the death of the mother. Among the Bemba also, although 'divorce is frequent...the father is never forgotten'. Richards continues:

It is extraordinary to see grown men and women, children of parents long since divorced and parted, making long journeys to visit their father and to give him presents. Extraordinary, too, to listen to the calm assurance of the father, living perhaps some 300 miles away, 'They will come back one day. How can they forget their father?' (Richards 1934: 276).

An Ashanti father has no legal authority over his children. As Fortes says:

The spiritual tie believed to unite father and child is a ritual symbol of the moral aspect of their relationship. Ashanti say that a man has no hold over his children except through their love for him and their conscience. A father wins his children's affection by caring for them. They cannot inherit his property, but he can and often does provide for them by making them gifts of property, land or money during his lifetime or on his death-bed (by written will nowadays). To insult, abuse or assault one's father is an irreparable wrong, one which is bound to bring ill luck....While there is no legal obligation on a son or daughter to support a father in old age, it would be regarded as a shame and an evil act if he or she did not do so. And, as with all kinship ties, the bond with the father is given tangible expression in funeral rites. It is the sons and daughters...own and classificatory, of a man and the brother's sons and daughters of a woman who provide the coffin (Fortes 1950: 268).

Ashanti parents play an important role in the marriages of their children. The consent of both parents, though not legally compulsory, is in fact indispensable for any marriage to take place. Gifts must be given by the bridegroom to the bride's parents in recognition of their 'labours in nurturing her and of their concern for her well-being'. With regard to his daughter's marriage, a father receives as much honour and consideration as his wife's .brother, his daughter's legal guardian, and, in fact, Fortes says the former carries greater weight than the latter (Fortes 1950: 269). A Bemba father also is always consulted about the marriage of his daughter, even if he has been divorced from her mother for some time. He can claim part, even half, of any marriage payment made for her (Richards 1950: 227).

The Ashanti say (as do the Bemba and the Trobrianders) that no man loves his sister's children as much as his own children. In this connexion, Fortes states:

Chiefs, in particular, stress this. The more sons and sons' sons a chief has, the more secure does he feel. As their social standing depends on him and as they have no rights to his office, they will support him in all circumstances. They are his most trusted followers, and important chiefs appoint their own and their brothers' sons and sons' sons...as titled councillors to attend closely on them. In the old days, men say, a youth preferred to follow his father to war rather than his mother's brother (Fortes 1950; 269).

Among the Bemba as well, a chief or a man holding high office is helped in his duties by his son or grandson rather than by his uterine nephew. Richards quotes the following statement by one of the chief's hereditary councillors:

'Why may my *mwipwa* [sister's son] not see my sacred relics? Because he will succeed me. He is the same as me....It would be a slight to the spirits while I am still alive. Besides, why should I show things to him who will one day get everything of mine? I am not going to teach him. I shall teach only my sons. My *mwipwa* can learn from other people when I am dead. How do you suppose I learnt myself?' (Richards 1934: 278).

The sons of Bemba chiefs, Richards says, have definite rank although they cannot, of course, be members of the royal clan. While young, they live at their father's court, 'carefree, irresponsible, and spoilt in every way'. When they grow older, they are given villages in their father's territory, live near him and get his constant support. There are even some large tracts of land which are regularly inherited by chiefs' sons. 'The Makasa, for instance, one of the biggest of the sub-chiefs, is always the eldest son of the Paramount Chief, and fulfils an important role in tribal affairs, while the headmen of his territory are always sons of former Makasa and their succession is therefore practically patrilineal' (Richards 1935: 278).

The relations of father and child among the Ashanti are 'rooted wholly and solely in the fact of paternity' (Fortes 1950: 267). There is no corporate organization based on the father's line, and though an Ashanti has strong ties with his father's kin, there is not the same sense of 'inescapable obligation' about this as there is about the social ties derived through his mother.

As will be seen, much that has been said about the ties of patrifiliation among the Ashanti and the Bemba is equally valid for the Trobrianders. It should be emphasized that, as among the Ashanti and the Bemba, a Trobriand child has strong ties with his father's kin but that the father's matrilineage, as a corporate group, is not involved, and there is no concept of a father-line.

The obvious importance of the role of the father in this 'matrilineal'system was one of the aspects of Trobriand society which most interested and puzzled Malinowski himself. His explanation of this situation, which he thought an anomaly, was primarily in terms of a conflict between the 'legal' principle of 'Mother-right' and the co-existing 'natural' principle of 'Father-right'. 'Thus' he concluded, 'round the sentiment of Father-love there crystallizes a number of established usages, sanctioned by tradition and regarded as the most natural course by the community. Yet they are contrary to strict law or involve exceptional and anomalous proceeding....If opposed and protested against in the name of the law, they must give way to it' (1926a: 111). [1]

Powell has also noted the importance of the role of the father in the Trobriands. His explanation is that a man, in his relationships with his wife and children, acts for the most part as the representative and spokesman of his wife's brother. According to this viewpoint, the mutual obligations of father and children are not, in structural terms, actually between the father and his children, but are rather between the children and their mother's brother, with the father acting largely as an intermediary. However, a close examination of the ethnographic facts arouses doubts whether either of these explanations is sufficient to account for the complex and far-reaching system of rights, obligations and ties incurred through patrifiliation.

II. THE ETHNOGRAPHIC DATA

A. Marriage rules

Our authorities state that 'clan' exogamy is the fundamental marriage rule of the Trobrianders. Trobriand clans, however, are rather amorphous entities. They are not corporate groups and are not, in fact, exogamous units. Although disapproved of, occasional marriages do take place between persons who are members of the same clan, but of different subclans. The effective marriage rule is subclan exogamy. Marriage with a man's true father's sister's daughter is stated by Malinowski to be the preferred form of marriage but, as has been pointed out, actual occurrences of patrilateral cross-cousin marriage are rare and largely confined to families of chiefs, where they serve special purposes (Leach 1958: 138).

Marriage in the Trobriands takes place primarily between people who call each other by the kinship term, *tabu*. As Leach says, *tabu* is a marginal kinship category referring to 'remote and potentially hostile relatives with whom Ego has no direct economic bonds but towards whom an attitude of "friendship" is expected' (Leach 1958: 144). The females in his own generation who are *tabu* to a male ego include the daughters of his father's sisters, the daughters of his father's sisters' husbands' brothers, the sisters of his sisters' husbands, the girls of the subclan of his mother's mother's husband, the girls of the subclan of the wives of his mother's mother's brothers, as well as other remote relatives. The marriage preference is for remote or non-relatives rather than for close relatives. As Leach points out, when a man marries a *tabu* relative, both she and her immediate kinsmen cease to be *tabu* and come into more closely bounded categories; marriage being thus 'a device whereby the dangers of *tabu* are for the time being exorcised' (Leach 1958: 145).

B. *Residence*

In discussing the ties and obligations between Trobriand fathers and their children, it is important to know what spatial relationships are correlated with them; that is, what are in fact the Trobriand practices of residence. It is well known that a boy is normally expected to cease to sleep in his father's house at adolescence and to move to a bachelor's house which, apparently, may be in either his father's or his mother's brother's subclan hamlet.[2] After his marriage, he is supposed to live in his mother's brother's (i.e. his own) subclan hamlet and to remain there for the rest of his life. In actual fact, of course, the picture is much more complicated. According to Powell, only 40 % of the male household heads in the Omarakana village cluster lived in their own subclan hamlets, while 26 % lived in their fathers' subclan hamlets, and 5 % in their wives' fathers' subclan hamlets. The remaining 29 % were scattered in the subclan hamlets of their wives, their sister's husbands, their daughters' husbands, and their mothers' mothers' husbands (Powell, Table 2 a).

It is unfortunate that we have residence figures only for the villages in the Omarakana cluster, because as Malinowski and Powell have both pointed out, the pattern of residence there is affected to some extent by the presence of the chiefly subclan, the Tabalu. The proportion of men living in their own subclan hamlets is probably higher outside this area.

It is also unfortunate that there is no breakdown by age in the residence figures. We should like to know which stages in the domestic cycle these households resident in the husbands' fathers' subclan hamlets represent.

However, it seems clear that there is a significant proportion of men—not all of them chiefs' sons by any means—who live as adults in their fathers' subclan hamlets. They are, in this case, however, 'strangers' and not 'owners' of the subclan hamlets in which they reside. Although they may own land there, they cannot pass it on to their children or to their heirs. They are there on sufferance of the owning subclan members and may be expelled at any time by the latter. This is what occurred in the case cited by Malinowski, of Namwana Guya'u, the son of To'uluwa, the paramount chief of Omarakana. Namwana Guya'u was expelled from his father's village by To'uluwa's maternal nephew and heir, although the chief himself strongly disapproved of the expulsion (1932: 10–12).

Women, of course, are less likely to remain as adults with their paternal relatives, as they normally go to live with their husbands. But it is to the homes of their parents and very often to the homes of their other paternal kin that women go for refuge when they have left their husbands or are in trouble. A divorced woman may take up residence, in particular, with her father's sister.

Powell also made a study of the kinship connexions between the fifteen adult dependants in the Omarakana village cluster and the heads of the house-holds in which they lived. Three of the nine males and two of the six females, or exactly one-third of the adult dependants, were living in the households of persons related through patrifiliation either to them or to their spouses (Powell, Table 2).

Another factor which complicates the Trobriand residence pattern is that almost half of all young children are 'adopted', that is transferred more-or-less permanently from one household to another. According to Powell's survey, eighty-six out of 176 children had been adopted in this way; sixty-three of the eighty-six were adopted by members of their own subclans, and twenty-three by persons who were not members of the adoptees' subclans. Of the latter, twelve adoptions were made in virtue of a relationship of patrifiliation either to the child or to a member of his subclan. Only boys were so adopted, as it is thought that if girls were to be adopted by persons of other subclans, their children might be lost to their subclans as effective subclan members. What is interesting here is not that more children are adopted by their subclan kin than by others, but that there should be any young children adopted by persons from other subclans. In Powell's survey, five boys were adopted by their fathers' elder brothers, one by his father's younger brother, one by his father's sister's son, four by their fathers' sisters, and one by his mother's father (Powell, Table 12). It is also interesting to note that when a couple is divorced, the children do not necessarily go to live with their mother. Usually, of course, this is what happens but sometimes the children may remain with their father. Powell cites the case of a 6-year old boy who refused to accompany his mother when she left his father. Though the mother tried to get custody of the boy, he was allowed to stay with his father, and this decision was supported even by the mother's brother (Powell: 359–62).

C. Marriage negotiations

In *The Sexual Life of Savages*, Malinowski described in some detail, though unfortunately at times rather vaguely, the Trobriand system of marriage negotiations. There is a strict taboo that a man must have nothing to do with the love affairs of his sister, and that her other maternal kinsmen may be concerned only very little in these affairs. Thus Malinowski says:

The careful avoidance by a man of any knowledge about his sister's amorous prospects is, I am certain, not only an ideal but also a fact. I was over and over again assured that no man has the slightest inkling as to whom his sister is going to marry, although this is the common knowledge of everyone else. And I know that nothing remotely touching upon the subject would be uttered within earshot of him (1932: 439).

Whether or not a man's ignorance about his sister's marital prospects is as complete as Malinowski affirms, it is quite evident that it is not the woman's brother or other maternal kinsman who makes the arrangements for her marriage. Malinowski says elsewhere:

Since her brother is strictly forbidden to take any interest in her sexual affairs, including her marriage, and her mother's brother has also to keep aloof from these matters, it is, strangely enough, her father who is her guardian as regards matrimonial arrangements (1927a: 72).

Although he thought it strange, Malinowski is quite definite about the role a father plays in his daughter's marriage. He says: 'the strict taboo...debars them [a girl's maternal kinsmen] from any *control* over her matrimonial plans' (1932: 72) (my italics). And again, he says specifically: 'the father has *control* of his daughter's marriage and love affairs' (1932: 447) (my italics). Malinowski describes the sequence of events in a Trobriand marriage as follows:

If a girl's 'family' approves of the boy who has been courting her, her father may take the initiative by saying to the boy: 'You sleep with my child: very well—marry her' (1932: 73). Or the girl's 'family' may ask the boy for small gifts, 'an equally unambiguous indication that he is accepted' (1932: 73). Whether it is the girl's father or the young couple who takes the initiative, the act of marriage is the same. It occurs when the girl, instead of returning in the morning to her father's house (where she has lived from shortly after birth until her marriage), simply remains with the boy in his *father's* house, taking her meals there and accompanying him throughout the day. It is significant that although a Trobriand boy is supposed to move out of his father's house at adolescence, it is nevertheless in his father's house that his marriage takes place.

There is no other rite, no other ceremony to mark the beginnings of wedlock. From the morning on which she has remained with the bridegroom, the girl is married to him, provided, of course, the consent of the parents has been given. Without this... the act constitutes only an attempt at marriage. Though utterly simple, this act of remaining with the man, of openly sharing a meal with him, and of staying under his roof, has a legally binding force. It is the conventional public declaration of marriage (1932: 75).

Two people in the Trobriands cannot establish a marriage by themselves. Consent must be obtained and marriage presents must be given. The crux of the problem here is to interpret what Malinowski meant in each case by 'the girl's family', 'the boy's family', 'the parents', etc., and to see who must consent to the marriage and who gives the marriage presents to whom.

The first marriage gift, called *Katuvila*, must be given on the day the young couple remain together or on the morning of the next day. In his table of marriage gifts, Malinowski lists: '(i) *Katuvila*—cooked yams, brought in baskets by the girl's parents to the boy's family' (1932: 76). Then he goes on to explain in detail:

(i)   *Katuvila*—cooked yams in baskets

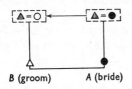

B (groom)   A (bride)

(ii a)   *Pepe'i*—uncooked yams

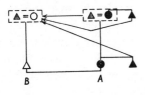

(ii b)   Redistribution of *Pepe'i*

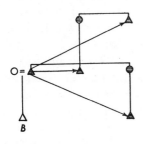

(iii)   *Kaykaboma*—cooked
vegetables on platters

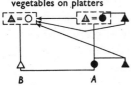

(iv)   *Mapula kaykaboma*—cooked
vegetables on platters

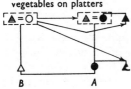

(v a)   Gathering of valuables for
the *Takwalela Pepe'i* gift

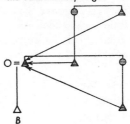

(v b)   *Takwalela Pepe'i*—valuables

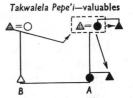

(vi)   *Vilakuria*—large quantity
of uncooked yams

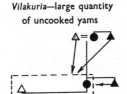

(vii)   *Saykwala*—fish

(viii)   *Takwalela vilakuria*—valuables

Fig. 3. Presents given at marriage.

The girl's family have to make the first offering to signify their consent to the marriage. Since their agreement is absolutely essential, this gift in conjunction with the public declaration of the union of the partners, constitutes marriage. It is a small gift, a little cooked food brought in baskets and offered by the girl's father to the boy's parents. It is set down in front of their house with the words *Kam Katuvila*, 'thy *Katuvila* gift' (1932: 76).

Thus it appears that the gift which constitutes marriage is given by the girl's father to the boy's parents, and that it takes place in the boy's father's subclan hamlet.

The second marriage gift, called *Pepe'i*, is a larger present given soon afterwards, usually on the same day. The girl's 'father, her maternal uncles, and her brothers who now for the first time emerge from the inaction imposed on them by the specific brother–sister taboo, each bring a basket of uncooked yam food, and offer it to the boy's parents' (1932: 77). The third gift, *Kaykaboma*, is a gift of cooked vegetables, 'each member of the girl's family' bringing one platter to the boy's parents.

These first three gifts, says Malinowski, 'express the consent of the girl's family, and are a sort of earnest of their future and more considerable contributions' (1932: 79). The whole series of marriage gifts is apparently not always given. Of these first three gifts, Malinowski says only one (either *Katuvila* or *Pepe'i*) must be given at all costs. Thus it appears that the consent of the girl's father must be obtained, as he gives both *Katuvila* and *Pepe'i*, but that the consent of the girl's maternal kinsmen is not absolutely necessary. As will be seen later, in actual practice consent is normally granted or withheld by both the girl's father and her maternal relatives, but in the rare case where they disagree, the girl's father's consent alone is sufficient.

There are three examples cited in the Trobriand literature (two described by Malinowski and one by Powell) where some or all of the girl's relatives did not consent to her marriage. In the first case, as described by Malinowski, Mekala'i, a boy 'with no wealthy relatives or powerful friends to back him up' made an attempt to abduct the step-daughter of the headman of Kabululo and to retain her in his parents' house in Kasana'i. 'On the first afternoon of their joint life, the headman of Kabululo simply walked over to Kasana'i, took his abashed and truant step-daughter by the hand and led her back to his own house; that was the end' (1932: 74).

The other case cited by Malinowski was that of Ulo Kadala.

He wooed a girl during my first stay in Omarakana and was refused by her parents. The couple attempted to settle down to married life, but the family pulled the girl back by force. Ulo Kadala still continued his faithful courtship. On my second visit to Omarakana two years later, the girl came to the village once more and took up her abode in the house of Isupwana, the adoptive mother of Ulo Kadala, a stone's throw from my tent. This second attempt at marriage lasted, I think, for a day or two while To'uluwa was making some not very energetic efforts towards reconciliation. One afternoon the parents arrived from the neighbouring village, and laid hold of the girl and unceremoniously carried her away. The procession passed in front of my tent, the wailing girl led by her father and followed by vociferous partisans, who hurled abuse at each other. The girl's people said quite explicitly what they thought of Ulo Kadala, of his laziness, his incapacity for doing anything properly, and his well-known greed. 'We do not want you, we shall not give her any food.' This argument clinched the refusal, and that was the last attempt which the two young people made (1932: 74–75).

Powell quotes this case as an argument to show that it is the subclan kin of the girl, and not her father, who have the ultimate right to give or refuse consent to her marriage. Thus he says:

When Malinowski wrote that a girl's 'family' or 'people' prevented her from marrying Ulo Kadala, saying to him: 'We do not want you, we shall not give her any food,' her father may have been in accord with the pronouncement, but it is clearly an ultimatum from the girl's maternal kinsmen collectively.... (Powell: 349).

This is, however, quite patently *not* a case where the girl's father *may* have disapproved of her marriage but a case where he, as well as her maternal kinsmen, *did* disapprove; it was, after all, her father who was leading her home. Now let us see what happened in a case where the girl's father approved of her marriage, but her maternal kinsmen did not.

It is described by Powell during the course of an examination of the relationships of *Urigubu* donors to their recipients.

Bwabwau...gardens for [i.e. gives an annual *urigubu* gift to] Vanoi, Mitakata's heir designate, who is married to Bwabwau's eldest daughter. [Mitakata was the paramount chief of Omarakana in 1950–51.] This marriage involves a breach of clan exogamy, both Vanoi and his wife being Mailasi, though his subclan is Tabalu and hers Mokaraybida. Bwabwau was in bad odour with his affines, especially his daughter's classificatory brothers, for permitting the marriage against their wishes, and they had refused to garden for the girl [i.e. give her an annual *urigubu* gift]. She had no uterine brothers old enough to garden for her out of personal affection despite the disapproval of the rest of their subclan. The marriage was also opposed by Mitakata, and his inability to prevent it is a measure of the present weakness of his position. He tried to bring pressure to bear on Bwabwau through the Lobwaita senior men through his influence as their affine, and consequently Bwabwau is out of favour with his wife's and his own subclans and with the chief as well (Powell: 102–3).

Here then is an extreme case where a father consented to his daughter's marriage—a marriage which was a breach of the law of clan exogamy and which was to no less a personage than the heir of the paramount chief of Omarakana— and the marriage took place, despite the disapproval of the girl's subclan kin (and incidentally the disapproval of the boy's subclan kin and the girl's father's subclan kin as well). This seems to be a clear refutation of Powell's thesis that a girl's subclan kin have the ultimate say in her marriage by refusing her *urigubu* gifts. In this case the problem was solved by the girl's father's supplying her annual *urigubu* gift.

It appears, then, that normally a girl's father and her maternal relatives both express their consent to her marriage in the first three marriage gifts; however, in a case of disagreement, the girl's father's consent alone may be sufficient.

Now we return to the series of marriage gifts. The fourth gift, *Mapula Kaykaboma*, is a repayment of gift (iii), *Kaykaboma*, and is given by the boy's 'family' to the girl's 'family', almost immediately after the *Kaykaboma* is received. *Mapula Kaykaboma* consists of cooked vegetables on platters and is identical in all respects to the *Kaykaboma*. Malinowski does not say more specifically who gives and who receives the gift of *Mapula Kaykaboma*. However, he says: 'The return offering of food [gift number (iv)], made immediately by the boy's family, is a characteristically Trobriand answer to a compliment' (1932: 79). From this statement it seems reasonable to infer that gift number (iv) is given by the recipients of gift number (iii) (the boy's parents) to the donors of gift (iii) (the girl's father, maternal uncle and brothers).

The fifth marriage gift is a very important one. When gift (ii) (*Pepe'i*) was received by the boy's parents, the boy's *father* 'made a small distribution of it among his own relatives' (1932: 77). The boy's father now prepares a gift of valuables of the *vaygu'a* type (large, polished axe-blades of green stone, necklaces of polished spondylus shell disks, and armlets of conus shell—the valuables which are used in the *Kula*). The boy's father's 'own relatives' to whom he distributed food from the gift of *Pepe'i* now bring him other valuables to add to his own. All these he presents to the girl's 'family' as gift number (v), *Takwalela Pepe'i*, a repayment of *Pepe'i*, gift (ii). It is not clear who on the girl's side receives the valuables. Malinowski says they are 'given by the boy's father in repayment of gift (ii) to the girl's father' (1932: 76). Seligman, on the other hand, says:

the boy takes the girl to spend the night with him in his father's house; the next day the bridegroom's father sends a considerable present to the girl's relatives. In one instance occurring at Lobua village, the bridegroom's father sent a pair of armshells...and two steel axes....When Makuniga, the *toriwaga* of Osiwasiu village, was about to marry, his people sent three ceremonial axe blades, one pair of armshells and one *sapisapi* necklace...this present was actually delivered to the bride's mother who, it was said, kept the armshells for herself but distributed the axeblades and necklace to her sisters and brothers (1910: 708).

Gift number (v), *Takwalela Pepe'i*, is considered to be a repayment for gift (ii) (*Pepe'i*) which was given to the boy's parents by the girl's father, maternal uncle and brothers; it is even presented in the same baskets in which the *Pepe'i* gift was received. Thus, it seems probable that both Malinowski and

Seligman are right in that *Takwalela Pepe'i* would be given to both the girl's father and to her maternal relatives. It appears to be a gift to the relatives of the girl who have consented to the marriage and have thereby pledged their future support. Thus, in a case where the *Katuvila* was given but the *Pepe'i* was not, it would seem reasonable to infer that the girl's father would be the sole recipient of the valuables. It is again unfortunate that there is no information as to what actually happens in these different cases.

What is important here, however, is that the *Takwalela Pepe'i* and the other gift of valuables, *Takwalela Vilakuria*, which will be discussed later and which is also given by the boy's father, are 'the only really substantial gifts from the bridegroom's family to the bride's...[and] exert a definitely binding force on the husband, for if the marriage be dissolved, he does not recover them save in exceptional cases. [3] They are about equivalent in value to all the other first year's gifts put together' (1932: 79). It is thus a man's father, aided by his own subclan kin, who pays for his son's marriage. Only in this light does the following statement of Malinowski's make sense: 'A man is almost entirely independent with regard to matrimony, and his marriage, which will be a matter of constant and considerable effort and worry to his wife's family, will continue to lie completely outside the sphere of his own people's concerns' (1932: 72).

The marriage gifts from the boy's side to the girl's side must be paid by someone, and it can be seen that the reason it is outside the sphere of 'his own people's concerns' is that it is the concern of his father's people.

The valuables which are given by the boy's father are not returnable even in case of divorce. Malinowski says that if the marriage ends in divorce and the wife remarries, 'the new husband must present a valuable object (*vaygu'a*) to his predecessor, in recompense for the one given to the wife's family at the beginning of the first marriage. The new husband must also give another *vaygu'a* to his wife's relatives, and he then receives from them the first annual harvest gift—*Vilakuria*—and subsequent yearly tribute in yams' (1932: 125). Thus, however many husbands a woman may have, her relatives keep all the valuables given them from each marriage.

After the *Takwalela Pepe'i*, there is a long pause in the exchange of gifts which lasts until the next harvest. During this time, and while the couple's own house is being built, the wife usually remains with her husband in his father's house. This statement of Malinowski's is corroborated by Powell who says that the two couples who were married while he was there were both still living in the husbands' fathers' houses when Powell left the Trobriands (Powell, 60).

The sixth in the series of marriage gifts is given at the next harvest. It is listed in Malinowski's table of marriage gifts as '*Vilakuria*—a large quantity of yam-food offered at the first harvest after the marriage to the boy by the girl's family' (1932: 76). There are several problems connected with the *Vilakuria*, which is the main gift that comes from the girl's side. Every harvest thereafter the couple will receive a substantial *urigubu* gift of yams from relatives on the girl's side; the *Vilakuria* is thought to be the first of these *urigubu* gifts. The consent of the girl's family to the marriage is a pledge to provide, among other things, this annual *urigubu* gift to the couple. It is not clear, however, who gives the *Vilakuria*. Malinowski describes the giving of the *Vilakuria* as follows:

The girl's family give a present of considerable value at the next harvest (that is, the first harvest after the marriage), and from then on at every harvest they will have to help the new household with a substantial contribution of fresh yams. The first present of this sort, however, has a special name (*vilakuria*), and is surrounded by a ceremonial of its own. Prism-shaped receptacles (*pwata'i*) are constructed of poles, in front of the young couple's yam-house, and the girl's family, after selecting a large quantity, a hundred, two hundred, or even three hundred basketfuls of the best yams, arrange them in these receptacles with a great amount of ceremony and display (1932: 78).

It is a woman's brother and/or her other male maternal relatives who are supposed to give the annual *urigubu* gift to their sister's household, and thus it would seem that they must also be the donors of the *Vilakuria* gift. And it is quite clear that the woman's maternal kinsmen are, in fact, involved in the giving of the *Vilakuria*. However, it appears that the girl's father is also concerned with the *Vilakuria* gift. This is evident in the following passage from *The Sexual Life of Savages*:

Paluwa, the father of Isepuna, worried good-humouredly as to how he might collect sufficient food to offer to a chief's son, his daughter's future husband; and he discussed his troubles with me at length. He was faced by the difficulty of having three daughters and several female relatives, and only three sons. Everybody's working power had already been taxed to provide food for the other married daughters. And now Isepuna was going to wed Kalogusa, a man of high rank in his own right, and also a son of To'uluwa, the paramount chief. All his people exerted themselves to the utmost to produce as big a crop as possible that season, in order to be able to give a fine *Vilakuria* present. And To'uluwa, the bridegroom's father, on his side revealed to me his own anxiety. Could he provide a worthy counter gift? Times were hard, and yet something fine had to be given. I inspected several of the chief's valuables, and discussed their respective suitability with him (1932: 80).

Here we have a description of the girl's father's worries about how to provide the *Vilakuria* gift, and of the boy's father's concern about the gift of valuables to be presented from the boy's side. It is true that this is a case which involves the families of high-ranking chiefs and might, on this account, be considered to be extraordinary. Trobriand chiefs, unlike commoners, are polygynous; a chief must have a wife from each of the subclans in his tributary district. As the sister's husband of all the men in his district he receives *urigubu* harvest payments and services from the male relatives of each of his wives. However, Malinowski says explicitly: 'The marriage of a chief does not differ from that of a commoner, except that his wife is brought to him by her parents openly, and that the gifts exchanged are more substantial' (1932: 114)

Also, we see that the next of the marriage gifts listed by Malinowski is '(vii) *Saykwala*—gift of fish brought by the boy to his wife's *father* in repayment of (vi) (the *Vilakuria*)' (1932: 76) (my italics). Malinowski says, immediately following his description of the *Vilakuria* gift:

This gift [the *Vilakuria*] also must be repaid without any too great delay. Fish is considered a proper counter-offering. In a coastal village, the husband will embark with his friends on a fishing expedition. If he lives inland, he has to purchase the fish in one of the coastal villages, paying for them in yams; the fish is laid in front of the girl's parents' house, with the words, '*Kam Saykwala*' (thy *Saykwala* gift) (1932: 78).

It is thus quite clear that the young husband must give the *Saykwala* gift as a repayment for the *Vilakuria* he has received, to his wife's father, who then, presumably, must have given at least part of the *Vilakuria* gift.

The Trobriand custom of infant betrothal, although rare and almost entirely limited to the families of chiefs, is significant with regard to the question of the responsibility of a girl's father for her *Vilakuria* gift. Infant betrothal usually takes place between patrilateral cross-cousins. A chief presents a valuable to his sister's husband and requests that his sister's infant daughter be betrothed to his own son. The request may not be refused. After the initial presentation of the valuable, the first four of the marriage gifts are given as in an ordinary marriage. Malinowski says that the *Vilakuria* gift is then given at the next harvest, by the girl's father on behalf of his son, who is a child, to the boy's parents (i.e. the chief and the boy's mother) who receive it on behalf of their son, the future bridegroom. As the brother of the future bride is an infant, someone else must take responsibility for his obligations; the person who does so here is his father. A chief can also request that his sister's daughter's daughter be betrothed to his own infant son. In this case the chief's sister's son would be old enough to give the *Vilakuria* gift but he does, not; it is still paid by the chief's sister's husband—the grandfather of the future bride.

An infant betrothal may be repudiated by the children when they grow up, and the marriage would then not take place. In such a case, the presents are not returned. If the marriage does take place, only two gifts—*Vilakuria* and *Takwalela Vilakuria*—are exchanged. This is said to occur just as in ordinary marriages.

This last of the initial series of marriage gifts, the *Takwalela Vilakuria*, is described in the list of marriage gifts as: 'a gift of valuables handed by the boy's father to the girl's father in repayment of (vi) (the *Vilakuria*)' (1932: 76). It is, however, not always given. *Takwalela Vilakuria* is given if the young husband is very rich, or if, on the other hand, he is very poor and the gift of *Takwalela Pepe'i* had not yet been given. It is again unclear who receives the *Takwalela Vilakuria*.

It seems fairly clear that the *Vilakuria* gift may be given by either the girl's father or her male subclan relatives or both. Hence the best supposition seems to be that the *Takwalela Vilakuria* may be given to either the girl's father or to her maternal relatives, or to both, depending upon who the donors of the *Vilakuria* were in the particular case.

It is significant that not all of these eight marriage gifts are equally indispensable. Of the first three, as was mentioned before, only one (either *Katuvila* or *Pepe'i*) must be given. Of the rest, Malinowski says, *Vilakuria* and *Saykwala* are never omitted, while either *Takwalela Pepe'i* or *Takwelela Vilakuria* are absolutely obligatory. There are thus four absolutely essential gifts; the girl's father and maternal relatives, but in exceptional cases of disagreement only her father, must express consent to the marriage by a small gift of food; valuables must be given by the boy's father; the *Vilakuria* gift must be given by either the girl's male subclan relatives or her father or by both, and the young husband must give a repayment of fish to the girl's *father* for the *Vilakuria* gift.

It thus appears that, to a large extent, a Trobriand father controls his children's marriages. For his daughter's marriage it is his consent which is, in the last analysis, what is required; he arranges the marriages and contributes substantial amounts of food in marriage payments. As we shall see later, in many cases he and/or some of his subclan kinsmen also contribute year after year to the annual *urigubu* payment presented to his daughter and her husband. For his son's marriage, the father, aided by his own subclan kin, makes the substantial payment of valuables which is required from the boy's side.

This interpretation of the givers and donors of the marriage gifts appears to be supported by a statement of Malinowski's in the *Argonauts* where he speaks of 'a series of mutual gifts exchanged immediately after marriage by a man and his wife's father (*not matrilineal kinsmen in this case*)' (1922: 184) [4] (my italics).

Powell seems to agree with Malinowski's description of the marriage gifts, as he refers to 'the gifts exchanged by the fathers at the inception of marriage as described by Malinowski' (Powell: 351), without suggesting that the gifts as described by Malinowski were incorrect in any way.

This is not to suggest that the subclan kin of the bride and groom, and particularly of the bride, do not play important roles in the marriage. Clearly they both can and do. What has been emphasized here is that although Trobriand subclans are corporate matrilineal groups, a marriage, in all its aspects, is the concern not only of the subclans of the bride and groom, but also of their respective fathers.

In any particular marriage the question of whose consent is most important and of which of the girl's relatives give what proportion of her marriage gifts is undoubtedly influenced by the rank, wealth and personality of the persons involved. What we have been concerned with here is the normative role of the Trobriand father with regard to the marriages of his children.

D. *Obligations engendered by marriage*

Once a marriage has taken place, and the marriage gifts have been exchanged, the parties concerned are bound to one another for at least as long as the marriage lasts by a network of reciprocal rights and obligations. We can begin with the rights and duties exercised within the domestic unit of husband, wife and children. The husband has the right to his wife's exclusive sexual services and to her domestic services. She must also look after him when he is sick, mourn for him when he is dead and carry his jawbone for some years afterwards. The husband, for his part, must care for, protect, and garden for his wife, look after her when she is ill and mourn for her when she is dead. Both husband and wife have an obligation to care for their children; the father's duty to nurse, feed, protect, and educate his children, however, is said by the Trobrianders to be a repayment by the husband to his wife for her sexual services.

Yet it appears that there is also a definite and clearly formulated idea of reciprocity between father and children. Malinowski says: 'The Father... has definite claims, reciprocal claims, that is, on the services of his children, and above all of his sons' (1935: 205). Thus, for example, as part of the mortuary rites for a dead man, his sons must suck his decaying bones. It is said of this: 'It is right that a child should suck the father's ulna. For the Father has held out his hand to its excrement and allowed it to make water on to his knee' (1932: 133). It is clearly stated as well that children must care for their parents in old age because the parents cared for them as children. [5]

Aged people apparently are not automatically taken care of by their subclans and must be looked after by their own children. According to Powell, couples who find themselves with no children and beyond childbearing age 'become anxious lest they should be left in their old age without children of their own (i.e. whom they had personally brought up) to care for them. So they would go, usually to a junior subclan kinswoman of the wife, and solicit...a child to...bring up as their own' (Powell: 357).

Thus it should not be forgotten that although in one sense it is said that the Trobriand father cares for his children as a payment to their mother, yet at the same time there exists the clearly defined concept of reciprocity of obligation between a father and his children.

Now we must consider the ties outside the domestic group, which are engendered by a marriage. The wife's subclan and, as we shall see, quite often her father's subclan kin as well, must fulfil *urigubu* obligations to the wife and her husband. These include not only the annual harvest payment but many sorts of services as well. A man may call upon his wife's male relatives for assistance in undertakings requiring communal labour. He may also call upon them on many other occasions as, for example, when he is transporting and unloading his *urigubu* gift to *his* sister and her husband, or when he is making *pokala* to an older man (i.e. presenting services and/or gifts to an older man who is in a position to return them in the form of titles, property or a particular service). When a man is ill, his wife's male relatives must keep watch over him to protect him against sorcery (i.e. they do not sorcerize him —they being the people considered most likely to do this); in feuds or emergencies they must come to his aid, and finally, on his death, the bulk of the mortuary duties fall to his affinal relatives.

Essentially, a man has the key to the yam houses of his wife's relatives. If one of N's wife's male relatives, M, has had his yam house well stored by *his* wife's relatives, then N and his wife may present M with a valuable and M must then give N the contents of one of the compartments of his storehouse. If N should give M two valuables, M must then give N the contents of two of the compartments of his storehouse. There is no question of the valuables being equivalent to the yams; Powell says specifically that the valuable is a token payment (Powell: 402). This 'untying of the yam house', as it is called, should be of particular importance in the case of headmen and chiefs who have need of large supplies of food to pay for their various chiefly activities.

A man thus acquires by marriage an economic lien on his wife's relatives who must present him with food and services. A chief, of course, has this lien on the relatives of all his wives, i.e. on all the members of his district.

These obligations terminate upon divorce or after the period of mourning for the death of the first spouse, unless the wife should die leaving sons. In this case the sons, or, if they are too young, their mother's brother, will usually present the widowed father with *urigubu* gifts so long as he does not remarry.

The husband's obligations to his wife's relatives are rather more tenuous. He cares for his wife, enables children to be born to his wife's subclan and cares for these children. In addition, he must repay the annual harvest gift he receives by definite periodic gifts of valuables, called *youlo*. When a man's wife's relatives render him services, he must give them gifts of food in return. His wife's relatives may also call upon him for assistance in undertakings of various kinds. What sorts of undertakings these are, however, are not described beyond the fact that they are not so extensive as the services that his wife's relatives are obliged to render to him.

In Vakuta, the husband must give a gift of valuables to his wife's relatives before the latter will harvest, transport and store their *urigubu* gift to him. Otherwise, the husband must do the harvesting and transporting himself as, in Vakuta, the donor's *urigubu* obligations extend only to the growing of the food.

Among high-ranking people these periodic gifts of yams and valuables, the *urigubu* harvest payment and the *youlo*, play an important part in the political and economic structure of the Trobriands. Malinowski points out the tendency to intermarriage between the chiefly families of the central plains of Kiriwina where food is especially plentiful and those of the coastal areas where the valuable shell ornaments are produced. He says:

In the old days the Sinaketans, who specialised in the fishing of spondylus shell and the manufacture of the red shell-discs used to marry women from Kiriwina.... People of rank in Kiriwina were able to supply the Sinaketan husbands of their sisters with a large quantity of food. The Sinaketans in return gave to the paramount chief and to other notables what to them was of greater importance, necklaces and belts of shell discs (1935: I, 290–1).

It is not sufficient then, at least in certain cases, to look upon the relationship between a man and his wife's relatives as an essentially one-sided affair whereby the husband receives much but returns only token gifts.

Now that we have seen what the obligations are which arise from marriage, we must investigate more closely who the people are who are actually involved in this life-long series of prestations and counter-prestations.

Malinowski had a fixed idea that the annual harvest gift had to be given to the couple by one or more of the wife's male subclan kin, except in the case of a chief where the wife's father might contribute as well to her *urigubu* gift. Malinowski, therefore, classified the *urigubu* gifts which he recorded into 'genuine', 'pretence', 'agnatic', 'affinal' and 'spurious' *urigubu*, although noting that the Trobrianders themselves made no such distinctions. If we consider, as the Trobrianders apparently do, that all *urigubu* harvest gifts are equally genuine, we can then see that a substantial minority of the *urigubu* payment is made by the wife's paternal relatives and sometimes by the husband's paternal relatives as well.

Powell says that in a normal year a householder of commoner rank and average status, in his prime, and in good repute, would expect to receive about fifty baskets of yams from his peer in his wife's subclan. He would expect about the same amount from his wife's father who 'not infrequently' gives him *urigubu* gifts as well (Powell: 78).

Malinowski records an *urigubu* gift given to a man named Tobuguya'u of Yalumugwa by his wife's brother's son, who had taken over his father's obligation on the latter's death. Malinowski calls this 'spurious *urigubu*', saying it 'is one of the encroachments of the patrilineal principle upon the system of maternal descent' (1935: 1, 387). However, there seems to be no reason to consider it as anything but genuine *urigubu*, and as we shall see, it is quite common for persons related by patrifiliation to the wife or to other members of her subclan to contribute to her *urigubu* payments.[6]

In 1918, only four of To'uluwa's thirteen wives were *not* given substantial *urigubu* gifts by their paternal relatives. This was, it is true, an exceptional year in that the amount of food presented as *urigubu* payments was about four times as great as in an ordinary year. However, Malinowski says specifically that the donors and receivers remained much the same from year to year. In such an exceptional year, therefore, it is only the amount of food and not the number of donors which varies significantly. In 1918 To'uluwa's wives received *urigubu* gifts from the following persons related to them or to one of their subclan members through patrifiliation: Katupwena, from her own father and from two of his subclan members; Namtawa, from one of her father's subclan members; Tubwoysewaga, from three of her father's subclan members; Bomawise, from her father's maternal nephew and from a man who had adopted her brother's son; Bokuyoba, from a man who had the same father as she but not the same mother, from a second man because his father and hers belonged to the same subclan, and from a third man, Malinowski says 'as a patrilineally inherited duty' because his father before him used to fill this same storehouse. Isupwana received *urigubu* gifts from her father's maternal nephew, from the husband of a woman who had the same father as she but not the same mother, from another man 'styled her son, where the relationship was on the paternal side', from a classificatory father 'because in ancient times some relation existed between the giver and Isupwana's father', and from a 'son' of Isupwana because his village and her father's are contiguous and have the same local subclan. Bomapolu and Seburada each received *urigubu* gifts from their fathers' maternal nephews, and Seburada from her father's younger brother as well (1935: 1, 398–411).

Of the *urigubu* presents made by Omarakana cluster householders and recorded by Powell in 1950–1, twenty-two out of 124 presentations were made in virtue of a relationship of patrifiliation either to the recipient or to a member of the recipient's subclan. These included one gift to a father's sister's son, one to a father's brother's daughter, three to mothers' brothers' daughters, sixteen to own daughters and one to a brother's daughter (Powell, Table 13). Of the *urigubu* gifts received by Omarakana householders, forty-five out of 209 were given in virtue of a relationship of patrifiliation either to the wife or to another member of her subclan (thirty-two, of which twenty-seven were from the wife's father) or to the husband or another member of his subclan (thirteen).

These figures include the gifts given both to the chief and to the other Omarakana cluster householders. When the figures are further broken down, it becomes apparent that it is definitely not only chiefs who receive *urigubu* payments from persons related to their wives' subclans by patrifiliation. Of the 209 *urigubu* gifts received, the chief received seventy-six, of which fourteen were given because of a relationship of patrifiliation (thirteen related thus to the wife or to a member of her subclan and one to the chief). The other householders received 133 *urigubu* gifts of which thirty-one were given by persons related by patrifiliation to members of either the husband's or the wife's subclans (nineteen on the wife's side, twelve on the husband's) (Powell, Table 14). Thus the chief received a lower percentage of his *urigubu* gifts from persons related by patrifiliation to members of his or his wives' subclans than did the other householders.

Both in 1918 and in 1950–1 there were a significant number of *urigubu* gifts given by other affinal kin as well, such as, for example, husbands of a wife's sisters.

Thus, it appears that although *urigubu* gifts from persons related through patrifiliation or affinity to members of the subclans of both husband and wife very rarely constitute the entire *urigubu* payment received by a householder and never constitute a majority of the gifts given or received in a village, they nevertheless always form a substantial minority of these *urigubu* payments.

E. Magical obligations

As we might expect from the general postulations about complementary filiation, one of the most important aspects of the relationship between a Trobriand father and his children is in the sphere of magic.

The ceremony and magic of a Trobriand woman's pregnancy are carried out by members of her father's subclan. The first pregnancy ceremony is especially elaborate, and payment for the work and magic of the girl's father's female subclan relatives (her *tabula*) is made by the girl's own subclan kin. Malinowski says about a girl's first pregnancy:

We have already seen on an earlier occasion of great importance in the life of a girl, namely when her marriage is about to be concluded, that it is the father, and not her official guardian, the mother's brother, whose consent is decisive and who has to supervise the whole affair. Again, in this later crisis, it is the father and his matrilineal kinswomen who take the active part. The father summons his sister, his mother, and his niece, and says to them: 'Well, come to my house and cut the *saykeulo* [the pregnancy cloak] for your niece, my daughter'. The father's sister then takes the lead, and rouses as many of her kinswomen as possible to help in the work. ...The *saykeulo* is always made in front of the father's house, or if he be a chief, on the central place of his village (1932: 180).

Four pregnancy garments are made by the girl's father's maternal kinswomen. When they are finished, the garments are magically endowed by their makers with certain properties and powers designed to improve the personal appearance of the wearer, and especially to whiten her skin.

On the day following the making and charming of the robes, the pregnant woman is publicly bathed and magically adorned by her father's sister and other paternal relatives. When the beauty magic has been performed on the pregnant woman, the *saykeulo* is placed on her shoulders by one of her *tabula*. The latter then usually recites some magic against the dangers of pregnancy and childbirth in order to protect the pregnant woman from the special evil of sorcery which is always dreaded at a confinement.

In full dress and covered with the long fibre mantle, the pregnant woman is then carried by two of her *tabula* to her father's house where she is placed on a small platform erected there. Malinowski says, however, that a woman of chieftain's rank is customarily taken by her *tabula* not to her father's but to her maternal uncle's house and seated upon a platform there. In either case, she remains on the platform from about three to five days (not including the nights) and there she is washed and food is put into her mouth by her father's subclan kinswomen.

The prevalent Trobriand opinion, Malinowski says, is that the purpose of the first pregnancy ceremony is to whiten the skin of the woman. The idea that whiteness as such is desirable is expressed in all the aspects of the ceremony. The *saykeulo*, for example, is said to be used to keep the sun off the skin. Other reasons given by the Trobrianders for the first pregnancy ceremony are that it makes for a quick and easy birth, that it assures the health of mother and baby, and that it is necessary for the proper formation of the foetus.

Immediately following the first pregnancy ceremony, payment is made to the girl's paternal relatives by her maternal kinsmen.

The work, the magic, and the ritual are performed by the female relatives of the father. In the distribution of food (*sagali*), which immediately follows the ceremony, it is the mother's brother, the brother, and the other maternal kinsmen of the young woman, who do the distributing. If she is a woman of small importance, this distribution takes place before her father's house. But if she, or her father or husband be a person of high rank, it is carried out on the central place of the village. The procedure is the same as in the mortuary and other ceremonial distributions. The food is divided into heaps and every heap is allotted to a single person, his or her name being called out in a loud voice. After the first pregnancy rites, each one of the *tabula* who has been working at the robe and taking part in the ceremony receives a heap of food. Besides this, the givers of the *sagali*...usually select some specially large and fine yams, or a bunch of bananas or areca nut, and carry the gift to the house of the paternal aunt, and perhaps to those of one or two other relatives as well (1932: 189).

The pregnant woman's father, himself, has an important role to play in protecting his daughter during her pregnancy. At the above-mentioned *sagali*:

The father of the pregnant woman—who has nothing to do with the *sagali*—chooses some specially good food and carries it, *on his own account*, to certain women who are known to possess a form of black magic of which pregnant women stand in great fear. 'Black' this magic is, literally as well as metaphorically, for by addressing the *mwanita* (black millepede), the sorceress is able to make a pregnant woman's skin black, as black as the worm itself. The father's gift...is intended to forestall and arrest any evil intentions which the sorceress might harbour (1932: 190) (my italics).

It should be noted in this connexion that a woman does blacken her skin when she becomes a widow and goes into mourning. Her father's payment to the sorceress at the first pregnancy ceremony can be thought of, among other things, as protection against her becoming a widow at this time, and thus as an assurance that the child will have a father to care for it.

The food the woman's father presents to the sorceress must have been provided by the pregnant woman's own subclan, as they bring all the food to the *sagali*. Despite the fact that it is their food, however, they cannot, themselves, take it to the sorceress; only the woman's father can do this.

A father's magical protection of his daughter does not stop at her first pregnancy but continues throughout their lifetimes and is even extended to include her children as well. This latter point is well illustrated by a story related by Malinowski in the *Argonauts*. It was told to him by the woman to whom it happened.

When she was a little girl, a woman...came to her parents' house and wanted to sell a mat. They did not buy it, and gave her only a little food, which, as she was a renowned *yoyova* [sorceress] and accustomed therefore to deferential treatment, made her angry. When night came, the little one was playing on the beach in front of the house, when the parents saw a big firefly hovering about the child. The insect then flew round the parents and went into the room. Seeing that there was something strange about the firefly, they called the girl and put her to bed at once. But she fell ill immediately....Next morning, added the Kiriwinian mother, who was listening to her daughter telling me the tale... 'she was dead already, but her heart was still beating'. All the women present broke out into the ceremonial lamentations. The father of the girl's mother, however, went to Wawela, and got hold of another *yoyova*, called Bomrimwari....(1922: 243).

Bomrimwari managed to find the little girl's insides and returned them to her, whereupon she recovered. A substantial payment was then made by the child's parents (i.e. presumably by her father) to the *yoyova*.

Only by a comprehension of the extent of a Trobriand father's magical relationship to his children and his children's children can it be understood why such a seemingly remote person as the girl's mother's father should have been the one to arrange her cure in this case.

Returning to the customs of pregnancy, it should be noted that the ritual bathing, the ceremonial investment with the pregnancy mantle and the magic of whiteness and of beauty, are performed only before the first child is born.

But making the skin as white as possible by ordinary means, including the use of the mantle, is a feature of every pregnancy. For all subsequent pregnancies, the *saykeulo* is made by the woman herself—or it may be given by a *tabula* and repaid by her as a private transaction. The mother's *tabula*, however, have essential ritual tasks to perform after each baby is born.

All childbirths take place either in the woman's father's house or in her mother's brother's house, never in the house of her husband. Soon after the delivery, a string must be twisted by one of the mother's *tabula* and tied around the mother's chest. It is again one of the mother's female paternal relatives who, some three days after the birth, must knead off the remaining piece of the baby's umbilical cord. After about a month the new mother's *tabula* ritually wash her and rub her skin with leaves charmed by the beauty spell used in the corresponding rite during the first pregnancy ceremony. The woman then goes out with the baby and makes the round of the village, 'receiving from friends and her father's relatives small gifts of food called *va'otu*. After she has finished the round, there is a mimic driving home...of her by her *tabula*...and here she has to remain for another month in seclusion' (1932: 197). This house to which she is driven back by her *tabula* is the house where the baby was born, and not the young mother's husband's house.

It is obviously insufficient to claim that the woman's father and his subclan kin perform all this magic as representatives of the woman's own subclan. The crucial point here is that only members of her father's subclan have the magical power to perform these ceremonies of pregnancy and childbirth and that the woman's own subclan is therefore absolutely dependent upon her father and his subclan kin for the increase of their own subclan. They must, of course, pay for this service, but they are nonetheless dependent upon it.

All this is not to deny the magical protection of a woman and her children by her own subclan members. This, of course, exists as well. At the actual childbirth, for example, it is primarily the mother's male subclan kin who guard the house and keep watch against sorcerers. The essential point is that the young mother and her children need magical protection both from the mother's own subclan and from her father's subclan. Neither by itself is sufficient.

It is evident, however, that the woman's father and his subclan kin have important magical powers necessary to protect her from the dangers of pregnancy and to assure the health and proper formation of the baby. The woman's father's female subclan kin play an essential role in the birth of each of her children and are largely responsible for making the infant into a social person.

It is interesting to note that a woman's father's spirit may even be responsible for her pregnancy. Malinowski quotes the following Trobriand statement about a woman's becoming pregnant:

A child floats on a drift log. A spirit sees it is good-looking. She takes it. She is the spirit of the mother *or of the father* of the pregnant woman. Then she puts it on the head, in the hair, of the pregnant woman, who suffers headache, vomits, and has an ache in the belly. Then the child comes down into the belly, and she is really pregnant (1932: 148) (my italics).

As is well known, the Trobrianders do not see any direct connexion between copulation and procreation, and a father is considered to be related to his children only affinally, as their mother's husband. However, the Trobrianders have certain beliefs about the father's role in the formation of children, which indicate that a rather complex relationship is actually involved.

Austen points out that even though the father is not thought to have contributed towards the formation of the foetus, he is believed to have helped to develop the already formed foetus. Thus he says: 'The man apparently feels that he has some participation in helping to bring about the arrival of the child because his body has kept warm the body of the woman while the foetus has been developing' (Austen: 112).

It is thought that a child has the flesh of its mother but the face of its father. A child is said to take after its father in features (as a pig does after its father), because the father has been in such close contact with the mother that his physical features have become impressed upon the child (Austen 1934: 112–13). The possibility of a person's resembling a member of his own subclan is emphatically denied by the Trobrianders—even to the extent that two sons of the same parents will both be said to look like their father but to bear no resemblance whatsoever to each other.

This idea of their physical resemblance seems to be associated with the emotional tie between children and their father's subclan members. Malinowski describes how, after a man's death, his kinsmen and friends come from time to time to visit his children in order 'to see his face in theirs'. They give presents to the dead man's children and sit looking at them and wailing. This is said to soothe their insides because of 'seeing once more the likeness of the dead' (1927b: 90).

A further idea of a father's relationship to his children is gained from the following statement by Malinowski:

The husband, even one who has several wives, must abstain from all conjugal or extra-conjugal intercourse until the baby and its mother go out for the first time. A breach of any of these rules is said to bring about the death of the child (1932: 197).

Thus, a woman's successful reproduction is dependent again upon her husband as he can bring about the death of the child. This is, of course, the same pattern found among the Bemba.

Continuing to examine the relationship between a Trobriand father and his children, it is interesting to note that Seligman was told that in the old days a Trobriander did not eat his father's totems and would not have married into his father's clan (1910: 683).

It should also be noted that the incest taboo between father and daughter does not disappear upon divorce or death of the wife. The father also continues to be addressed by his children as *tama*, meaning father [or as Leach says, 'a domiciled male of my father's subclan hamlet' (Leach 1958: 132)], even after divorce or after his wife's death. It is quite evident that, as among the Ashanti and the Bemba, the ties of patrifiliation do not cease upon divorce or upon the death of the mother.

Austen gives an example of Trobriand thought about the father–daughter relationship:

[There was] an argument over the ownership of a betel palm, the father claiming a tree said to belong to his daughter, whose mother he had divorced. The people who were close by considered that the father 'had no shame' in disputing the ownership of a tree which his daughter, whom he had helped to develop in the womb, was, rightly or wrongly, claiming as her own (1934: 112).

An interesting sidelight on this whole matter appears in a statement recorded by Powell. During a discussion with some Trobrianders about their ideas of reproduction, he noticed that some parts of the account varied from what had been told to Malinowski. When Powell questioned them on the discrepancies, they said that both accounts were 'true' bút 'different'.

Malinowski's, they said, was 'men's talk', valid in formal situations, e.g. in matters of land ownership and the like; the account given to me was 'women's and children's talk', that is it was what *fathers or their sisters* told children as they became old enough to take more than a childish sexual interest in the opposite sex (Powell: 278) (my italics).

Thus it appears, interestingly enough, that children are told about sexual matters by their fathers or their fathers' sisters.

Having seen the importance of a father's magical relationship to his daughter, we must now examine his magical relationship to his son.

The essence of Trobriand magic is the spell. As Malinowski says, the words act because they are primeval, because they have been properly handed down in an unbroken filiation of magic, because they have been correctly learned by the new magician from his predecessor, and *because they are carried out by the sociologically determined person* (1935: II, 223). What is interesting to see is who these sociologically determined persons actually are.

According to Malinowski, there are two kinds of magic in the Trobriands: 'matrilineal' and 'patrilineal'. 'Patrilineal' magic, which may be transferred either from father to son or from ' stranger' to 'stranger' includes such types of magic as the formula for evil magic and its cure, magic initiating a man into certain crafts, canoe-making charms and love magic (1916: 172). 'Matrilineal' magic, which is more important by far, is bound up with a given locality and is supposed to be transferred from mother's brother to sister's son; it includes the all-important magic of the sun and the rain, of gardening, fishing and of war (1916: 171).

FILIATION AND MARRIAGE IN THE TROBRIANDS

Despite the fact that 'matrilineal' magic is supposed to belong to a particular subclan and to be, in fact, one of its most important possessions descending from generation to generation within the subclan, Malinowski states that 'more than half of the outstanding younger magicians have obtained their powers by paternal gift and not by maternal inheritance' (1927a: 121). That this patrilineal transfer of magic is not merely a recent innovation caused by European contact can be demonstrated by a genealogical study of Trobriand magical filiation. The Garden Magician of Omarakana whom Malinowski knew was Bagido'u, of the Tabalu subclan. His predecessor had been Yowana, his father, who was of the Kwoynama subclan. Yowana, in turn, had been preceded by his father, Purayasi, a Tabalu man. It has been pointed out Bagido'u was in fact the proper heir in the third generation to Purayasi, being the sister's son of Purayasi's sister's son (Fortes 1957: 183). However, the fact that Bagido'u ultimately received the magic, as he should have, does not explain why it passed for three generations from father to son instead of from mother's brother to sister's son.

It is not only in Omarakana that most of the important magic passes from father to son. Navavile, the Garden Magician of Oburaku, inherited his position from his father, as did other Trobriand Garden Magicians, notably Motogo'i and Kayla'i (1935: 1, 371). Kayla'i was the son of M'tabalu, the chief of Kasanai. While M'tabalu was alive, Kayla'i wielded the magic of the gardens and was even temporary officiating wizard in the great magic of the rain and sun. This is the most powerful of all Trobriand magic, as it is believed to cause famine or good harvests throughout the Trobriands, and is therefore the most important possession of the Tabalu subclan. Malinowski says: '[after M'tabalu's death] Kayla'i's position...remained unimpaired. Nor is such a case an exception due to decay of ancient law' (1935: 1, 362). Here then is an extreme case, where the most powerful of all Trobriand magic was wielded by the chief's son, a man who was therefore not a member of the subclan which owned the magic.

It should be noted in this connexion that in each community several persons are instructed in the garden magic, though only one holds the position of Garden Magician. Thus, in Omarakana, besides Bagido'u, To'uluwa, Molubabeba and his son, Tokulubakiki, and Bagido'u's younger brothers, Towese'i and Mitakata all knew the garden magic, as did several Tabalu from the neighbouring village of Kasanai—Tokolebeba, Kwaywaya, and M'tabalu. Many Tabalu subclan members knew the garden magic, then, and each (being entitled by heredity to the magic) was at liberty to recite it privately. The person selected to be the Garden Magician and therefore to be responsible for all the Omarakana gardens, however, was Bagido'u, son of Yowana, son of Purayasi.

Malinowski says that

In native mythology and legal theory it is always the head of the kinship group owning a village who is the garden magician. This man, however, frequently delegates his duties to his younger brother, his matrilineal nephew, or his son (1935: I, 64). ...When the office is in the hands of the chief's son, he...only holds it as a delegate of the rightful head of the community (1935: I, 67).

Of course, according to this explanation, a chief's brother or sister's son would also hold the garden magicianship only as the chief's delegate. What seems important, however, is not that the Garden Magician is considered to be the chief's delegate, but that the magical filiation goes so often from father to son. Why are these the persons so delegated?

It is not only the important systems of magic which are handed down from father to son; ordinary persons often acquire magical knowledge from their fathers as well. In fact, Malinowski says: 'a man [is himself often] doubtful whether he had not been cheated out of some of it [the magic] in receiving it from his uncle or elder brother. Such a doubt was never in the mind of a man who had received his magic as a gift from the father' (1927a: 121). A man who receives magic from his father does not give a specific payment for it; if he wishes to receive it from a subclan kinsman, however, he must first present *pokala* to the older man.

When magic is passed down from father to son it is not a haphazard, makeshift or irregular arrangement; it is incorporated into the heart of the magic itself. Malinowski says of one magical formula, it

is undoubtedly the most important in all Omarakana garden magic, for the following reasons: it is performed on several occasions and on each is the essential spell of the complex ceremony in which it occurs; it figures in the two or three most important acts: the grand inaugural rite, the first and second burning, and at harvest...' (1935: II, 257).

In this spell, Malinowski says, 'the lineal predecessors in magic of the officiating *towosi* [Garden Magician]' are invoked (1935: I, 468). The invocation is as follows: '*Tubu-gu Polu, tubu-gu Koleko, tubu-gu Takikila, tubu-gu Mulabwoyta, tubu-gu Kwayudila, tubu-gu Katupwala, tubu-gu Bugwabwaga, tubu-gu Purayasi, tubu-gu Numakala*, and thou, new spirit, *tabu-gu Mwakenua, tama-gu Yowana*' (1935: I, 96; II, 256). Here, then, we see that in the most powerful formula of Trobriand garden magic (and this is true as well for all the other spells of garden magic cited by Malinowski which invoke ancestors) the persons who are called upon are either *tabu* or *tama* to the magician. *Tabu*, in this case, refers to ancestors on both the maternal and the paternal sides. *Tama* refers, of course, only to agnates. As we have said, Yowana was Bagido'u's father; Purayasi was Yowana's father. Malinowski says, 'Yowana was the father of my informant [Bagido'u], Mwakenua his grandfather' (1935: II, 262). Mwakenua must then have been Bagido'u's mother's father. In the most powerful spell of Trobriand garden magic, then, the magician invokes the aid of his father, his father's father and his mother's father. Again, we must emphasize that it is not only persons related to him by patrifiliation whom he calls upon. Some of the Garden Magician's own subclan ancestors are, of course, also invoked; Bugwabwaga and Numakala were subclan ancestors of Bagido'u. It is not known who the others mentioned were. It is clear, however, that the magician derives important magical powers through patrifiliation.

As we have seen, it is a woman's father and other members of his subclan who, to a very great extent, insure her fertility and procreation, and magically protect her progeny. Now we see the role of the paternal ancestors in magically insuring the fertility of the gardens. The word *tama* is a part of the magical spell itself. The father's magical power is thus invoked specifically, and by name, in order to insure the fertility of the gardens. It is interesting to note that the spell continues:

> The belly of my garden grows...
> The belly of my garden swells,
> The belly of my garden swells as with a child (1935: I, 97).

Thus it seems that the Trobrianders themselves have some sort of concept of fertility—at least that they connect a woman's pregnancy with the growing of food in the gardens. And the father, his subclan kin and his ancestors are called upon to insure this fertility—both of the humans and of the gardens.

F. Obligations after death

The network of rights and obligations binding together the parties to a marriage ends, for most of the persons involved, after an extensive period of mourning for the marriage partner who dies first.

When a person dies, his subclan kinsmen are not allowed to touch the corpse, and no member of the deceased's clan may display outward signs of mourning in costume or ornamentation. On a man's death, his widow, his children and his father (if he be alive) must cut their hair, blacken themselves and go into mourning. The widow's mourning costume, according to Seligman, is provided by her dead husband's sisters.

The corpse is washed, anointed, ornamented and caressed by relatives-in-law; the grave is dug and the corpse buried by the dead man's sons. The widow lies down, often with her daughter beside her, upon a layer of logs placed over the corpse. The body is twice exhumed and inspected for sorcery, and the bones are cleaned and sucked by the sons of the deceased. The dead man's subclan kinswomen then ceremonially wash the sons' mouths.

The widow, covered with soot and grease, must move into a small cage where she remains for six months to two years. During this time she is under the surveillance of her husband's matrilineal relatives who regard her mourning and its privations as their due. At the end of her period of mourning, she is washed, anointed and dressed in a new gaudy skirt by her dead husband's kinswomen; this act makes her marriageable again.

According to Seligman, a widower blackens himself and wears mourning for his dead wife in much the same manner as a widow does for her husband. Some or all of his mourning gear is given to him by his dead wife's sisters. It is unfortunate that there is so little information about what happens when a woman dies, the only data being that furnished by Seligman.

Thus, in the mortuary rites as in other life crises, the ceremonial role is taken by persons who are agnatically or affinally related to the central figure. Again, payment is made to them by the subclan members of the person involved.

In the mortuary ceremony, as described by Malinowski, the eldest male of the deceased's subclan acts as master of the ceremony. From his kinsmen and from his wife's relatives he receives considerable gifts of food, and to these he adds perhaps half the contents of his own storehouse. Seligman says that the dead man's yams are used as well. All the food is distributed at a series of *sagalis* to the widow, children and other relatives-in-law of the deceased, as payment for their mortuary duties. The food is then redistributed by the recipients among their subclan members and relatives-in-law.

Mortuary ceremonies are carried out only on the body of the deceased, for the spirit goes immediately to Tuma, the island of the dead. Even in Tuma, however, spirits are interested in what is happening among the living. There is one example quoted in the literature of a Trobriander's 'visiting' the spirits in Tuma (in a trance). When he 'returned', he said: '[In Tuma] your father and mother cry for you all the time; they want to see you; give me two sticks of tobacco and I shall go, see them, give them the tobacco. Your father saw me; he told me, "Bring the tobacco from Gomara" [his son]' (1916: 139). The other Trobrianders were highly sceptical about this visit to Tuma and considered it a fraudulent claim. It is, nevertheless, interesting to see that the father–child relationship is considered to continue even after death, and that a dead man would request tobacco not from his heir, but from his son.

It is commonly said that in the Trobriands a man inherits from his mother's brother or other senior subclan kinsman on the latter's death. What does this actually mean? What is, in fact, inherited by a man's heir? Possessions in the Trobriands include land, titles, valuables, magic, trees, food and personal possessions. On a man's death, his personal possessions (which are not described), it is said, may be given to anyone. His yams, as we have seen, go to his agnates and affines as part of the payment for their mourning services. His valuables, Powell says, are used in the first mortuary rite and are then distributed, again among his agnates and affines, in acknowledgement of their mourning services. Powell says that this is an element in the mortuary ritual and is not a form of inheritance (Powell: 414). Whether or not it is considered to be inheritance, it is clearly important to note that on his death, a man's valuables go to the persons who are his principal mourners, i.e. his widow and his children. As we have seen, the magic a man owns (which, by its nature of course, has to be transferred before his death), is supposed to be handed down to his heir but is in fact often given to his son. Coconut and areca palms are also supposed to be passed down within the subclan, but as Powell says, there is some flexibility in interpreting the rules here, because as the trees were originally planted by their first owners, the owners are felt to have a certain right of disposal over them 'despite formal claims by heirs' (1956: 415).

Thus, a man's personal possessions, his food, his valuables, his magic and his trees may be and often are left to his children. Subclan land, titles, and those valuables which are held in trust for the subclan—of which it appears there are very few indeed (1922: 94)—constitute the inheritance of his heir and of the other members of his subclan who have claims upon him. These latter possessions may be temporarily inherited by his son, but at most only for the son's lifetime. Unlike the first group, they cannot be passed on to the son's children or heirs. Nevertheless, it is evident that Trobriand inheritance is a complex affair, and that all of a man's property is not, by any means, simply inherited by his subclan heir.

III. CONCLUSION

It is evident from the above data that the ties of patrifiliation are exceedingly important in the Trobriands and that, in many respects, they follow a pattern which is consistent with that found in other 'matrilineal' societies.

In the great majority of 'matrilineal' societies, membership in a lineage, although of primary importance, is not sufficient by itself for the formation of a person's character or for the conduct of his social life. And thus, as Fortes says of the Ashanti, 'Paternity carries a very high value' (1953a: 7). Among the Ashanti, the Bemba and the Trobrianders, a child needs a father in order to grow up properly, and its father is essentially and intimately connected spiritually with the child.

As we have seen, Trobriand fathers are considered to have a definite role in the formation of their children; their magical protection is essential throughout the lives of their children; and the father–child relationship can exist unchanged even when, through divorce or death, the mother is no longer there as the connecting link (and the other ties between the two subclans have been terminated). It thus seems reasonable to infer that children can be considered, from the Trobriand viewpoint, as being the children both of their mothers and of their fathers—so long as it is realized that entirely different things are meant in each case. The fact that these are different relationships does not mean that they do not both exist. However, in such a discussion of the Trobriand 'father', 'mother', 'parents', it is essential to keep in mind that these

English words do not correspond to Trobriand categories, and the meanings inherent in the English word 'father' must not be superimposed upon the Trobriand father.

What we are interested in is the respective relationships of the father, and of the mother's brother as a representative of his subclan, to the children. As we have seen, both have rights in the children, and in a sense the children belong to both—though for different purposes.

A woman who has a child is involved in three separate but necessarily intertwined relationships. Her brother, as the male representative of her subclan, retains the rights over her powers of procreation. Her reproductive powers are the source of the continuity of his subclan; however, as we have seen, he does not hold exclusive rights over his sister's children. The woman's brother, moreover, is dependent for the increase of his own subclan both upon his sister's husband and upon her father. It is considered extremely bad for a woman to have children before she is married, and her subclan is thus dependent upon her husband for the children they need to continue the existence of their subclan. Also the husband and his kinsmen must care for and protect the children, both physically and magically, in order for them to grow to maturity properly.

On the other hand, the woman was enabled to produce the children in the first place because of the fertility which she received from her father. And her father, because of his relationship of patrifiliation with his daughter, extends his protection to her children as well.

A woman's own subclan is thus dependent for the increase of their subclan upon her husband (because of his relationship of patrifiliation with her children) and upon her father (because of his relationship of patrifiliation with her).

Of course, the actual relations among a particular woman's brother, husband and father will depend to a large extent upon their relative ranks and personalities, and certain parts of the basic pattern of relationships may be altered to fit the particular circumstances. Thus, for example, the first pregnancy ceremony varies to some extent according to who the pregnant woman is and who is interested in her marriage and her children. If she is of very high rank, her own subclan will have an exceptionally great interest in her and in her progeny. And in this case, the first pregnancy vigil is carried out on the platform of her mother's brother's house rather than at her father's house, as would be the case were she a commoner and not of such exceptional importance to her subclan.

In either case, however, she derives her powers of procreation from her father. A woman's paternal relatives not only empower her to have children; they also take the lead in making the child into a social person after it is born. And as it is ego's mother's father and the latter's sisters who take the major ceremonial role in making ego into a social person, so later, it will be ego's own sons and his father as well (if he be alive) who will play essential ceremonial roles in the ending of his life as a social person.

The respective roles played throughout his life by a man's subclan kinsmen, his relatives by patrifiliation and his affines are in some sense always in opposition, but they may vary considerably, depending upon the circumstances. It is generally thought to be the latter two groups which are potentially dangerous to a person [as we have seen, they are people who have magical powers necessary for his life and development, but as Leach says, 'a Trobriander would never forget that any magician may very easily become a sorcerer' (Leach 1958: 144)]. Thus a man's relatives by patrifiliation and his affines are the first to be suspected of sorcery if misfortune should befall him. On the other hand, Powell speaks of a chief's keeping his sons and his wives' male relatives in his own village in order to use them for protection against his own subclan kinsmen, should the need arise (Powell: 494).

In order to see clearly the relationships between a woman's brother, her husband and her father, we must again examine the marriage payments. These can be looked at in two ways. The first is as an exchange between the bride's side and the groom's side. The presents from the bride's side to the groom's side are perishable, and the bulk of them go to the young couple, while those given by the groom's side are valuables (hence non-perishable) and they are given not to the young couple but to the bride's elder relatives. This indicates, then, that the bride's relatives are being compensated for giving up some of their rights in the bride while the groom's relatives are not losing any essential rights over the groom.

The second way to look at the marriage gifts is to examine who on each side gives them and why. The bride's side receives valuables and pays out food, most of which goes to the young couple. The groom's relatives have therefore paid out valuables for which they have received nothing in return. What sort of reciprocity, if any, is involved here?

It is, as we have seen, the groom's father who makes the payment of valuables at the time of his son's marriage. There are two ways of looking at this, which taken together give a plausible explanation of the role of the groom's father. One explanation is that the father pays valuables for his son's wife as an obligation to his son who has helped him all his life, who has given him annual *urigubu* harvest payments, and who will care for him in his old age. But the father is not only fulfilling an obligation to his son. He is also repaying his son's subclan for the *Vilakuria* which *he* received from his wife's subclan kin on *his* marriage and for the annual *urigubu* harvest payments he has been receiving from them. For by this gift of valuables to his son's wife's relatives the groom's father makes sure that similar support will be given his son throughout his lifetime. Thus, on P's marriage to Q, P received a *Vilakuria* gift from X and subsequent *urigubu* harvest presents as well. After a while,

Z may have taken over X's obligations to P, but at any rate, P has been receiving large quantities of food from Q's subclan, and his repayments of valuables over the years have not been considered an equivalent return. Now, by paying valuables out of this circle—to A's relatives—P insures that B, a member of X's subclan, will be treated by A's relatives in the same way that he himself was treated by X and Z. We can thus see that there is a definite system of reciprocity involved here, but that it is a long-term system.

We must now consider the role of the bride's father. We have seen that at least part of the *Vilakuria* is often paid by him and that a substantial minority of the annual *urigubu* harvest payments given to the couple are made by persons related to the wife and sometimes to the husband by patrifiliation.

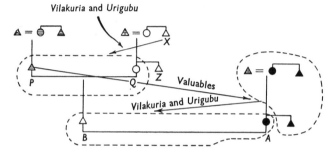

Fig. 4. Transfer of valuables from the groom's father to the relatives of the bride seen as part of long-term reciprocity between the groom's father and the groom's own subclan.

How then does this fit in with Malinowski's well-known statement that 'the *urigubu* is the endowment by its real head of the unit of filiation...the expression of the real constitution of Trobriand kinship grouping' (1935: 207)? If we say instead that while the *urigubu* is indeed one expression of the constitution of Trobriand kinship grouping, this real kinship grouping includes more than subclan relationship. The *urigubu* might rather be considered as the endowment to the domestic family by those persons and subclans which have interests in it and as an annual reminder of their claims upon it.

Under ordinary circumstances, the main interest in a household would be held by the wife's subclan, but the wife's father and his kin will often also have an interest in it, and the husband's subclan and members of the husband's father's subclan may be concerned as well. It is obvious that different numbers of persons and subclans will have interests in different marriages; more people will be concerned in a chief's marriage than in a commoner's, for example, and this will be reflected in the numbers and relationships of *urigubu* donors. This is true on a smaller scale as well, and since some marriages are of more importance than others, the former will receive *urigubu* gifts from more sources than the latter.

It seems more reasonable to consider the *urigubu* gifts from persons related to the recipients by patrifiliation and affinity as meaningful in their own right, rather than to declare *a priori* that they are 'spurious' and without consequence or to decide arbitrarily that the givers are merely representing the wife's subclan and are not interested in the marriage in their own right. If we think of the *urigubu* in this way, it accounts for cases such as the marriage of Vanoi to Bwabwau's daughter, where the *urigubu* gift was given entirely by the girl's father. Here the *urigubu* still represents the interests held in the marriage, although in this case they are different from the usual ones.

This essay was begun with the object of investigating and clarifying the jural significance of the father in Trobriand paternal, marital and affinal relations. [7] Re-analysis of Malinowski's ethnographic data and the supplementary information provided by Powell's more recent research has shown that the Trobriand father is invested with important, and, in some respects, decisive jural, economic and ritual roles, rights and responsibilities. These are different aspects of the recognition of complementary filiation in this 'matrilineal' social structure. In demonstrating this, we have seen that complementary filiation is a factor of crucial importance in the constitution of Trobriand society and in this respect fits the pattern found in other 'matrilineal' systems with which we have made some comparison.

NOTES

[1] References are to Malinowski's writings unless otherwise specified.

[2] 'Subclan hamlet' is used in this paper as defined by Leach (1958: 124–5). It is equivalent to Malinowski's 'village section' and refers to the households in a village and the garden lands associated with them, which belong to a single subclan. A village may be occupied by members of a single subclan, but multi-subclan-hamlet villages are more common.

[3] There is no information as to what constitutes such an exceptional case.

[4] It is curious that Malinowski should have said 'by a man and his wife's father' here, when, by his own detailed evidence, it is primarily the man's father and not the man himself who engages in the series of marriage gifts. It is possible, of course, that in certain cases a man, and especially a chief, might conduct the marriage negotiations in his own person. However, what is important to note here is that Malinowski says definitely 'not matrilineal kinsmen in this case'.

[5] The care a father gives his children is no small matter. Malinowski says: 'In ever so many cases, I could observe that when a child...was in trouble or sick; when there was a question of some one exposing himself to difficulties or danger for the child's sake, it was always the father who worried, who would undergo all the hardships needed, and never the maternal uncle' (1922: 71–2).

[6] Unfortunately there is no similar specific information about which of the wife's relatives render the services due to her husband.

[7] I should like to thank Professor Meyer Fortes and Dr Edmund R. Leach for many valuable and stimulating discussions of the problems raised in this paper. I am indebted to Dr H. A. Powell for permission to use his unpublished material. I should also like to thank both the Radcliffe College Graduate School for a fellowship held during the time of this research, and Newnham College for their hospitality during my year's stay in Cambridge.

BIBLIOGRAPHY

AUSTEN, L. (1934), 'Procreation among the Trobriand Islanders', *Oceania*, vol. 5.

BARNES, J. A. (1949), 'Measures of Divorce Frequency in Simple Societies', *J. R. Anthrop. Inst.*, vol. 79.

BARTH, F. (1959), 'Segmentary Opposition and the Theory of Games: a Study of Pathan Organization', *J. R. Anthrop. Inst.*, vol. 89.

CENTERS, R. (1949), 'Marital Selection and Occupational Strata', *Amer. J. Soc.*, vol. 54.

DJAMOUR, J. (1959), *Malay Kinship and Marriage in Singapore*, London.

DORJAHN, V. R. (1958), 'Fertility, Polygyny and their Interrelations in Temne Society', *American Anthropologist*, vol. 60, no. 5.

DUMONT, L. (1957), 'Hierarchy and Marriage Alliance in South Indian Kinship', *Occasional Papers, R. Anthrop. Inst.*, no. 12.

EVANS-PRITCHARD, E. E. (1951), *Kinship and Marriage among the Nuer*, Oxford.

FORDE, D. (1941), *Marriage and the Family among the Yakö in South-Eastern Nigeria*, London.

FORTES, M. (1949*a*), *The Web of Kinship among the Tallensi*, London.

—— (1949*b*), 'Time and Social Structure: an Ashanti Case Study', *Social Structure* (ed. M. Fortes), London.

—— (1950), 'Kinship and Marriage among the Ashanti', in *African Systems of Kinship and Marriage* (eds. A. R. Radcliffe-Brown and D. Forde), London.

—— (1953*a*), 'Analysis and Description in Social Anthropology', in *The Advancement of Science*, vol. 10, London.

—— (1953*b*), 'The Structure of Unilineal Descent Groups', *American Anthropologist*, vol. 55.

—— (1957), 'Malinowski and the Study of Kinship', in *Man and Culture* (ed. R. Firth), London.

—— (1959), 'Descent, Filiation and Affinity: a Rejoinder to Dr Leach', *Man*, vol. 59.

GLUCKMAN, M. (1950), 'Kinship and Marriage among the Lozi of Northern Rhodesia and the Zulu of Natal', in *African Systems of Kinship and Marriage* (eds. A. R. Radcliffe-Brown and D. Forde), London.

The Gold Coast Census of Population, 1948 (1950), London.

GOODY, J. R. (1956), *The Social Organisation of the LoWiili*, London.

—— (1958) (ed.), *The Developmental Cycle in Domestic Groups* (*Cambridge Papers in Social Anthropology*, no. 1), Cambridge.

—— (1959), 'The Mother's Brother and the Sister's Son in West Africa', *J. R. Anthrop. Inst.*, vol. 89.

—— (1962), *Death, Property and the Ancestors*, Stanford, California.

GOUGH, E. K. (1955), 'Female Initiation Rites on the Malabar Coast', *J. R. Anthrop. Inst.*, vol. 85.

—— (1959), 'The Nayars and the Definition of Marriage', *J. R. Anthrop. Inst.*, vol. 89.

GOULD, H. A. (1960), 'The Micro-demography of Marriages in a North Indian Area', *Southwestern J. Anthrop.*, vol. 16.

ISHWARAN, K. (1959), *Family Life in the Netherlands*, The Hague.

LEACH, E. R. (1957), 'Aspects of Bridewealth and Marriage Stability among the Kachin and Lakher', *Man*, vol. 57, London.

—— (1958), 'Concerning Trobriand Clans and the Kinship Category *Tabu*', in *Cambridge Papers in Social Anthropology*, no. 1 (ed. J. R. Goody), Cambridge.

LÉVI-STRAUSS, C. (1949), *Les Structures élémentaires de la parenté*, Paris.

LIPSET, S. M., and BENDIX R. (1959), *Social Mobility in Industrial Society*, London.

BIBLIOGRAPHY

Lowie, R. H. (1933), article on 'Marriage', in *Encyclopaedia of the Social Sciences.*

Malinowski, B. (1916), 'Baloma: Spirits of the Dead in the Trobriand Islands', reprinted in *Magic, Science and Religion, and Other Essays* (ed. R. Redfield), Glencoe, Ill.

—— (1922), *Argonauts of the Western Pacific*, London.

—— (1926a), *Crime and Custom in Savage Society*, London.

—— (1926b), *Myth in Primitive Psychology*, London.

—— (1927a), *Sex and Repression in Savage Society*, London.

—— (1927b), *The Father in Primitive Psychology*, London.

—— (1929), article on 'Marriage', in *Encyclopaedia Britannica.*

—— (1932), *The Sexual Life of Savages* (with special foreword to the third edition), London.

—— (1935), *Coral Gardens and Their Magic*: vol. I, *The Description of Gardening*; Vol. II, *The Language of Magic and Gardening*, London.

—— (1948), *Magic, Science and Religion, and Other Essays* (ed. R. Redfield), Glencoe, Ill.

Marches, J., and Turbeville G. (1953), 'The Effect of Residential Propinquity on Marriage Selection', *Amer. J. Soc.*, vol. 58.

Mauss, M. (1923–24), 'Essai sur le Don', *L'Année Sociologique*, series 2, vol. 1, Paris (transl. by I. Cunnison as *The Gift*, (1954), London).

Mayer, P. (1950), 'Gusii Bridewealth Law and Custom', *Rhodes–Livingstone Papers*, no. 18.

Meek, C. K. (1925), *The Northern Tribes of Nigeria*, vol. 1, London.

Mitchell, J. C., and Barnes J. A. (1950), *The Lamba Village*, in *Communications from the School of African Studies*, University of Cape Town.

Montaigne, M. *Essays* (first publ. 1580).

Phillips, A. (1953) (ed.), *Survey of African Marriage and Family Life*, London.

Powell, H. A. (1956), 'An Analysis of Present Day Social Structure in the Trobriand Islands', Ph.D. thesis, University of London.

Radcliffe-Brown, A. R. (1935), 'Patrilineal and Matrilineal Succession', reprinted in Radcliffe-Brown, *Structure and Function in Primitive Society* (1952), London.

—— (1950), Introduction to *African Systems of Kinship and Marriage*, London.

Rattray, R. S. (1927), *Religion and Art in Ashanti*, London.

—— (1929), *Ashanti Law and Constitution*, London.

Richards, A. I. (1935), 'Mother-right among the Central Bantu', in *Essays Presented to C. G. Seligman* (ed. E. E. Evans-Pritchard et al.), London.

—— (1940), 'Bemba Marriage and Present Economic Conditions', *Rhodes–Livingstone Papers*, no. 4.

—— (1950), 'Some Types of Family Structure amongst the Central Bantu', in *African Systems of Kinship and Marriage* (ed. A. R. Radcliffe-Brown and D. Forde), London.

Seligman, C. G. (1910), *The Melanesians of British New Guinea*, Cambridge.

Smith, M. F. (1954), *Baba of Karo*, London.

Smith, M. G. (1953), 'Secondary Marriage in Northern Nigeria', *Africa*, vol. 23.

Smith, R. T. (1956), *The Negro Family in British Guiana*, London.

—— (1955), *The Economy of the Hausa Communities of Zaria*, London.

Spiro, M. E. (1958), *Children of the Kibbutz*, Cambridge, Mass.

Stacey, M. (1960), *Tradition and Change: a Study of Banbury*, London.

Stenning, D. J. (1959), *Savannah Nomads*, London.

Trimingham, J. S. (1959), *Islam in West Africa*, Oxford.

Turner, V. W. (1957), *Schism and Continuity in an African Society*, Manchester.